PRAISE FOR *BECOMING KIM JONG UN*

"[This] excellent biography from former CIA analyst Jung H. Pak cuts through the regime's opacity and the fog of gossip to provide an excellent primer on the country's present-day leadership as well as hints of whatever might come next. The multigenerational drama of dynastic succession provides a fascinating cultural and historical backdrop. . . . [Pak] artfully trac[es] the DPRK leader's upbringing and political ascendancy. . . . *Becoming Kim Jong Un* moves between storytelling in intimate, elegantly written scenes and clear, well-argued policy analysis. Moments of color, humor and Kim family high jinks are the book's saving grace, making it more appealing than a dry lesson in geopolitics. As the Great Successor himself knows well, if you're hoping to captivate a broad, loyal audience, it helps to have some personal flair." —*Los Angeles Times*

"There's hardly a better time to read what could be the most definitive account of North Korea's supreme leader. Former CIA officer Pak shrewdly sheds light on the world's most recognizable mysterious leader, his life and what's really going on behind the curtain."
—*Newsweek,* "The 20 Must-Read Fiction and Nonfiction Books of the Summer"

"[An] expert assessment . . . an insightful analysis of perhaps the world's most dangerous dystopia." —*Kirkus Reviews*

"North Korea has long been regarded as a 'hard target' by the intelligence community—and with abundant good reason. Dr. Jung H. Pak has managed to shed more light on the current North Korea leader, Kim Jong Un, than virtually anyone else. She has adeptly and discreetly applied her experience as an intelligence analyst and managed to penetrate the opaque nature of North Korea, and in doing so has displayed her considerable skills in and mastery of the analyst's tradecraft. An important book, both for the professional expert and for those who simply want to gain insight into the hermit kingdom and its enigmatic leader."
—James Clapper, former Director of National Intelligence

"Jung H. Pak's sober but absorbing portrait of North Korea's leader should be the starting point for any scholar, journalist, or policy-maker trying to make sense of the most dangerous regime on earth. Pak ties together biography, national security analysis, and policy prescription with the precision one would expect from a scholar and former intelligence officer."
—Michael J. Green, former Asia adviser to President George W. Bush, director of Asian studies at Georgetown University, and senior vice president at the Center for Strategic and International Studies

"*Becoming Kim Jong Un* is the most complete account to date of a dictator who has too often been caricatured by the public. Highly read-able, thoughtful, and dispassionate, this book offers important insights into an enigmatic leader who will shape the destiny not only of the Korean Peninsula but of the Northeast Asian region and the world. It's the next best thing to receiving a top-secret CIA briefing."
—Sue Mi Terry, former CIA analyst and former Korea director at the National Security Council

"One of the nation's top North Korea analysts, Dr. Jung H. Pak, has delivered a rich and insightful volume surveying the rise to power of Kim Jong Un, a history of the Kim family, and the actions of the Pyongyang regime since its inception. Cogently and concisely treat-ing a broad sweep of issues central to North Korea, Dr. Pak makes an essential contribution to the collective understanding of one of the world's most dangerous and complex problems. It is a must-read for the expert and casual observer alike."
—Mark Lippert, former U.S. ambassador to South Korea

BECOMING
KIM JONG UN

A FORMER CIA OFFICER'S
INSIGHTS INTO NORTH KOREA'S
ENIGMATIC YOUNG DICTATOR

JUNG H. PAK

BALLANTINE BOOKS
NEW YORK

FOR J.B.H, N.E.H, AND W.B.H.

AND JOOMI

CONTENTS

———— ■ ————

AUTHOR'S NOTE

Following Korean, Japanese, and Chinese custom, surnames precede given names unless otherwise noted. There is no established standard on transliteration of the Korean language, which is why there are variations: Kim Jong-il, Kim Chong-il. Per the AP Stylebook, I write North Korean names as three words (Kim Jong Un), while South Korean names are two words, with a hyphen in the given names (Moon Jae-in). In the notes, I use the formulation that appears in the original source.

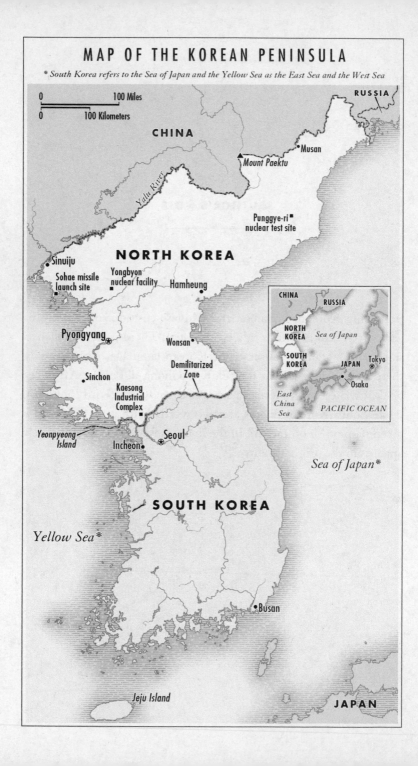

MAP OF THE KOREAN PENINSULA

* South Korea refers to the Sea of Japan and the Yellow Sea as the East Sea and the West Sea

0   100 Miles

0   100 Kilometers

RUSSIA

CHINA

Musan

▲ Mount Paektu

Yalu River

Punggye-ri ■
nuclear test site

NORTH KOREA

Sinuiju

Sohae missile
launch site ■

Yongbyon
nuclear facility

Hamheung

Pyongyang ⊛

Wonsan

Demilitarized
Zone

Sinchon

Kaesong
Industrial
Complex ■

Yeonpyeong
Island

Incheon

Seoul ⊛

SOUTH KOREA

Yellow Sea*

Sea of Japan*

Busan

Jeju Island

JAPAN

Inset map

CHINA

RUSSIA

NORTH KOREA

Sea of Japan

SOUTH KOREA

JAPAN

Tokyo ⊛

Osaka

East China Sea

PACIFIC OCEAN

PROLOGUE

———■———

Even by the standards of North Korea—consummate purveyor of propaganda—one could not have asked for better weather for the staging of Kim Jong Il's funeral on December 28, 2011. It was cold, bleak, and snowing. The white snow contrasted perfectly with the black of the hearse, the coffin atop it, and the mourners' attire, matching the melancholy in the people's hearts as they bade farewell to their beloved leader, who had ruled them since 1994, when the country's founder, Kim Il Sung, had died. As the funeral procession moved through the snow, the North Korean people lining the streets wept, fainted, and convulsed with grief, genuine or otherwise. Men and women, soldiers and workers, the young and the old beat or clawed at their chests and clung to one another for comfort or pounded the ground in anguish. The roar of this collective demonstration of sorrow was deafening, and it probably stirred even those in the crowd who did not feel this passion for the dead leader who had ruled with an iron hand.

Prominently leading the procession was the baby-faced Kim Jong Un—North Korea's new leader. He kept his composure, walking silently and mournfully, though his tense face and tears betrayed the real grief he must have felt. He was now, after all, an orphan; his mother had died of breast cancer when he was twenty years old.

Kim Jong Il, the dictator, father, and movie impresario, would have been pleased with every aspect of this final production.

KIM JONG IL'S DEATH on December 17, 2011, from "overwork," as the North Korean state media described it, was not a surprise. Everyone knew that Kim had health issues—he had suffered a stroke in late 2008—and that the time would probably come when his family's history of heart disease and his days of smoking, drinking, and partying would catch up with him. His father, Kim Il Sung, had also died of a heart attack. Still, the death was jarring.

At the time of the funeral, I was a relatively new analyst at the Central Intelligence Agency, having begun my job there in early 2009, soon after Kim's stroke. When he had made his first public appearance at the rubber-stamp Supreme People's Assembly spring meeting, he was shockingly thin, his once plump cheeks now crepey and clinging to his prominent cheekbones. His gait was slow and measured.

When Kim's death came, a palpable anxiety gripped the world. South Korea convened a National Security Council meeting as the country put its military and civil defense on high alert. Japan set up a crisis management team, and the White House issued a statement saying it was "in close touch with our allies in South Korea and Japan." At CIA headquarters in Langley, Virginia, I remember being watchful for any indications of instability in Pyongyang, as I began to develop my thinking about where North Korea might be headed under its youthful and inexperienced new leader.

The North Korean regime was quick to dispel any doubt or confusion about its next ruler. The state media, after dutifully exalting Kim Jong Il's "brilliant" life and leadership and his role as the "parent of the nation and a lodestar of the fatherland's reunification," immediately proclaimed that the future was secure under Kim Jong Un:

> At the head of our revolution today stands Comrade Kim Jong Un,
> the great successor. . . . All of the party members, the men and of-

ficers of the people's army, and the people should faithfully uphold the leadership of Comrade Kim Jong Un, they should firmly defend the single-hearted unity of the party, the army, and the people and should further strengthen it like steel. . . .

The path for our revolution is arduous, and the prevailing situation is harsh, but there is no force in the world that can block the revolutionary advance of our party, army, and people that are moving forward under the wise leadership of great Comrade Kim Jong Un.

The North Korean regime was not shy about lionizing the youthful and inexperienced new leader.

For Kim Jong Un, his father's funeral was the climax of a public succession that had begun in earnest just a few years before. The U.K. ambassador to Pyongyang reported that officials toasted Kim Jong Il and his son, the "young general," at national events. Octogenarian elites bowed deeply in front of Kim Jong Un on state television. The regime not only touted the continuity from Kim to Kim but also marketed the younger man as a reincarnation of his revered grandfather, down to the same dark suit and haircut, even girth.

But it wasn't clear whether Kim Jong Un wanted the burden of being North Korea's leader. If the elites did not accept him, instability, mass defections, a flood of refugees, bloody purges, even a military coup could ensue. Would a brash, reckless, untethered Kim wield his newfound power, including an inherited nuclear arsenal, in a fit of military adventurism? Was his goal to dominate North Korea's policy and behavior, or would he be more open to eliciting counsel from those around him?

Asia watchers predicted Kim's imminent fall, overthrow, or demise: "North Korea as we know it is over. Whether it comes apart in the next few weeks or over several months, the regime will not be able to hold together." Surely someone in his midtwenties with no leadership experience would be quickly overwhelmed and usurped by his elders. There was no way that North Koreans would stand for a second dynastic succession, unheard of in Communism, not to mention that his youth was a critical demerit in a society that prizes the wisdom that comes with age and maturity. North Korea was poor and isolated, unable to feed its people. Even if Kim did manage to hold on to his position by clinging to the country's nuclear and missile programs for legitimacy and prestige, the collapse of North Korea seemed more likely than ever.

As Kim solemnly marched alongside his father's hearse, he was accompanied by a ring of senior party and military officials, the so-called Gang of Seven. Their prestigious role in the funeral and symbolic placement around the new successor suggested that Kim Jong Un had the support of the old guard and the status quo would continue. Most experts saw these seven regime veterans as probable mentors for the young leader, at least for the near future, and some predicted an evolution of the Kim family's personality cult: Kim Jong Un would be a figurehead, and these "regents" would eventually call the shots in North Korea.

That was then. In the ensuing years, Kim would use the mechanisms of authoritarian control—repression and fear, co-optation of elites, and control of military and security forces—to consolidate his power and bolster the personality cult that had girded the legitimacy of his grandfather and his father as the sole leaders of North Korea. But Kim was not satisfied with simply maintaining this inherited infrastructure of control. In the journal *Asian Perspectives,* Patrick McEachern, an analyst in the U.S. State Department and an astute observer of North Korea, details how Kim centralized his power by reducing the institutional roles of the military and cabinet and placing the Korean Workers' Party under his singular leadership. Within the first two years of his reign, Kim purged, executed, demoted, and otherwise removed or marginalized five of the Gang of Seven, while jealously assuming key leadership positions himself. His innate flexibility and adaptability were in evidence as he sharpened his tools of coercion, using new technologies (cyber) and old (chemical and biological weapons), muscularly pressing forward to thrust North Korea into its place in the world as a nuclear-armed power capable of potentially striking the United States.

Despite the enormous influence that Kim Jong Un exerts over current geopolitics and the danger he poses to global security, most people know next to nothing about him. Fascination with North Korea has sparked a deluge of articles, documentaries, and expert interviews to meet the demands of a public hungry for information about the young dictator who dominates the news cycle, as well as interpretation of his actions. Unfortunately, most of the accounts and reporting are simplistic, lacking deep analysis and understanding of the historical and geopolitical contexts. The wonky Washington-speak of national security ignores both Kim's individuality and style and North Korean culture and politics, as if Kim's personality, perceptions, and preferences do not matter when we talk about how to solve the intractable nuclear problem.

I was at the forefront of shaping the understanding of the U.S. government and foreign partners on Korean Peninsula issues first at the Central Intelligence Agency and then as the deputy national intelligence officer for Korea at the National Intelligence Council. I led the U.S. intelligence community's production of strategic analysis and represented our views on the Koreas in White House policy meetings. I also provided direct analytic support to the National Security Council and advised the director of national intelligence and his senior staff on key developments and emerging issues. My own evolution as an analyst coincided directly with Kim's rise to power. I worked with talented colleagues whose dedication to the national security mission and analytic rigor inspire me to this day, and I owe them a debt of gratitude for teaching me how to write, think, rethink, and lead by example. This book is grounded in that accumulated knowledge about the development of North Korea under this new leader and how he became the Kim Jong Un of today. It tells the history of the regime, including its nuclear crises, through an accessible biographical lens and uncovers its leader's aspirations, outlook, and sense of self, as well as his likely perception of North Korea's place in the world. I conclude with recommendations on how the United States and the global community should approach the North Korea problem.

———

AS THE SNOW FELL and the mournful band music droned on, the young successor led the funeral procession to the Kumsusan Memorial Palace, where his father's embalmed body would rest in perpetuity next to that of his grandfather. Kim's sister, Kim Yo Jong, stood near him, her face wan and shoulders slumped in sadness.

Kim Jong Un had succeeded in his first task—organizing and presiding over a well-orchestrated funeral in the way that his father had for Kim Il Sung.

Then he got to work as North Korea's new leader.

BECOMING KIM JONG UN

ONE

FROM TEN-FOOT-TALL BABY TO INTERNATIONAL STATESMAN

NORTH KOREA IS WHAT CIA analysts call "the hardest of the hard targets." The nuclear-armed country is an enduring national security threat, but the regime's opaqueness, self-imposed isolation, robust counterintelligence practices, and culture of fear and paranoia provide at best fragmentary information, impeding the agency's ability to inform, predict, and warn with a high level of confidence. Some of the most mundane pieces of information, such as birthdays of key regime leaders or the Kim family's whereabouts on any given day, are hard to verify or even obtain. Although North Korea has allowed foreign journalists into the country, their movements and reporting are tightly controlled and vetted. Kernels of what might have been truth are often buried under layers of regime mythmaking, rendering it indecipherable.

Hard target or not, this is our job at the CIA. Our mission is to warn policymakers about threats to our national security, highlight potential opportunities to advance U.S. interests, and sometimes "make the call"—give the president and other U.S. officials an answer stripped of nuance and caveat to assist them in making urgent decisions. We analyze a vast array of information, from classified to open source, incorporating our knowledge of the adversary's history, culture, language, and past negotiations with the United States. In the career section of its website, the CIA specifies how intelligence analysts "must quickly sift through data that is often inconsistent and incomplete. This is like putting together the pieces of a puzzle received at different times, from different places, and with pieces of other puzzles mixed in." Recruits must "connect the dots" because the country and the president rely on them to analyze the information and make objective assessments, many of which will have profound consequences for the direction of policy.

When it comes to North Korea analysis, it is especially difficult to fit the puzzle pieces together. You know what the completed picture should look like when you are working on a jigsaw puzzle. You can match colors and separate out the corners and the flat edges to build the outline. As the picture takes shape, it becomes progressively easier to finish the puzzle.

Connecting the dots seems simple enough. But how do you know which dots to connect and in what sequence? What do you do with a stray dot (or two or a dozen) that doesn't fit the big picture but seems to be outlining a different shape? Kim Jong Un's decision in early 2018 to meet with the leaders of South Korea, China, and the United States and his comments about wanting peace after years of self-imposed isolation and belligerent behavior are an example of dots that deviate from the existing contours; many analysts are left wondering about which dots are now the ones to follow.

Intelligence analysis is difficult, and it's not intuitive. The analyst has to be comfortable with ambiguity and contradictions, constantly training her mind to question assumptions, consider alternative hypotheses and scenarios, and make the call in the absence of sufficient information, often in high-stakes situations, so that policymakers at the top rungs of our government can make decisions about our national security.

I soon learned that a CIA analyst's training is a never-ending process. My Langley colleagues and I were required to take courses to improve our thinking and cultivate habits that reduced the potential for overconfidence and complacency in our analysis. Walk into any current or former CIA analyst's office and you will find *Psychology of Intelligence Analysis,* a slim purple book by Richards Heuer, who worked at the CIA for forty-five years in both operations and analysis. Heuer's focus is on how intelligence analysts can overcome, or at least recognize and manage, the "weaknesses and biases" in their thinking processes. One of his key points is that analysts tend to perceive what they *expect* to perceive, and "patterns of expectations tell analysts, subconsciously, what to look for, what is important, and how to interpret what is seen." An analyst's established mindset predisposes her to think in certain ways and affects the way she incorporates new information.

Heuer's book is pretty much the bible for our line of work. It was presented to us during our first courses as new CIA officers and often referred to in subsequent training. It still sits on my shelf at the Brookings Institution, within arm's reach. When I happen to glance at the purple book, I am reminded about how humility is inherent in intelligence analysis—especially in studying a hard target like North Korea. It forces me to confront my doubts, remind myself about how I know what I know and what I don't know, weigh evidence, calculate my confidence level in my assessments, and evaluate how those unknowns might change my perspective.

KIM JONG UN: CRAZY FAT KID OR FEARLESS GIANT?

What, then, are the expectations and perceptions that we need to overcome to form an accurate assessment of Kim Jong Un and his regime? When the focus is on Kim's appearance, there is a tendency to portray him as a cartoon figure. The over-the-top rhetoric from North Korea's state media, Kim's own often outrageous statements, and the hyperbolic imagery and boastful platitudes perpetuated by the ubiquitous socialist art and architecture have all made it too easy to reduce Kim to caricature. The baby fat still apparent on his then twentysomething-year-old face, an unflattering haircut that made waves—so to speak—in the Western press, and shapeless jackets and voluminous too-short trousers that did little to hide his girth only fed the media narrative that this was a kid who should not be taken seriously. Kim has been called—including by U.S. presidents and other elected officials—"Little Rocket Man," "sick puppy," "crazy fat kid," and "Pyongyang's pig boy." An article in *The Washington Post* on December 23, 2011—just a few days after Kim Jong Un took up his deceased father's mantle of leadership—quoted a neuroscientist who suggested that Kim's brain had not fully matured. According to this expert, the frontal part of the brain, which is important in "restraining impulses and making long-term plans," has not quite finished growing and developing in one's midtwenties. This was frightening news, given the fact that a man with an apparently underdeveloped brain controlled his country's nuclear arsenal.

Indeed, there is a veritable industry of North Korea humor. The blog Kim Jong Un Looking at Things is made up entirely of photos of Kim, well, looking at things in various locations—a shoe factory, a fishery, a lubricant machine factory churning out what looks like greasy soft-serve ice cream—as he gives his now-familiar "on-the-spot guidances." There's Kim on top of a mountain, looking valiantly and pensively into the sunset. There's Kim majestically posing on a stallion. On January 18, 2016, soon after North Korea's fourth nuclear test—Kim's second as leader, and what he claimed to be the country's first hydrogen bomb detonation, more destructive than an atomic blast—he was portrayed as a chubby baby on the cover of *The New Yorker,* playing with his "toys": nuclear weapons, ballistic missiles, and tanks. The imagery suggests that like a child he is prone to tantrums and erratic behavior, unable to make rational choices, and liable to get himself and others into trouble.

A corollary assumption stemming from his youth was the idea that he was a reformer at heart and that because of his age his approach to the outside world could be shaped by external powers through engagement. When Kim Jong Il ascended to power in the early 1980s, the outside world had also speculated that he might be a reformer interested in modernizing his country. Citing an East

German embassy assessment from 1982, Don Oberdorfer, a *Washington Post* reporter and author of the book *The Two Koreas,* wrote that Kim endorsed more fashionable clothing choices and greater consumption of alcohol. These early signs turned out to be merely cosmetic changes, not indicators that the regime was looking to make fundamental reforms.

There were more tantalizing signs that Kim Jong Un yearned to integrate North Korea into the international community and free his country from the isolation that the regime had deepened over sixty-five years. Unlike his grandfather and his father, Kim had been educated for a few years in Switzerland. North Korean media released a video that showed him at a concert in Pyongyang in which Disney characters romped around the stage while video clips of *Dumbo* and *Snow White and the Seven Dwarfs* were projected onto massive screens, and a group of skimpily clad women played the violin. He also appeared in public with his wife, Ri Sol Ju, a first for a North Korean leader; Kim's father and grandfather avoided being seen in public with their wives or revealing too much about their personal lives. Each of these gestures was interpreted as a hopeful sign that Kim wanted to take North Korea in a new direction. His engagement with China, South Korea, and the United States since January 2018 has revived this line of thinking, even amid fresh reports about North Korea's progress in its ballistic missile and nuclear programs. Observers find the cognitive dissonance of Kim's actions both disconcerting and promising.

But pitted against this hope is the sense that we are certainly heading toward catastrophe. When one considers the frighteningly rapid advancement of North Korea's cyber, nuclear, and conventional capabilities, the countless rows of soldiers marching in impossible unity at military parades, and the belligerent threats, Kim is suddenly no longer the crazy fat kid but a ten-foot-tall giant with untold and unlimited power: unstoppable, unpredictable, undeterrable, omnipotent. His intercontinental ballistic missiles can reach Los Angeles. He threatened to turn the Blue House, South Korea's presidential residence, into a "sea of fire." He has a million-man army ready to march south to force reunification. He has dozens of nuclear weapons at his disposal. He called the U.S. president "mentally deranged" and threatened nuclear war.

KIM THE ENIGMA

Just as the drumbeat of a potential second war on the Korean Peninsula reached a crescendo in late 2017, following North Korea's brazen testing of intercontinental ballistic missiles, its largest ever nuclear test, and the ensuing war of words with President Trump, Kim decided to pivot toward diplomacy in 2018. Even as he vowed to mass-produce nuclear weapons in his annual New Year's address, he also expressed an interest in attending the Winter Olympics. For the first time since the division of the peninsula in 1945, a Kim family member set foot in South Korea—his sister, Kim Yo Jong. That breakthrough quickly set in motion a series of high-level summits with President Xi Jinping of China, President Moon Jae-in of South Korea, and President Donald Trump of the United States—the first between a North Korean leader and a sitting U.S. president.

In his pivot to engagement—and under intense media scrutiny of his every move—Kim transformed himself from a ten-foot-tall baby to a real, live human being, who walks, talks, and goes to meetings like everyone else. As we glean new insights from observing him without the soft, propagandistic filter of North Korea's media, the Kim puzzle pieces multiply. There he is sipping tea with President Moon, listening intently to President Xi, and delivering remarks to reporters in Singapore while sitting next to President Trump, as if he had been doing it all for years. He has a sense of humor. He dines with his wife like any other husband. He goes sightseeing in Singapore and takes selfies. He talks about wanting peace and prosperity for his people and the Korean Peninsula.

But the summitry of 2018 has led to passionate debates about Kim's intentions. His international debut has buoyed those with more dovish tendencies who have argued that Washington needs to alter its policy and provide security guarantees and economic benefits to slowly wean Pyongyang away from its nuclear weapons. Voices across the political spectrum have applauded the improvements in inter-Korean ties, celebrating the two Korean leaders' roles as primary drivers of the region's trajectory without Washington's interference. Longtime Korea watchers have maintained that Kim's engagement tactics are nothing more than sleight of hand to divert attention from North Korea's possession and ongoing development of ballistic missiles and production of fissile material, and to weaken the international appetite for sanctions implementation. Most former government officials and seasoned veterans of negotiations with North Korea agree that Kim is highly unlikely to give up his arsenal unless and until he believes that his commitment to nuclear weapons will risk his own survival.

What is clear from Kim's gambit is that he controls which puzzle pieces we get to fit together and which dots appear and then disappear. Kim's new visibility has forced me and many others—including, I suspect, my former colleagues in the intelligence community—to check our key assumptions. Are we too burdened by the history of failed negotiations and North Korean prevarication to have a clear perspective on current developments? Is Kim Jong Un as a leader fundamentally different from his grandfather and his father, both of whom tried to keep North Korea sealed off? Are those who tout engagement with North Korea and giving Kim the benefit of the doubt—including President Trump, who called him "honorable"—falling prey to what Richards Heuer called "vividness bias," in which direct interaction with Kim is given greater value than the other types of evidence to the contrary about Kim's intentions?

The stakes are high. Whether Kim is an overgrown baby or an aspiring international statesman hungry for regional peace has tremendous implications for our national and global security. We simultaneously underestimate and overestimate Kim's capabilities, conflate his capabilities with his intentions, and question his rationality, while assuming that he possesses a strategic purpose and the means to achieve his goals. It is precisely because of North Korea's ambiguity and Kim's manipulation of it that we continue to work on the puzzle that is his regime. Unless we understand the real Kim, the roots of the dynasty that shaped his outlook, and his personality and ambitions, we risk making policy decisions that could undermine our goal of a denuclearized North Korea.

■

TWO

GUERRILLAS AND GODS

KIM JONG UN WAS ten when his grandfather Kim Il Sung died from a heart attack on a sultry day in July 1994. For nearly fifty of his eighty-two years, the senior Kim had presided over North Korea as the father of the country. The personality cult of Kim Il Sung was deeply entrenched, and his son Kim Jong Il was recognized as the only legitimate heir to the revolution. "To North Koreans, Kim Il-sung was more than just a leader," wrote Bradley Martin, one of Kim's biographers. "He showered his people with fatherly love." It was clear that Kim had become a religion. The North Korean people genuinely believed in his greatness, and as the CIA's top North Korea analyst Helen-Louise Hunter described it in her 1999 book, *Kim Il-song's North Korea,* "like many religious believers, they may have their doubts, but they hold fast to the faith in spite of these doubts."

The spirit of Kim Il Sung seeped into every aspect of a North Korean's life. It touched all of the senses. His portrait was in every home, office, store, classroom, and building. Operas, musicals, and television shows proclaimed his genius; thousands of monuments and museums ensured that North Korean citizens were in constant touch with his spirit and totally surrounded by it. He was in their food and the air they breathed—and, they believed, it was his agrarian experiments that had resulted in bounty (never mind the generous amounts of aid that flowed from the Soviet Union, China, and the socialist bloc, especially East Germany). Of course, it was his martial prowess and brilliance that had liberated the Korean Peninsula from the Japanese imperialists and returned the land to the peasants and proletariat. He was the *suryong,* the Supreme Leader, and North Korea's "heart and the only center." His birthday, April 15, was declared a national holiday in the 1960s, taking on a Christmas-like atmosphere with festivals, fireworks, and gifts distributed by the state. Even in death, the "Eternal President" managed to transcend time: The North Korean calendar was revised to begin in 1912, the year of his birth, which became Year 1. The cult of Kim Il Sung was not a natural phenomenon, however; it took decades of careful indoctrination.

The anguished cries of "Father" heard at Kim Il Sung's funeral reflected the regime's success in crafting and reinforcing a personality cult and a paternalist state. In this "family," the father's authority is paramount, while his love and benevolence are unquestioned. In exchange, the children must be loyal, respectful, and act only in the interest of the family and the father, subsuming the self in the higher collective good. Kim had the legitimate power to punish children who were disloyal, or not loyal enough, and also to help the children redeem themselves. After all, without Kim Il Sung, they as a nation and as a people would not exist, which schoolchildren learned in their textbooks and through lectures about their "father's" heroic deeds and adventures.

Because children tend to believe in legends more than adults do, to ten-year-old Kim Jong Un his grandfather was probably larger than life. But unlike other children, Kim must have felt the revolutionary blood coursing through his veins and experienced not only pride but also a sense of reflected greatness by virtue of his birth and biology. It must have been overwhelming, like knowing you were related to George Washington or Abraham Lincoln or Santa Claus or Jesus Christ.

Luckily for Kim Jong Un, his grandfather laid the spiritual, ideological, and physical foundations of power, using brutal repression when necessary. But as successful as he was, Kim Il Sung probably could not have become a god without having been a guerrilla first.

KOREA UNDER SIEGE

Today the United States considers North Korea to be a top national security priority, but fifty years ago, most Americans would have dismissed such a concept: that a country about the size of Mississippi or Pennsylvania (and half the area of the United Kingdom), 6,700 miles away from Washington, D.C., could be the focus of geopolitical concern and a primary source of tension in Northeast Asia.

Before 1945 there was no North or South Korea—just one nation on a peninsula that juts off eastern China, with Russia to its north, separated from the Japanese archipelago by the sea to the east. An American missionary who arrived in 1885, when Korea was still a sovereign country, though besieged by its more powerful neighbors, felt as if he had been suddenly transported back to the Middle Ages. Another missionary mused that Korea seemed to be "2,000 years removed from the twentieth century." Isabella Bird Bishop, an intrepid British explorer, was shocked by Korea's overwhelming stench and squalor. The "meanness" of Seoul, the capital city, was indescribable, and her description of conditions was uncharitable.

> An estimated quarter of a million people are living "on the ground," chiefly in labyrinthine alleys, many of them not quite wide enough for two loaded bulls to pass . . . and further narrowed by a series of vile holes or green, slimy ditches, which receive the solid and liquid refuse of the houses, their foul and fetid margins being the favourite resort of half-naked children, begrimed in dirt, and of big,

mangy, bleary-eyed dogs, which wallow in the slime or blink in the
sun.

Paradoxically, impressions of Korea included not only negative
conditions but also romanticized attributes. American missionaries,
eager to inject optimism into their readers back home—in part to
encourage donations—argued that the Koreans were kind people,
hospitable to a fault, a population ripe for Christ. The land itself,
they claimed, was truly God's creation, with abundant flora and
fauna. Boasting of the advance of Christianity, Horace Underwood,
one of the first American missionaries to Korea, wrote in 1908,
"Veritably it has seemed like a chapter from the Acts of the Apos-
tles."

It was this understanding of Korea—backward but pliant and
eager for tutelage—that justified its status as a geopolitical football
and ultimately as a colony of Japan, which Bishop described as neat
and clean compared with Korean streets littered with decaying garbage. The Japanese legation's compound within Seoul's walls was
"in acute contrast to everything Korean," with its neat and bustling
shops and clean and dainty houses "where thrift reigns supreme."

For the first half of the twentieth century, Korea was a battle-
ground on which China, Russia, Japan, and Western powers fought
for domination using economic, political, and military means. Japan
clashed with China in the First Sino-Japanese War of 1894–95 and
then with Russia in 1904–5 over control of Korea. Throughout its
history, Korea has attempted to fend off foreign invasions, driving
away Westerners, ignoring Japan, and maintaining lukewarm ties
to China, earning its moniker "the hermit kingdom." However, as
nations sought markets and hegemony in the nineteenth century,
this imperialist impulse added to Korea's own domestic problems.
Peasant rebellions, soldier revolts, intellectual ferment, and failed
attempts at reform led to the peninsula's eventual colonization by
Japan from 1910 to 1945.

The United States helped lay the groundwork for the Japanese
annexation of Korea in the second year of the Russo-Japanese War,

when President Theodore Roosevelt recognized Japan's domination of Korea in the secret Taft-Katsura Agreement of July 1905, in part to check Russian expansionism and to gain Tokyo's recognition of U.S. control of the Philippines. Roosevelt's entrusting Japan to take control of Korea reflected his overall favorable impression of the country. For the U.S. president, Japan, with its evident modernization, representative Diet, written constitution, and military mettle, was superior among the Asians. Roosevelt went on to win the Nobel Peace Prize in 1906 for his role in mediating the Treaty of Portsmouth, which ended the Russo-Japanese War but ushered in four decades of brutal Japanese colonization of the Korean Peninsula.

The crucible of Japanese domination of Korea and the ensuing Japanese quest for military and political domination of East Asia gave rise to Kim Il Sung.

THE BIRTH AND ASCENT OF A GUERRILLA

North Korea's Eternal President was born Kim Song Ju—Kim Il Sung was his nom de guerre—in Pyongyang, just two years after annexation by Japan in 1910. His father, Kim Hyong Jik, was born in 1894 during the last throes of the Joseon dynasty and before Korea succumbed to foreign powers; he married Kim's mother, Kang Pan Sok, when he was fifteen years old and she was seventeen.

Like many other Koreans who railed against Japanese colonialism, Kim Hyong Jik joined the independence movement and was punished for his activism. His son would witness both his beloved father and his uncle go to jail for their nationalist activities and suffer the effects of their incarceration. Kim recalled his first visit to the prison, "a place of death and deadly venom." He hardly recognized his father; every visible part of his body was swollen and bruised. Profoundly affected by the sight, Kim wrote in his memoir that seeing his father in prison was one of the most significant moments of his life, and that the "scars and wounds on Father's body pained me physically and I swore to get even with the Japanese devils, that were not human beings at all, but Satan." To honor the patriarch of the family, Kim swore to "give his all to the struggle to liberate the country at any cost."

Given the political and economic environment of the time, Kim's parents had short, difficult lives—his father died at thirty-one and his mother at forty. They left little money to support their children. But whatever legitimate connection the Kims had to the nationalist and revolutionary fervor of the time, their son amplified their roles and that of his entire lineage; for example, he claimed that his great-grandfather had participated in the fight to repel the ill-fated U.S. merchant ship *General Sherman,* which was attacked and destroyed in Pyongyang in 1866 when it attempted to open the country to trade, and that his grandfather had fought against imperial Japan.

Although Kim Il Sung's image and history have been polished and embellished in the regime's hagiography, by all objective accounts he was a bona fide Korean nationalist fighter, a ruthless killer of the hated Japanese, one of several leaders who gained fame and followers during that fraught period in Korea's history. He earned his reputation as an efficient killer of Japanese police and soldiers in Manchuria, which had been occupied since 1931. During the 1930s and '40s, he led guerrilla bands of fifty to three hundred men through hot and humid summers and icy, brutally cold winters. Kim and his brigade of Chinese and Koreans reportedly killed the leader of the Japanese Special Police, who had been trying to track him down in Manchuria, along with scores of Japanese officers and other law enforcement personnel.

The historian Bruce Cumings has noted that Kim "represented a younger generation of revolutionary nationalists filled with contempt for the failures of their fathers and determined to forge a Korea that could resist foreign domination." In his memoir of more than two thousand pages, Kim put it this way:

My life began in the 1910s when Korea had suffered the worst tragic calamities. By the time I was born, Korea was already under the Japanese colonial rule. . . . The Korean people seethed with anger and wept with sorrow over the loss of their nationhood. . . . Korea in those days was a living Hell, unfit for human habitation. The Korean people were, in all aspects, walking stiffs; their spirits were dead.

This massive volume, published just before his death, takes on an almost Homeric rhythm, recounting the heroics of Kim and his followers, the depths of his despair as he shivered without a blanket on the Manchurian battlefield, and the heights of his optimism when encountering the kindness of villagers. His stories are captivating and graphic, highlighting the smells and sounds of battles, the broken bodies, the cruelty against Koreans—eyes pierced by sharpened sticks, fingers and heads cut off by roving bandits or as punishment for revolutionary activities, decapitated heads staked as a warning to others. "It was my misfortune," he wrote, "to be born in an era of evil events and to grow up seeing the worst of the Japanese savagery. These left indelible marks on my memory and shaped my future activities." Having experienced repression and witnessed brutality from an early age, Kim raged at the "elite of Korea" who let the nation fall.

While other nations went about in mighty warships and rode shiny trains, our feudal leaders rode filthy scrawny donkeys wearing horse-hair hats and wasted several hundred years in a stale state of stupor and suffocating economic stagnation. They kowtowed to foreign gunboat diplomacy and opened up the gate for foreign invasion and exploitation; Korea became an easy prey for the imperialists.

But rather than confront the Japanese troops who were determined to root out Korean guerrillas—many of whom perished—Kim and his small group of fighters fled to the Soviet Union in 1940, where he studied under Soviet military officers and rose to the rank of captain in the Red Army's Eighty-eighth Brigade. Although Kim apparently spent World War II in a rear unit far away from the

fighting—in contrast to the regime narrative of his fearless and re-
lentless assault against Japanese forces—at the tender age of thirty-
three, the chubby-faced, ambitious, brutal, anti-Japanese guerrilla
triumphantly returned to North Korea intent on becoming its new
leader.

After intense jockeying among other Korean nationalists, Kim
was installed as the leader of the northern half of the Korean Peninsula by the Soviet Union in 1945, when it was provisionally divided
along the thirty-eighth parallel, with the United States controlling
the southern half. The division was arbitrary, cutting across seventy-
five streams, twelve rivers, more than a hundred country roads,
eight highways, and six rail lines, according to the U.S. Army's history of the war in Korea. He had been away from Korea for twenty
years, but as a native of Pyongyang, the charismatic Kim, with his
nationalist and Communist credentials—but not least because of his
apparent loyalty to the Soviet Union—fit the bill for Moscow. Kim
declared the founding of the Democratic People's Republic of Korea
on September 9, 1948, after purging potential challengers, organizing a robust surveillance and security apparatus to root out dissent,
engaging in systematic violence, and adopting reeducation programs to ensure his domination. He was no mere Soviet puppet,
however, and the fact that he was a survivor, a savvy political opera-
tor, and an able manipulator of Beijing and Moscow contributed to
his ascendance and longevity.

Fresh from the fields of combat, flush with the new powers that
he'd wrested from his challengers, and confident about the support
of his Soviet backers, Kim sought to reunify the Korean Peninsula.
Perhaps his still youthful exuberance contributed to this confidence,
or he saw an opportunity to make his bid before the division fully
gelled, or he was driven by a messianic zeal that only he could make
Korea whole again. It was probably all of these things. Indeed, the
international environment seemed to support his conviction that he
had freedom of action. Washington's interests lay in the Western
Hemisphere, including reconstructing Europe and limiting the ex-
pansion of the Soviet Union; it did not view the security of South

Korea as a strategic concern. George Kennan, the architect of the postwar containment policy, argued in 1948 that the United States should "get out of [Korea] as gracefully but promptly as possible." His conclusion that the peninsula held no strategic interest was later shared by Secretary of State Dean Acheson and the Joint Chiefs of Staff. From Kim's perspective, Communism seemed to be on the winning side of history, while Europe was in tatters. Mao Zedong and the Chinese Communists finally prevailed in their civil war, defeating the Nationalists led by Chiang Kai-shek in 1949. The Soviet Union successfully detonated an atomic bomb that same year, elevating itself as a nuclear power alongside the United States.

For Kim Il Sung, the time seemed ripe to unify the divided Korean Peninsula under Communism.

KIM'S HUBRIS

North Korea attacked the South on June 25, 1950. One hundred thirty-five thousand well-equipped and well-trained Korean People's Army troops, many thousands of them veterans of the Manchuria guerrilla campaign, poured south of the thirty-eighth parallel and easily captured Seoul within three days. By the end of that summer, the North Korean army had taken control of almost all of South Korea, except for a small corner of land in Busan, on the southeast coast of the peninsula. Just a week before the invasion, the CIA had provided strategic warning about North Korea's intentions to invade and that the North had the military superiority to overwhelm the South to achieve "its main external aim of extending control over southern Korea." President Truman ordered U.S. troops into action, and within three months the United Nations forces had outflanked Kim's armies and begun a drive northward past the thirty-eighth parallel. That was enough to trigger a reaction from China; over the course of the conflict, the newly established Communist nation would deploy as many as three million troops in support of North Korea. On July 27, 1953, an armistice was signed, and the first "hot war" of the emerging Cold War ended in a stalemate that deepened the division of the Korean Peninsula and cemented the U.S. commitment to defend South Korea. As the Pulitzer Prize–winning journalist David Halberstam concluded in his book *The Coldest Winter,* "Korea was a place where almost every key decision on both sides turned on a miscalculation."

Miscalculation based on false assumptions and hubris led to the brutal conflict, and those actions taken seven decades ago still resonate today. Kim Il Sung thought his army would be met by cheering crowds, sparking a revolution, and he and his Soviet sponsors calculated that the United States would not fight back. Not heeding Chinese warnings or the presence of Chinese fighters on the battlefield, a confident United States led by General Douglas MacArthur pushed north of the thirty-eighth parallel, toward the Yalu River, eliciting a massive Chinese counteroffensive that pushed the U.S. and South Korean armies to retreat southward. The Chinese offensive and the escalation of the war in the winter of 1950 placed political pressure on President Truman to consider using the atomic bomb to keep the conflict short and contained. General MacArthur was a strong advocate of deploying the bomb, even in China, and openly challenged Truman's authority. Despite MacArthur's removal for repeated insubordination, Truman kept the nuclear option on the table well into 1951.

The war's casualty figures speak only superficially to the human toll and tragedy. Nearly three million Koreans—10 percent of the overall population of the two Koreas—were dead, missing, or injured. Around 900,000 Chinese fighters, 500,000 North Korean soldiers, and 400,000 United Nations Command troops were killed or wounded. Nearly 34,000 U.S. troops lost their lives, with about 110,000 wounded, missing, or captured. All actors committed atrocities, including mass executions of political prisoners and the killing of civilians. North Korea abducted South Koreans and conscripted them into the North Korean army, while people at home whom the regime considered anti-Communist were executed. The United States dropped more bombs on North Korea than it had in the entire Pacific theater in World War II. The historian Charles Armstrong wrote that the U.S. Air Force used 635,000 tons of bombs on Korea compared with 503,000 tons during World War II in the Pacific. Even battle-hardened General MacArthur, shortly after he was relieved of his duties by Truman, testified in the Senate, "I have never seen such devastation. I have seen . . . as much blood and disaster as any living man, and it just curdled my stomach, the last time I was there. After I looked at that wreckage and those thousands of women and children and everything, I vomited." A veteran of the Korean War who was involved in the infamous massacre at No Gun Ri—where American soldiers killed hundreds of Korean civilians—decades later recalled, "On summer nights, when the breeze is blowing, I can still hear their cries, the little kids screaming."

The war destroyed everything in North Korea. American bombings leveled factories, hospitals, schools, roads, homes, dams, farms, and government offices; by 1952, there was nothing left to bomb. As Armstrong argued, the three years of B-29 raids—and the fear of Washington's potential use of the atomic bomb—were etched deeply into the collective consciousness of North Koreans, and this sense of anxiety and fear of outside threats would continue for decades after the war. Millions of people were displaced, families searched desperately for missing loved ones, and orphans cried over their parents' lifeless bodies as barely pubescent teens found themselves responsible for their younger siblings. The July 1953 ceasefire brought a close to the fighting—which Kim claimed the United States had ignited—but technically left the two Koreas at war to this day and made permanent the cruel separation of families.

While people lived in tunnels and caves to escape the bombings, Kim Il Sung was busy packaging the devastation and death as a victory in the "Fatherland Liberation War," claiming success in expelling the U.S. imperialists and South Korean toadies who "trampled underfoot and burnt everything in all quarters . . . butchered innocent people en masse [and] kicked children and pregnant women into the flames and buried old folks alive." If there was failure, it wasn't his fault but that of those who were not sufficiently faithful to the revolutionary spirit as embodied in his Manchurian guerrilla experience. The North Korean people believed this. They had witnessed and suffered through the attacks and trusted that their only savior was Kim Il Sung. But then again, they had no choice but to accept the regime's account and to help rebuild the country.

So, by the time he turned forty, according to the regime narrative, Kim Il Sung had been solely responsible for ousting the Japanese imperialists from the Korean Peninsula. He had routed the American "jackals" and the South Korean "puppets" in Seoul, wrapping himself in savior mythology. Sung-Yoon Lee, a professor at Tufts University's Fletcher School of Law and Diplomacy, wrote that Kim Il Sung "even in failing to achieve his ultimate goal— liberate the South and unify the peninsula under his rule— profoundly 'revised' the geostrategic importance of the Korean Peninsula from a minor, forgotten outpost on the tip of the Asian mainland to a major powder keg on a key strategic strip of land in Northeast Asia." Lee added that Kim's belligerent approach over the decades of his rule only inspired his patrons in Beijing and Moscow to "placate him with bigger blandishments."

Kim Il Sung also certainly learned some valuable lessons from the Korean War. The United States now considered the Korean Peninsula a strategic national security interest, determining that it would defend South Korea with military force, if necessary. It also became apparent that China would fight back against U.S. encroachment. Kim now realized that North Korea's position among China, the Soviet Union, and the United States presented him with an opportunity to turn the powerful players against one another to Pyongyang's advantage.

Yet the disastrous war and his country's reliance on China— which took leadership of the conflict and stationed forces in North Korea until 1958—required Kim to intensify his efforts to cement his control. In the mid- to late 1950s, Kim reinforced his campaign to make himself the sole leader of North Korea, purging suspected challengers for "disloyalty" and wiping out mention of the role of the Chinese People's Volunteer Army in defending the regime,

while purging, exiling, or executing pro-China and pro-Soviet officials. The backing of Joseph Stalin had made it easier for Kim to
create a highly personalized autocracy, but the denunciation by the
new Soviet leader, Nikita Khrushchev, of his predecessor's personality cult, reign of terror, and failed policies augured problems for
Kim. As documented by the Russian scholar Andrei Lankov, in
1956, during what would be the only significant internal challenge
to Kim Il Sung, top North Korean party members aligned with the
post-Stalin Soviet Union and China united to condemn Kim for his
amassing of power, accusing him of being responsible for straying
from socialism for his personal benefit. When Kim continued to
purge his opposition, Moscow and Beijing further intervened by
sending a delegation to press Kim to reverse the purge and restore
his government's pro-Soviet and pro-China North Korean blocs.
But that just gave Kim the latitude to label his opponents as factionalists and therefore tainted by foreign influence.

At the same time, Kim was realistic about his dependence on the
largesse of Moscow and Beijing. He cajoled his way out of trouble,
pledging to make improvements to mollify their concerns. Kim also
recognized that his patrons' nervousness about North Korea's stability, Pyongyang's position as a bastion of Communism in East Asia,
and the Sino-Soviet split in 1956 over doctrine and the two powers'
diverging geopolitical interests allowed him the freedom to maneu-
ver and assert his autonomy. Driven by self-importance, nationalism, paranoia, and venal opportunism, Kim seized the occasion to
fortify his rule and to set off on his own ideological course—what
the professor of Korean studies James Person called an "indigenous
version of Marxism-Leninism."

BUILDING THE CULT OF KIM IL SUNG
In a 1955 speech, Kim introduced his concept of Korean-style socialism and began to indoctrinate the population in the notion of *juche,*
roughly meaning self-reliance, aimed at solidifying his rule. For
one, he used it to highlight his "Korean-ness" and the opposition's

impurity and presumed subservience to foreign powers and to bolster his self-declared position as the *suryong,* the unitary leader of North Korea. Second, *juche* justified hardships and motivated the people to work with greater zeal to rebuild the country after the war and channeled North Korean nationalism and xenophobia toward a worship of Kim as the defender of their way of life. Externally, Kim's assertion of his country's autonomy, but without breaking from the socialist camp, allowed him to pit Moscow and Beijing against each other, flattering and deferring to his more powerful neighbors when it was conducive to extracting more aid.

Juche and *suryong* as they have evolved seem like a hodgepodge of existing concepts: Christianity (Kim had come from a Christian family, reflecting the missionary presence in Korea), filial piety, the hierarchy and familial relationships of Confucianism, and Communism (especially Stalinism and the cult of personality). But at the same time, the intensely nationalist bent of Kim's *juche* was a rejection of Stalinist internationalism, and his deification of the *suryong* shared commonalities with the imperial cult following the Meiji Restoration of the emperor that came to define Japan's prewar and wartime nationalist ethos. These ideas also reflected Kim's desire to create ideological and institutional walls to prevent outside interference and maintain his unitary leadership.

Perhaps Kim Il Sung's view of the world as a hostile place was a belief he could not have escaped, given the environment in which he was raised. Born into imperialism, he never experienced a sovereign, independent Korea or a stable home life because of his parents' early deaths. He knew hardship and deprivation, fear and uncertainty. In the struggle for national and individual survival—which often conflicted—it was difficult to know who was trustworthy. To outlast better-known and better-educated Korean nationalists, Kim had to coerce, cajole, steal, and kill on the political and military battlefields. He elevated his small circle of Manchurian guerrillas, endowing them with power and privilege, knitting together webs of political and military loyalty to ensure his primacy for the foreseeable future. Once in control, he restructured society and all aspects of its relationships, familial and institutional, to tighten his people's bond to their leader.

Beginning in the late 1950s, Kim's obsession with power and loyalty drove his regime's efforts to categorize every citizen by their *songbun,* or background, putting them in three general groups—the "core," "wavering," and "hostile" classes—based on whether they were loyal revolutionaries (the core) or landowners, capitalists, or collaborators of Japanese imperialism. This project required multiple government investigations to check every individual's background. These classifications were inherited and dictated what types of privileges one would be granted or denied. One's caste decided where one would go to school, whom one would marry, where one would work. It would be unwise, for example, to marry someone from a lower category because that would taint one's family and have an impact on the opportunities available to one's offspring. Thus, it was in the individual's interest to subsume personal desires and demonstrate loyalty to Kim in order to survive and thrive.

Yet in spite of the rigid classification system that Kim imposed on his citizens, he also believed education was an important tool for building a stable nation of followers devoted to him. From the very beginning, Kim focused on using education to craft regime narratives that elevated himself and his partisans, while teaching the masses proper socialist ideology. Over time, the education system focused less on Communism and shifted increasingly to the deification of Kim Il Sung, his family, and the guerrillas he fought alongside. The shift was particularly evident in the wake of Kim Jong Il's entry onto the political stage, when the son happily fed his father's appetite for accolades and vastly expanded the persona of the Kim family.

The founder's focus on children and education is indicative of the regime's calculated effort to raise good, loyal North Koreans. The CIA analyst Helen-Louise Hunter noted that North Korea's education system was intended, according to Kim Il Sung himself, to "serve the existing social system." Kang Chol-hwan, the prominent defector and author of *The Aquariums of Pyongyang: Ten Years in the North Korean Gulag,* remembered the 1960s of his childhood as happy. Kim Il Sung was "a kind of Father Christmas" who would send cakes and sweets and every third year would provide a school uniform, a cap, and a pair of shoes. His school curriculum included the usual arithmetic, music, and art, but above all children were taught to revere Kim Il Sung:

> We learn[ed] by rote answers to questions such as: On what day and at what hour was Kim Il-sung born? What heroic feats did he perform against the Japanese? What speech did he give at such-and-such a conference, on such-and-such date? Like my fellow pupils, I thought cramming myself with such important facts was perfectly normal, and doing it gave me great pleasure. An education of this sort resulted in a wellspring of admiration and gratitude for our political leaders and in the willingness to sacrifice everything for them and the homeland.

Hunter wrote that Kim's tireless crisscrossing of the country to meet as many people as he could—riding buses and subways, visiting collective farms, factories, and schools—showed "his special genius for establishing personal rapport with his people" and wooing them with his larger-than-life personality. A CIA document from January 1983 compared Kim's campaign to win hearts and minds to that of an American politician: "Thinking of North Korea as about the size of Pennsylvania, it is easy to imagine the relationship that a charismatic governor of such a state might develop with his people over a period of 40 years, if he spent 150–200 days on the road each year." Such efforts paid dividends by reinforcing the cult of personality and the lasting reverence that even North Korean defectors hold for the country's founder.

In Kim Il Sung's North Korea, it was also important for the children to be prepared to battle their external enemies. Kang recalled that like all his classmates, he joined the Pupils' Red Army. The children formed ranks and marched with fake machine guns. "Right away we felt we were Kim Il-sung's little soldiers," he wrote.

High schoolers, he added, had more serious training, as they "memorized emergency air-raid instructions, learned to hide from enemy planes, and to steer the population to the nearest air-raid shelters." Victor Cha, the former Asia adviser in the George W. Bush administration, has pointed out that North Korean children learn conjugation by reciting "We killed Americans," "We are killing Americans," and "We will kill Americans," and learn arithmetic by adding or subtracting the number of dead Americans.

This style of education has persisted through the generations. Yeonmi Park, a defector who was born in 1993, a year before Kim Il Sung died, said she and her classmates would line up during recess "to take turns beating or stabbing dummies dressed up like American soldiers." The process of dehumanizing and demonizing the United States bled into the language. Park recalled, "We could never just say 'American'—that would be too respectful. It had to be 'American bastard,' 'Yankee devil,' or 'big-nosed Yankee.' If you didn't say it, you would be criticized for being too soft on our enemies." The purpose of a Western education is to develop critical-thinking skills and cultivate civic-mindedness, as well as to prepare students to become productive members of the workforce and society; in contrast, a North Korean education is intended to instill doctrine, an unchanging and unyielding "truth" based on the Great Leader's definition of reality. He is the sole authority of moral behavior and the only source of enlightenment, both in Kim Il Sung's day and today, as his son and grandson have derived their legitimacy and authority through their blood ties to the country's founder.

The North Korean regime was triumphant, claiming to its people that they lived in a socialist paradise powered by their *juche* can-do spirit, but at the same time Koreans were a "uniquely vulnerable child race in the Leader's protective care," as described by the North Korea analyst B. R. Myers. And that childlike purity necessitated an education system that propagated a perpetual state of crisis to keep the dangerous and polluting outside forces at bay. The guerrilla wars of the Japanese occupation and the total war of the Korean conflict against the United States were replayed with zeal.

Nevertheless, their independence should not be taken for granted, as the external threats continued to loom, given the presence of U.S. troops just miles away along the Demilitarized Zone separating the two Koreas.

To young Kim Jong Un, his grandfather was a hero for the ages. By the time Kim Il Sung died, his ten-year-old grandson no doubt already recognized to some degree his part in North Korea's destiny. As famine loomed and millions faced starvation, no expense was spared for the pomp and circumstance of a pricey funeral—the embalming by Russian specialists alone reportedly cost $1 million, with an additional $800,000 per year for maintenance costs. For young Jong Un, a direct descendant of the Sun of Korea, heir to the anti-Japanese, anti-U.S. struggle, raised in a culture of paranoia, violence was a part of his grandfather's legacy. He would benefit from a political system that his grandfather designed and his father reinforced, placing him at the pinnacle of the social pyramid, with all of the accompanying entitlements. The country's survival—and the Kim family's legitimacy—depended on Jong Un's embrace of this reliance on violence and inherited privilege, for only then could this young guerrilla become a little god in service of his founder.

THREE

THE INHERITANCE

I N 1992, AT HIS eighth birthday party, Kim Jong Un dressed up not as Batman or Superman, as boys in the United States might, but as a little general in a uniform decorated with one star. Real generals wearing real uniforms with real stars bowed to him—something that a typical boy certainly would never expect. "It was impossible for him to grow up as a normal person when the people around him were treating him like that," his aunt Ko Yong Suk said in an interview with *The Washington Post* years after she and her family defected to the United States.

We don't know who gave Jong Un the made-to-order general's uniform. Perhaps it was a gift that Kim Jong Il bequeathed to all of his sons—he had at least three we know of, the other two being Jong Un's half-brother, Jong Nam, and his full brother, Jong Chol. Or perhaps it was a deliberate move by his ambitious mother, Ko Yong Hui, one of Kim Jong Il's favorite mistresses, who was probably seeking to elevate her two sons amid the likely jockeying for position behind the scenes. After all, by the time of this birthday celebration, Kim Jong Il had long been designated as his father's successor and it would have been a prudent move for Ko Yong Hui to position Jong Un and Jong Chol as the potential future heirs and assert their status above the generals.

But while Jong Un lived a life of privilege and ease in one of the Kim family's many villas and mansions, replete with servants, amenities, and toys, the country's future and Kim Jong Il's success as the new leader of North Korea were anything but guaranteed. North Koreans were no strangers to adversity, but in the early 1990s, Pyongyang faced economic, humanitarian, and security challenges, while its aging leader was planning for a potentially destabilizing succession of power to his eldest son. The collapse of the Soviet Union and the Communist bloc deepened North Korea's isolation even as it needed a continuous infusion of economic assistance. Its traditional allies and primary benefactors, Moscow and Beijing, were looking to strengthen ties to Washington and Seoul. South Korea had emerged by then as an economic powerhouse, having hosted the 1988 Olympics. North Korea's dire food situation was well on its way to disaster; in just a couple of years, a famine would kill between six hundred thousand and one million people, or 3 to 5 percent of the population, the result of decades of the regime's mismanagement of the economy and callous disregard for its people, exacerbated by extreme weather. Adding yet another dimension to this challenging environment was the brewing confrontation with the United States over North Korea's covert nuclear weapons program.

The child Jong Un would not have concerned himself with these problems. It was up to his father, Kim Jong Il, to learn how to play on this new strategic chessboard. Luckily, he had two decades of apprenticeship to a master who had ruled for nearly five decades and laid the foundations for the Communist world's first dynastic succession.

THE SUN AND THE RISING SON

The first few pages of Kim Jong Il's official biography have the flavor of the Book of Genesis, with its plethora of "begats" highlighting the genealogies of important individuals. Published in 1998, a respectable four years after the death of his father, the biography is plodding, lacking the drama and action of Kim Il Sung's guerrilla days and the heady years after liberation from Japan. There would be multiple official biographies over the course of his tenure, sharpening, revising, and embellishing Kim's superhuman exploits. Minus his father's military credentials, charisma, and good looks, and burdened by the uncertainty of an unprecedented hereditary succession in the Communist world, Kim Jong Il required an official biography that emphasized his bloodline and a genealogy—bolstered by mythology and semi-truths—to elevate his legitimacy as the new leader. The genealogical account of Kim's birth was most likely intended to imbue it with a sense of inevitability, a foreordained act of supernatural proportions, and to set him up as a key driver of the country's destiny and the only proper vehicle for the continuation of his father's will.

The 1998 biography highlighted Kim's impeccably patriotic family and his essential Korean-ness. Kim was born on Mount Paektu, a significant location in Korea's history, on February 16, 1942. His father was "the father of the Korean nation," his mother was a "communist revolutionary fighter . . . who devoted her whole life to the struggle for the restoration of the country and the freedom and happiness of the people." His grandfather, a "leader of the anti-Japanese national liberation movement, was a pioneer in shifting the direction from the nationalist movement to the communist movement in Korea." His grandmother and uncles were "revolutionary fighters who dedicated their lives to the cause of national restoration." Myths that were supposed to be taken as truth or believed as an article of faith peppered official accounts of his birth: a double rainbow and a new star appeared in the sky; a swallow foretold it. Kim was walking when he was three weeks old and talking by eight weeks; he could change the weather by making marks on a map. Official biographies claimed that even as a kindergartner Kim "had a thorough knowledge of the globe" and stood by his father's side during the Korean War providing counsel while American planes swarmed overhead and bombs rained down. In her haunting memoir, Yeonmi Park recalled that she and her classmates learned that Kim Jong Il had supernatural powers: He wrote fifteen hundred books as a college student, and, when he was very young, covered the road with sand to make it a smooth ride for his father. "Even when he was a child," she wrote, "he was an amazing tactician, and when he played military games, his team always won because he came up with brilliant new strategies every time." She and her classmates, like good little soldiers, also played military games, "but nobody ever wanted to be on the American imperialist team, because they would always have to lose the battle."

But Kim Jong Il wasn't born in 1942 on Mount Paektu. The Kims' first son had a Russian nickname—Yura—and he was probably born in 1941 in a Russian military camp in Siberia, where Kim Il Sung was in the Eighty-eighth Brigade. In the early 1980s, the regime changed his birth year to 1942 to better align with 1912, the year of his father's birth.

Jong Il's mother, Kim Jong Suk, was a guerrilla, a member of the women's unit in the fight against the Japanese, though not a supernatural figure, as regime hagiography portrays her. Jong Suk married Kim Il Sung in 1940 and was his first recognized wife. She was a teenager when she joined Kim's unit in 1935 and worked as a kitchen helper; at one point she was arrested by the Japanese for stealing food and supplies. Although Jong Suk suffered through the indignity of her husband's wandering eye and his previous marriage, Kim Il Sung in his memoirs extolled his wife's compassion, faithfulness, and devotion. "She snatched me from the jaws of death on several occasions," he wrote admiringly. She dried his clothes against her warm body and cut off her hair to line her husband's boots to keep his feet warm. And she never wavered in her revolutionary zeal, nor assumed an equal status with Kim Il Sung, whom she called Commander or Premier. In a 1999 interview, her contemporary Lee Min called Jong Suk "quite a beauty. . . . Her face was that of a princess but her complexion was dark on account of her many years in the field. Her eyebrows were black and her eyelashes were long, making her truly attractive." Lee added that Jong Suk was "quick, generous and had many talents" and contributed to morale by cooking, sewing, and acting and singing in shows that Kim Il Sung produced while he was in Siberia. Less flattering accounts of her claim she was "an illiterate with a dogged character."

Kim Jong Il's early childhood was disrupted by the Korean War and marked by twin tragedies: His brother, nicknamed Shura, died in 1947 at the age of three, and just two years later his mother succumbed to complications of childbirth—she was only thirty-one. Eight-year-old Jong Il was devastated; his younger sister, Kyong Hui, was still a toddler. A year or so later, when the war made the country too dangerous for the Kim family, Jong Il and his sister had to move out of their home in Pyongyang, ultimately settling in China. It didn't help these two small children who had just lost their mother and the comforts of home when their father quickly married Kim Song Ae, more than a decade his junior, with whom he had been having an affair while Jong Suk was alive. They had two sons who competed with Jong Il for their father's attention. Jong Il reportedly complained later in life that he had had a lonely childhood because his father was so busy. He initially refused to call his father's new wife "mother" and spent more time at his paternal uncle's house. The situation was frustrating for the Great Leader, who reportedly grumbled, "My whole attention is given to playing mediator between my wife and my son. . . . He bursts in fury at his stepmother and even at me."

Nevertheless, Kim 2.0 enjoyed all of the privileges and deference that came with being the first son of the country's top leader. By every account, the Kims lived in luxury. Despite the wholesomeness that the regime attributed to Kim Il Sung, lauding his sacrifices and suffering for the people, he quickly settled into a life of comfort and ease more typical of an authoritarian who had absolute power and all of his country's resources at his disposal. By the 1960s, North Korea had benefited from a decade of generous economic aid from the Soviet Union, China, and the Eastern European countries, and members of the Kim family undoubtedly appropriated large sums to satisfy their avarice. The most prominent member of the regime's inner circle to defect in the 1990s, Hwang Jang Yop, reported that Kim and his family had "special royal villas"—possibly a hundred of them between Kim and his son by the middle of the decade. "Any place deemed to boast the slightest scenic beauty is designated as a site for one of these royal villas," said Hwang. Secured by small armies of bodyguards, sentries, and servants, "these were elaborate palaces, with swimming pools, tennis courts, crystal chandeliers, and ballrooms, surrounded by moats and man-made lakes." Ensconced in these lavish mansions with toys and servants at his disposal, and without a mother—the only person besides his father who could have imposed any semblance of discipline—Jong Il became a mini tyrant. Hwang recalled that he was "a conceited child who flaunted his status as the son of the highest ruler among his friends. This tendency to do whatever he liked worsened as he grew and turned into the overvaulting ambition to make his father's power his own."

As an adolescent in the 1950s, Jong Il hated authority and talked back to teachers, yet he could be charming; he threw over-the-top parties for his friends, zipped around Pyongyang on a motorcycle, and wore fashionable clothing none of his peers could afford or acquire. His schoolmates said the Great Leader's son was "artistic, passionate, and social," while Hwang said that his first impression of Kim was that of a "smart, curious, and ambitious youth." (In fact, a senior South Korean official who met Kim Jong Il in 2000 at the first inter-Korean summit also concluded that Kim was "emotional and intuitive, rather than rational or logical.") Jong Il and his friends were known to drive cars at fast speeds through the empty roads late at night, according to Helen-Louise Hunter, who mused, "One can imagine the exhilaration of these relatively spoiled young people driving fast down a deserted highway at night—with no fear of getting caught for speeding." The younger Kim gained a reputation not only for recklessness, cruelty, and womanizing but also for political savvy and bureaucratic acumen. He honed these skills in the competition for his father's affection and favor, especially given his stepmother's ambition to elevate herself, her sons (in particular the older of the two half-brothers, Pyong Il), and her branch of the family ahead of his own. Despite Jong Il's complaints about his loneliness and the fraught relationship with his stepmother, his father was highly invested in his eldest son's education; teachers were ordered to give him extra lessons and special attention.

Jong Il lacked not only the gravitas, affability, and avuncular nature of his famous father but also the Great Leader's physical stature: At five foot two or three, he was about six inches shorter than Kim Il Sung. But Jong Il possessed a skill that outweighed his disadvantages: his ability to satisfy his father's craving for adulation. For those surrounding the country's founder, including his son, "feeding [Kim Il Sung's] enormous appetites and ego provided full-time and never-ending work." Even as a teenager, Jong Il sought to demonstrate his devotion and filial loyalty. Hwang recalled that young Kim accompanied his father on a trip to the Soviet Union in the late 1950s, where he took care of the Great Leader's itinerary, took notes of the day's events, and polished his shoes, leading a touched Kim Il Sung to remark, "My son is truly the best! I can trust no one else but him."

As North Korea's leader faced his mortality and began to consider who might replace him, he kept mum on publicly naming a successor until 1980. However, he had started grooming his eldest son as early as the 1970s, as noted in a declassified 1978 CIA document. Jong Il was then the leader of the influential Organization and Guidance Department of the Korean Workers' Party Central Committee, which meant he had the power to "coordinate sensitive personnel matters, including promotions, transfers, and demotions for party functionaries from the national to the local level." The CIA assessment also claimed that "perhaps the most potent political weapon" for the younger Kim was "his evident role as chief interpreter, protector, and propagandizer" of his father's thoughts.

Jong Il sought to use all the tools of repression to solidify his primacy in the succession struggle. The 1978 CIA assessment stressed these efforts: "By guiding the movement to indoctrinate all of society with [his father's] thoughts, the younger Kim is in a position to evaluate the ideological rectitude of party officials and, more important, to censure or demote those who are found lacking." And as the "keeper of the faith and as the secretary in charge of organizational affairs," Kim used his unique position as the eldest son and his growing bureaucratic power to build his base. He exiled his half-brother Pyong Il to faraway posts and discredited his uncle and the Kim Song Ae side of the family.

It was an unending project. "In order to show his father that he was the most loyal, he singled out people near Kim Il Sung," Hwang said. "Arguing that these people were not loyal and citing doubts about their ideology or competency, he would relentlessly attack and remove them." He adopted his father's example of doling out privileges and positions to ensure loyalty and unabashedly using nepotism to guarantee that the Kim family would remain the ruling dynasty by installing his family members in the regime's top positions. At the same time, he gave plum assignments to the adult children of the guerrillas in his father's circle to further legitimize the hereditary transfer of power and provide continuity from the founding generation to the next. This had the effect of deepening the investment that the younger generation had in perpetuating the Kim dynasty, with Jong Il as the unquestioned leader. Still, in a 1982 paper titled "The Dynasty Takes Shape," the CIA assessed that Kim Jong Il "will not be able to replace his father in image, role, or charisma."

Perhaps all too aware that he lacked his father's star quality, Kim made up for it in visible gifts. To remind the people of their loyalty to the Sun, the Great Leader, their Father, Kim Jong Il doubled down on the cult of personality, blanketing North Korea with tens of thousands of pieces of art, photographs, statues, exhibits, and monuments. For his father's seventieth birthday, in 1982, Jong Il unveiled the *Juche* Tower, which was made of 25,550 granite blocks, one for each day the Great Leader had lived by that time, and surpassed the height of the 555-foot-tall Washington Monument by 2 feet. An instant landmark in Pyongyang because of its size and historical and political significance and capped by a glowing orb, the tower looks like a massive torch, triumphantly reaching for the heavens. That same year, the Arch of Triumph—modeled after the one in Paris, but thirty feet taller—celebrated Kim Il Sung's return to Pyongyang in 1945, marking the location where he was introduced to the people by the Soviet military. The monuments not only commemorated the country's founder but also cemented his son's future status.

GLAMOROUS GUERRILLAS

Jong Il also harnessed the power of film and literature to build and solidify his position as the son of North Korea's most famous guerrilla, as well as to play to his father's ego. Soon after graduating from Kim Il Sung University, twenty-five-year-old Jong Il volunteered to be the cultural arts director of the Propaganda and Agitation Department. He used this position to marry his love of film with his political ambition, exploiting the power of cinema to constantly refresh the cult of personality and reinforce the regime's narratives about the centrality of Kim Il Sung in the country's history, present, and future. The younger Kim was a known movie impresario, a fan of James Bond and Rambo movies and the actress Elizabeth Taylor. He reportedly owned twenty thousand DVDs and videos, saw every Academy Award–winning movie, and was upset when James Bond was captured and tortured by North Koreans in *Die Another Day*. (The regime released a statement decrying the film as "insulting to the Korean nation.")

For a sheltered, relatively shy young man who lived in the shadow of his father, film was a gateway to the outside world and a means to play god in the small part of the universe that he controlled. And while many of his peers outside North Korea were rebelling against the establishment, demonstrating, marching, and fighting for civil rights and national independence in the tumult and upheaval of the 1960s and '70s, Kim was busy trying to please his father and strengthen the status quo in North Korea. He recognized the power of cinema to shape perceptions, play on the emotions, and create uniformity of thought based on the shared experience of moviegoing. His films told emotional, heart-wrenching tales of noble North Koreans who fought and resisted Japanese imperialism with unwavering faith in Kim Il Sung and Communism.

But Kim was unsatisfied with the state of North Korean films and wanted to make them more modern, so he ordered the January 1978 kidnapping of a famous South Korean actress, Choi Eun-hee, in Hong Kong. Six months later, North Korean agents also abducted her ex-husband, Shin Sang-ok, a celebrated South Korean movie director, when he went to look for her in Hong Kong. The couple secretly taped Kim Jong Il complaining that "in South Korea, they have better technology. They are like college students and we are just in nursery schools." In his high, squeaky voice, he also lamented, "We don't have any films that get into film festivals." The couple delivered. They made nearly twenty films during their eight years in captivity, satisfying Kim's desire to develop North Korea's film industry. To garner fame, he allowed the couple to travel to various film festivals; during one of those trips, they escaped to the U.S. embassy in Vienna.

Kim made movies with the aim of winning the hearts and minds of average North Koreans, to encourage them to worship his father and, by extension, himself, but clues to how Kim envisioned his role in North Korea could be found in his favorite Western films. As recounted in London-based filmmaker Paul Fischer's book *A Kim Jong-Il Production,* Shin said that Kim was "like any ordinary young man. He liked action movies, sex movies, horror movies."

But in the context of North Korea, Kim 2.0's preference for James Bond and Rambo takes on a particular meaning. Shin recalled that Kim often had trouble seeing Bond and Rambo movies as fiction and viewed them more as "social realist docudramas." Clever, charming, sexy, and arrogant, James Bond is someone most men might admire. Bond was a world traveler, jet-setting from Paris to Istanbul to the Caribbean to North Korea, bedding dozens of the world's most beautiful women, eating caviar and drinking champagne, and driving the fastest cars with the latest technology. The embodiment of the consumerist culture, he created desire for those products and that lifestyle. Sean Connery's Bond, six foot two and muscular, was a composite of the commandos that Ian Fleming, the author of the Bond books, had met during his service in intelligence during World War II. A glamorous guerrilla, perhaps, in Kim Jong Il's mind, James Bond single-handedly outfoxed, outcharmed, and outhumored every type of villain. But if Bond was too perfectly coiffed at all times, Rambo was raw masculinity, fighting in tattered clothing and defeating better-equipped and more numerous foes, often using makeshift weapons, the element of surprise, and sheer grit.

The twin images of Bond and Rambo probably resonated with Kim Jong Il because, like his father and the regime's hagiography, they taught him just how glamorous guerrilla warfare could be. Victory is these heroes' unwavering destiny. North Korea's postwar guerrilla tactics during Jong Il's grooming process were likewise calculated to enhance his father's martial credentials and to allow the pampered son to revel in the reflected glory of those aggressive acts. In the late 1960s and early 1970s, North Korea had the fourth-largest standing army in the Communist bloc, with around four hundred thousand personnel. In the 1970s, as the succession process ramped up, the country's armed forces were boosted to around six hundred thousand, with a corresponding increase in their capability and mobility through upgrades in conventional weapons systems. Additional investment in its one hundred thousand highly trained commando units enabled North Korea to insert thousands of operatives deep into South Korea, according to a declassified 1979 CIA assessment.

From the 1960s to the 1980s, North Korea conducted a series of deadly terrorist acts: attempting a botched infiltration of South Korea's Blue House, shooting down a U.S. reconnaissance plane, killing the South Korean president's wife, digging a series of tunnels through the Demilitarized Zone in an effort to infiltrate the South, and ambushing a South Korean delegation in Burma, killing nearly everyone in the president's cabinet. CIA intelligence analysts concluded that the military buildup was consistent with an overall reunification strategy that Kim Il Sung kept as a core objective of the North Korean state. According to the 1979 intelligence estimate, the military buildup indicated a "three-pronged approach by strengthening the North as a revolutionary base for reunification, promoting the growth of revolutionary forces in South Korea, and working to gain support from other revolutionary forces around the world." The military emphasis—a push to constantly invoke its guerrilla past—had "effectively subordinated all of North Korea's domestic and foreign policies to the overriding goal of national reunification under North Korean control."

As the political scientist Samuel Huntington has pointed out, for all of these aggressive moves, guerrilla combat "is a form of warfare by which the strategically weaker side assumes the tactical offensive in selected forms, times, and places." Since World War II, nuclear weapons have allowed the "weak [to] compensate for conventional inferiority." By the time the elder Kim announced his son as his successor in 1980, North Korea's fortunes were already in steady decline as a result of decades of economic mismanagement, isolation, and the violent suppression of any perceived or real dissent. Both Kims privately acknowledged North Korea's waning prospects, but rather than admitting the problems and undertaking economic reforms, the regime chose its survival above all else, encasing itself in the ideology of *juche, suryong,* and, under Kim Jong Il, *songun,* or "military first." Their tools were coercion, violence, repression, and propaganda to create a culture of fear. Stoking anti-Americanism and memories of the all too recent horrors of Japanese colonialism and the Fatherland Liberation War, they kept their people pliant.

NUCLEAR DREAMS

When Kim Jong Il took over after Kim Il Sung's death in 1994, the world that his father created had crumbled. This privileged and shielded son of a dictator, with no war experience, had to manage a complex strategic environment in which his country's traditional protectors and allies, China and Russia, had abandoned North Korea in favor of engaging with the West and South Korea. The end of the Cold War in the early 1990s meant that Pyongyang had to be much smarter and more agile in its dealings with the outside world. Meanwhile, South Korea, which since its founding in 1948 had been governed by a series of authoritarian leaders, had embraced democracy. Thanks to its impressive export-oriented policies and its alliance with the United States, it had galloped past the North in economic development.

And yet, ironically, world events only seemed to confirm the prudence of North Korea's self-imposed isolation and repressive practices. In the late 1980s, as the USSR started to crumble, Kim Il Sung's old friends in the Soviet bloc were overthrown and killed by their own people, as in Romania, or began opening up to the West. In South Korea, the dictator Park Chung-hee was murdered by his own intelligence chief and the last authoritarian president, Chun Doo-hwan, eventually stepped down. Democracy prevailed, albeit in fits and starts. South Korea also vaulted past the North in conventional military capabilities. The Soviet Union and China had been important sources of matériel as well as economic assistance on which Pyongyang had relied. As their aid began to dissipate, the Kims were no longer able to continue modernizing their military or feeding their people. A December 1991 National Intelligence Council (NIC) memorandum stressed that "shortages of food and fuel were widespread, due largely to a meager harvest and the breakdown of concessionary trade arrangements with the Soviet Union and Eastern Europe." China, too, facing its own more pressing domestic problems and tired of North Korea's shenanigans—such as the Burma bombing—had begun to tamp down its aid.

North Korea was alone, and it could rely on no one else for its survival. Kim Jong Il almost certainly realized that given these circumstances, it would be to North Korea's detriment to integrate too much with the outside world. Instead, he and his father isolated the country and made it a priority to safeguard internal stability through strengthening security mechanisms to root out and discourage dissent at the local and national levels, maintain a culture of fear to ensure loyalty, and keep support among the elite by tethering their livelihood to the sustainment of the Kim family dynasty.

Terror, repression, and isolation were not enough, however. As Jonathan Pollack, an expert on Northeast Asia, cogently argued, "Kim Il-sung viewed nuclear power as a talisman that would affirm the country's standing as an advanced scientific and industrial power," and might have started his nuclear ambitions as early as the 1960s, doggedly requesting information or assistance from East Germany, the Soviet Union, and China. And why *shouldn't* North Korea have nuclear capabilities? Kim Il Sung and his son undoubtedly asked. By the late 1960s, the United States, the Soviet Union, the United Kingdom, France, Israel, and China had nuclear weapons, followed by India and Pakistan in 1974 and 1998, respectively. And South Korea had also made advances in the nuclear realm. South Africa had operated a nuclear weapons program since the 1970s, but dismantled it in 1990.

Throughout the 1990s, the intelligence community in the United States and South Korea sounded the alarm about North Korea's covert nuclear weapons program and developing ballistic missile capabilities. In February 1993, the director of the CIA said that North Korea might have produced enough fissile material for at least one nuclear weapon, and a 1999 NIC paper assessed that, after Russia and China, North Korea was "most likely to develop ICBMs capable of threatening the United States" by 2015. The defector Hwang Jang Yop said in 1997 that North Korea was capable of "scorching South Korea with nuclear weapons, chemical weapons and rockets."

Compounding the concern was that North Korea exported ballistic missiles, conventional weapons, and laborers to countries in Africa, the Middle East, and South Asia, creating "an immediate, serious, and growing threat to US forces, interests, and allies . . . and . . . significantly alter[ing] the strategic balances [there]," according to the 1999 NIC analysis. Not that the regime was hiding its missile sales to these countries. In 1998, after denying U.S. charges for years, the North Koreans boldly declared that "we will continue developing, testing and deploying missiles" and demanded that the United States lift sanctions and "make a compensation for the losses to be caused by discontinued missile export."

The nuclear and missile programs provided North Korea with added insurance for regime survival at a critical moment in the country's history, given the succession from father to son and the challenging strategic environment following the end of the Cold War. Luckily for North Korea—and unluckily for the United States, its allies, and the vast majority of North Koreans who continued to suffer under the Kim regime—nascent nuclear weapons capabilities gave this tiny country strategic relevance on the international stage. Through alternating cycles of provocation and diplomacy, North Korea sought to maintain the element of surprise, demonstrating its capabilities through the testing of nuclear armaments and ballistic missiles, then employing a charm offensive to defuse tensions and to buy time to further perfect its weapons program.

Kim Jong Il had decades of tutelage under his father to learn these skills of manipulating the internal and external environments, outlasting two U.S. presidents, and the ups and downs of nuclear negotiations. By successfully creating an alternate reality, carefully wrapping his father's image and his own in multiple layers of mythology and heroism, he was able to persuade the North Korean people to live as if they were unaware of their country's declining fortunes and growing poverty. Sycophancy, nepotism, Kim's dogged commitment to replacing his father, and the personality cult formed a powerful combination that helped to secure the Kim family's dynastic fortunes and legitimacy. Kim himself had a front-row seat in shaping and adapting to North Korea's new surroundings. The next generation, however, would not have this luxury to educate itself or to learn fully the extent of North Korea's problems.

FOUR

THE SON RISING

K IM JONG IL DIDN'T just love movies and making them; he also loved the women who starred in them. Like his father, he was known as a womanizer, attending wild, lavish parties with loyalists and, over the course of his life, hundreds of young women. Imagining him in this role brings a rather discordant image to mind, given his ubiquitous beige jumpsuit, big glasses, and bouffant teased to make him look taller. Defectors previously close to the Kims reported lurid details of these infamous parties that went well into the wee hours. Champagne, cognac, and caviar overflowed the tables, while naked dancing girls entertained the attendees.

As the ultimate puppet-master host, Kim Jong Il would command partygoers to dance, sing, or drink. Young girls plucked from outlying villages, picked for their beauty and youth—both Kims had an affinity for teenagers, as if they could become immortal by having sex with them—entertained the guests with singing, dancing, and massaging. Their parents willingly, naïvely, or helplessly "donated" their daughters to the Kims, convinced that they were either serving their country or improving their livelihoods and their daughters' future prospects by sending them to the capital. Many defectors described the regime's use of "joy divisions" in which these teenagers were trained and then dispatched to Jong Il's holiday homes or hunting grounds. Of course, their parents couldn't possibly turn down the Great Leader or the Dear Leader, even if they'd wanted to.

Like his father, Jong Il had multiple wives and consorts whom he housed in mansions and villas sprinkled throughout Pyongyang. And like the Great Leader, he seems to have compartmentalized his home life from his work life, keeping his family away from the public by cloistering them in private, secure housing. Father and son most likely did so in an effort to keep the spotlight on themselves, to tamp down any rumors of other potential sources of power, and to underscore the ideology of a paternal leader, whose only "family" is the entire country.

THE THREE SONS

Because the regime's continuity was based on the Kim genealogy, a crucial duty for the Dear Leader was to designate which of his three sons by two favored consorts would be his successor, and then to prepare that son to rule North Korea.

The mother of his eldest son was Song Hye Rim. Beautiful and glamorous, she was a famous North Korean actress who traveled to international film festivals and was already married to a prominent novelist. She was born in South Korea, but her Communist parents left for the North during the Korean War. Her background and relationship with Jong Il are sketchy, as so many things are about North Korea. But one can imagine a twentysomething Jong Il, already in love with cinema, besotted by a leading actress who was four or five years older. As the son of a dictator with absolute power, he cared little for convention or rules. He demanded that she divorce her husband and leave her family so that he could have her complete devotion. They lived together, but it is unclear if they actually married. No one but Song herself would be in a position to know how she really felt about Jong Il, though one can imagine that Kim showered her with gifts and compliments—Americans who met him said that he could be quite charming. Song's sister, who used to live with the couple in the early days of their relationship, wrote in her memoir that Kim and her sister shared similar artistic tastes and preferences and watched movies together. She also remembered that Hye Rim described him as a "meticulous and humorous comedian." Song's nephew Li Il Nam, a frequent visitor to the residence who defected in 1982, recalled, "From what I heard, my aunt was disappointed in her [first] marriage and was quite taken by Kim Jong-il." In 1971, Song gave birth to a prized first son named Jong Nam.

Kim kept his relationship with Song and his little family away from his father, for fear of his disapproval—she was born in South Korea, after all, and divorced—and to avoid jeopardizing his chances during the delicate succession process. Kim adored Jong Nam, who was born when Kim was around thirty years old. He was a chubby little boy, with full cheeks, thick legs, and a bit of a paunch peeking over his waistband in a country where most boys his age were undernourished. They lived in a mansion, reportedly staffed by servants, hundreds of bodyguards, and a handful of cooks. The young boy lived in luxury; he wore diamond-studded watches and was surrounded by piles of toy guns, modern gadgets, and video games. He had a ten-thousand-square-foot playroom and crates of toys sent by North Korean diplomats stationed in Europe and East Asia who had been tasked with procuring the latest in childhood playthings. Jong Il jealously guarded his precious secret with the help of apparatchiks who feared devastating reprisals if any information about the mother and child leaked. To keep things contained, Jong Nam was tutored at home rather than attending school. The situation understandably caused friction between the boy's parents; Song threatened to reveal their secret to Kim Il Sung, according to her niece Li Nam Ok, who defected from North Korea in 1992. Li said that Jong Il warned Song off with a pistol.

Despite his official second marriage in 1973 or 1974 to a woman his father approved of—his first in the late 1960s reputedly ended in divorce—Kim spent most of his time with his son. He co-slept with him and spared nothing to keep the isolated boy happy, according to Song's nephew. Li Il Nam described how the pampered boy was allowed to read South Korean novels and watch South Korean and Japanese television shows, pastimes that would have landed any other North Korean in a gulag. Jong Nam once ordered his servants to kidnap a South Korean comedian he liked and bring the man to his villa to entertain him. The kidnapping didn't happen, but the incident shows the extent of Jong Nam's privilege and his view of how much power his father wielded. In fact, even though Kim's agents didn't carry out the abduction, Li said they found a North Korean farmer who resembled the comedian and trained him for months to impersonate his routines. One of Jong Nam's cousins wrote in his memoir that the little prince "ruled the roost" and was "the king and the commander of the house."

The one thing little Jong Nam did not have was freedom. The only playmate his age was his cousin Li Nam Ok, the daughter of his mother's sister, who came to live with them to keep the family company. She would later say that Jong Nam accepted the situation because he never questioned his father. Having once been a prominent actress, his mother suffered from her isolation in a gilded cage; she sought treatment for depression and other mental and physical ailments in Moscow for extended periods. Jong Nam found some respite from the stifling atmosphere in North Korea when his father sent him to school in Moscow and Geneva between 1978 and 1988. He returned to Pyongyang when he was eighteen.

Covetous though he was of his secret family, Kim had already turned his amorous attention elsewhere. He had taken up a new lover, Ko Yong Hui, a Japanese-born actress who quickly bore him two sons and a daughter: Jong Chol (1981), Jong Un (1984), and Yo Jong (1989). Born in Osaka in 1952, Ko was part of the Korean diaspora with her family during the first half of the twentieth century and the era of Japanese colonization of Korea. At the end of World War II, approximately two million Koreans were living and working in Japan, having been conscripted by the Japanese government to fill the labor shortage or voluntarily moving there to seek economic opportunities. Ko's family moved to Pyongyang in 1961 as part of a program by the regime to repatriate ethnic Koreans living in Japan.

Ko, a beautiful young woman with large eyes and a delicate oval face that would grow fuller over the years as she got older and plumper, was a dancer in the Mansudae Art Troupe when she caught Kim Jong Il's admiring eye in the early 1970s, right around the time that Kim Jong Nam was born. Ko reportedly convinced Jong Il to exile her competition, Song, to Moscow, reflecting her determination to keep her own children first in line for succession. The defection of Song's sister and niece, whom he had trusted to take care of Jong Nam in Europe, might have factored into Kim's decision to scratch his first love from his life—now tainted with the disloyalty of her kin—and made him more receptive to Ko's maneuverings.

By the time that Jong Nam returned to Pyongyang in 1988, his father was busy with his new family and the affairs of state, since he had by then been publicly appointed as Kim Il Sung's successor. Jong Nam began working in various government posts.

The firstborn's presence in Pyongyang in proximity to the two other sons began to engender much speculation about who might potentially succeed Kim Jong Il. The odds favored Jong Nam, as the eldest, yet he would not be the one groomed for several reasons. For one, the elder Kim might have judged that Jong Nam was tainted by foreign influence based on reports from his son's guardians and staff appointed to keep watch over him. Kim had been enraged and frustrated with his son's behavior over the years. While in Geneva, Jong Nam would frequent nightclubs and hang out with Western women, leading his father to threaten to banish him to work in one of North Korea's dreaded coal mines. In the early 1990s in Pyongyang, Jong Nam, probably during a night of heavy drinking, blindly fired a gun in a club for foreign guests at the Koryo Hotel. In 2001, international media reported that Jong Nam had been detained in

Japan with a fake passport in a failed attempt to go to Tokyo Disneyland, an embarrassment for his intensely private father and for a regime sensitive to such public humiliation. By many accounts, Jong Nam regularly enjoyed partying, traveling, shopping, and womanizing, and these impulses appear to have outweighed his desire to govern the isolated nation. Still, this kind of playboy behavior was not inherently disqualifying since Kim Jong Il similarly indulged himself throughout his life.

More concerning to his father was that Kim Jong Nam had reportedly suggested North Korea undertake policy reform and open up to the West, a reflection of his extended studies abroad and his unhappy isolation as a child forced to grow up alone in a gilded prison. This opinion angered his father. In a 2012 interview with a Japanese reporter, Jong Nam recalled, "I grew further apart from my father because I insisted on reform and market-opening and was eventually viewed with suspicion." He tried to explain their estrangement: "My father felt very lonely after sending me to study abroad. Then my half-brothers Jong-chul and Jong-un and half-sister Yo-jong were born and his adoration was moved on to them. And when he felt that I'd turn into a capitalist after living abroad for years, he shortened the overseas education of my brothers and sister."

The lives and education of Jong Chol and Jong Un are even more shrouded in mystery, with the most significant observations coming from Kenji Fujimoto, a pseudonym adopted by Kim Jong Il's sushi chef, who became the boys' playmate after being admitted into the leader's elite circle. Fujimoto recalled that the two young boys were referred to as princes and the daughter as a princess. Like Jong Nam, both boys were tutored at home until they were dispatched to an expensive school in Bern, Switzerland, in the 1990s. The cumulative tuition at the school for a student enrolled from kindergarten to the twelfth grade was $300,000, which suggests that the Kims' classmates were from powerful and wealthy families.

Jong Chol, the older of the two, was deemed not tough enough to succeed his father, although his mother reportedly once suggested to Kim that Jong Chol should be the heir. Fujimoto described him as gentle and interested in music. One of Jong Chol's friends recalled that he "is not the type of guy who would do something to harm others. He is a nice guy who could never be a villain." His friends included classmates from the United States and South Korea. He liked basketball, especially watching Dennis Rodman, and would don a replica Rodman uniform when he played the game with his friends. Jong Chol enjoyed action movies, particularly those featuring the actor Jean-Claude Van Damme, whom the thin boy admired for his physique. He and his younger brother were not stellar students by any means, and like so many other boys in their teens were more interested in playing than studying. According to Thae Yong Ho, a high-ranking North Korean diplomat in London who defected to South Korea in 2016, Jong Chol was more interested in attending Eric Clapton concerts, partying, and shopping in London and elsewhere. Thae was in charge of escorting Jong Chol and revealed that the princeling was very polite and quite a talented guitar player.

Unlike the temperate, music-loving Jong Chol, Jong Un was competitive and tough. In 1996, when he was twelve, he joined his brother at the International School of Berne, where a classmate recalled that "his English was bad at first. He had a strong accent and was given extra lessons." Jong Un studied German and English, and was reportedly good in math. But apparently because he was unable to succeed at the private school, according to one South Korean scholar, in 1998 he transferred to the less demanding Schule Liebefeld Steinhölzli, a German-language public school near Bern, where he studied until he returned to Pyongyang in early 2001 at age seventeen. Fujimoto described Jong Un's mother as not being strict about her sons' education and said that the two boys were never forced to study.

Jong Un's friend and classmate Joao Micaelo, who knew him as "Un Pak," the son of a North Korean diplomat, said years later, "We weren't the dimmest kids in class but neither were we the cleverest. We were always in the second tier. Un tried hard to express

himself but he was not very good at German and became flustered
when asked to give the answers to a problem. The teachers would
see him struggling ashamedly and then move on." Jong Un was apparently unbothered by his less than stellar scores. "He left without
getting any exam results at all. He was much more interested in
football and basketball than lessons," said Micaelo. Perhaps he just
wasn't interested in the school's curriculum, which included course-
work in Swiss history since 1291 and the evolution of democracy
there, civil rights leaders Martin Luther King, Jr., and Nelson Man-
dela, and human rights. But the competitiveness he lacked in the
classroom showed up in spades on the basketball court. "He was
very explosive," one friend said. "He could make things happen. He
was the playmaker." Another friend said Jong Un was tough and
fast: "He hated to lose. Winning was very important." He especially
loved Michael Jordan. He would draw his picture over and over
again, and harbored hopes that playing basketball would make him
taller. Ra Jong-yil, a former senior South Korean intelligence official, supported this schoolmate's impression, claiming that the Dear
Leader had long preferred his youngest son because of his aggressiveness, which gave him the temperament to run a country.

A former teacher said that Jong Un was a "friendly, gentle,
young Asian boy" who struggled to form close relationships with
his peers because of the language barrier. One of the few pictures of
Jong Un with his classmates at the public school shows him in the
middle of the back row. While the other students have their arms
wrapped around one another in a joyful embrace, leaning in toward
the camera, mouths open in wide smiles and glee, Jong Un stands
straight, with his arms at his side, directing a cautious look at the
camera. Living under a pseudonym in Switzerland, he was not a
North Korean "prince" but just the son of an embassy official, like
many of the other kids. It must have been hard for the teenager,
who had been raised in palatial mansions in Pyongyang, to do without the adulation and deference to which he had become accus-
tomed.

"We lived in a normal house and acted like a normal family," recalled his aunt Ko Yong Suk, who took care of the two boys in Switzerland. "I encouraged him to bring his friends home, because we wanted them to live a normal life. I made snacks for the kids. They ate cake and played with Legos." If Jong Un needed to act a bit restrained at school and keep his temper under control, he unleashed his imperial self at home, where the family's wealth was on full display. Micaelo recalled that unlike other embassy kids, Kim "lived in a flat in a nice residential area near the school . . . surrounded by the best gadgets that the rest of us kids couldn't afford—TVs, video recorder, a Sony PlayStation. He had a cook, a driver, a private teacher." During school vacations, Jong Un and his family went swimming in the French Riviera, skied in the Alps, and enjoyed the thrills at Euro Disney and Tokyo Disneyland. Trips home meant going back to enjoy the family's vast estates with horses, swimming pools, bowling alleys, even luxury vehicles adapted so that the boys could drive them from a young age. Summers were spent on the east coast of North Korea at their private resort on the beautiful beaches of Wonsan.

Of course, Kim was not a normal boy from a normal family. Worried about how they would fare in Kim Jong Il's new regime, his aunt and caretaker defected to the United States in 1998. And indeed, under its new leader, their country was about to enter its most dangerous period since the Korean War.

THE FAMINE

While the Kim princes were tucked away in a cocoon of privilege and indulgence, whether in one of the family's villas in Pyongyang, in resorts on the coast, or in western Europe in the mid- to late 1990s, average North Koreans were in the throes of one of the most devastating human-made disasters in history—the famine that reached its peak from 1995 through 1998. Although exact numbers are hard to verify, six hundred thousand to one million people died as a result, while the Kim family continued to spend lavishly on luxury items and on the military. As the anthropologist Sandra Fahy and others have argued, North Korea's famine—what the regime called "the arduous march" to anoint it with a revolutionary flavor—was entirely preventable. Fahy claims that avoiding the famine would have required the regime's abandoning its international isolation and loosening its grip on power. But instead, the government gave priority to its own survival, using the *juche,* or self-reliance, and *son-gun,* or military-first, ideologies to justify leaving the people to fend for themselves.

According to the interviews Fahy held with North Koreans who survived the famine, food was used as a political weapon and reward, distributed according to loyalty, gender, age, and geography—consistent with their *songbun,* the regime's elaborate caste system constructed to ensure faithfulness to Kim Jong Il and the cult of Kim Il Sung. High government officials and those who lived in Pyongyang—only those with elite status had the privilege of living in the capital—received more government rations, while those in the isolated, rural northeast and the youngest, aged, and disabled were allotted the least.

Kim Jong Il was unwilling or unable to adapt to the new geopolitical landscape that followed the end of Soviet aid and concessionary loans from China. For example, trade with the Soviet Union, which accounted for more than 50 percent of North Korea's total trade, decreased from $3.25 billion in 1990 to around $100 million by 1994. Both the confrontation with the United States over its nuclear program between 1992 and 1994 and the domestic uncertainty surrounding the succession process probably factored into the regime's decision not to address the famine, the causes of which were clearly rooted in its reliance on foreign aid, unsustainable farming practices and outdated equipment, bad agricultural policies, and accumulating debts. Korea experts Stephan Haggard and Marcus Noland have revealed that the regime's public distribution system, which distributed food nationally in monthly or biweekly allotments, was unable to fulfill its mandate, steadily cutting rations to the extent that the government had to launch a "Let's eat two meals a day" campaign. The flood of 1995 exacerbated the suffering, but the regime blamed the weather much more than was truly the case.

Although the international community responded to the famine with $2 billion in food aid over the course of the following decade, Kim stubbornly clung to North Korea's old ways, refusing to acknowledge wrongdoing or misguided policies and ignoring the frustrated requests from international monitors of the incoming aid to ensure that it went to the most vulnerable populations. Instead, 10 to 30 percent of international donations did not reach their intended destinations, as local, party, and military officials siphoned off the items for personal use or to sell in the markets for profit, according to Haggard and Noland. Meanwhile, as his people were starving, Kim chose to purchase luxury items for himself and loyalists and funnel the regime's funds toward ballistic missile development and other big-ticket military hardware, highlighting that his ultimate priority was his own survival and the perpetuation of North Korea as a garrison state.

Internally, the regime blamed others for the people's suffering. One defector told Fahy, "This is what they taught the people: . . . 'America, the international community, and the puppet South Korea are ceaselessly preparing for war. We have to tighten our belts to build up the national defense, to build up the economy.' . . . And for that, the citizens suffered through hell, not anticipating the rain and snow storms that came and destroyed the farms. 'Let's tighten our belts and forward march!' That is the way they propagandized it."

When the worst of the famine struck the population, leading to understandable crimes such as stealing grain or corn from a field, the regime sought to punish rather than help. Sandra Fahy's interviewees recounted public executions for these desperate acts of survival. Dozens of witnesses told her that these criminals had their heads completely shot off, "the hot blood" creating a mist as it rose into the cold winter air. When asked why the head was targeted, the defectors told her that "it was because the criminal's thinking was wrong: the criminal was thinking like a capitalist."

During the 1990s, the stories of suffering continued to leak out, as defectors provided accounts of the horrible toll the famine took on the country. Corpses piled up near train stations; roving bands of starving orphans stole what they could or collapsed when they couldn't find anything; women turned to prostitution in an attempt to survive and feed their families. People of all ages, including children, foraged in the woods to find roots, mushrooms, and other wild plants, often with tragic consequences when they would unwittingly eat poisonous varieties. One defector recalled that the hungry died on the streets and corpses were left out in the open. Another said, "The sound of the children crying out for something to eat in the evening, they were like frogs croaking, crying." A woman who defected described taking a train in 1997 and realizing that a fellow passenger was dead; she said that she and the other people on board were "blasé" about the corpse, suggesting how famine deaths became just a part of people's daily lives. People ate garbage, rats, frogs.

For Kim Jong Il, who took over the country just as the worst effects were being felt, the timing of the famine could not have been worse. For many North Koreans, the disaster defined the transition from his father's rule to his, exacerbating the challenges that he faced as the new leader without the guerrilla background to burnish his credentials. The timing of Kim Il Sung's death, Fahy wrote, "marked a distinct before-and-after for many North Koreans, who consequently placed recollections of pre-1994 as 'not that bad,'" while the Kim Jong Il years were seen as starting the downturn in the economy and food security.

The intelligence community was aware of the internal and external stresses on the new leader, issuing warnings about the potential for a North Korean collapse. Senior U.S. officials were openly predicting that his regime would fail. In 1996, CIA director John Deutch, in his testimony to the Senate Select Committee on Intelligence, expressed his concern about such a possibility in the near term because of the "incredible economic problems that the country faces." And earlier that year, General John Shalikashvili, the chairman of the Joint Chiefs of Staff, told *The Washington Post,* "We are now in a period where most who watch the area would say it's either going to implode or explode—we're just not quite sure when that is going to happen." In 1998, a group of CIA analysts and outside experts convened by the agency assessed that the Kim Jong Il regime could not "remain viable in the long term," the majority doubting that "the current, deteriorating status could persist beyond five years."

KIM JONG UN RETURNS HOME

Kim Jong Un was most likely unaware of all the challenges his father faced or his country's tenuous circumstances, given his youth and his years abroad; he returned to Pyongyang in 2001. It must have been jarring to finally move back to Pyongyang after living in a small, multinational town in Switzerland and jet-setting from the Alps to the Riviera. While he was a small fish in a big pond in the milieu of a triumphant post–Cold War Europe, shy, quiet, hiding his real identity, he was a big fish in a tiny pond in North Korea. Teams of teachers, tutors, cooks, assigned playmates, bodyguards, relatives, and chauffeurs had developed Kim's sense of entitlement and tried to shield him from the realities of North Korea and the world even beyond his childhood years. But there were signs that the teenage Kim could not unsee what he had witnessed and learned in Europe.

In the mid- to late 1990s, the West was in a celebratory mood. After five decades of the Cold War, in which the United States and the Soviet Union had locked horns in an ideological confrontation, the West rejoiced in the collapse of the Soviet Union, seeing the event as a victory for liberal democracy and capitalism. The American political scientist Francis Fukuyama famously declared "the end of history." The United States and Vietnam, where a hot war had punctuated the era of cold peace, normalized ties in 1995, a reconciliation that seemed to demonstrate to most observers that the world would now be marked by peaceful coexistence, with Washington as the global leader. Indeed, armed conflict decreased dramatically in the period between 1992 and 2003, and champions of globalization believed that mankind was on a linear path of progress with Western-style governance and economic models leading the way in knitting together the international community. Time and history did not seem to be on the side of North Korea, the last bastion of Communism, isolationism, and its particular brand of Korean ethnocentrism based on the personality cult of Kim Il Sung.

It was during this period, during his summer vacation in August 2000, when Kim Jong Un was beginning his new life in Pyongyang, that he had a conversation with the sushi chef Fujimoto, which demonstrates that he clearly took note of the contrast between his home country and his travels and studies abroad. According to Fujimoto, Jong Un said, "Why are goods so insufficient and rare in DPRK's department stores and regular stores, in contrast to those in Western countries?" He also inquired about the fate of average North Koreans: "How are our people managing their lives?" Jong Un admitted to Fujimoto that he admired the economic success of China and Japan: "I heard from my father that China is doing very well in many fields, including industry, commerce, hotels, and agriculture," he said, and marveled at Japan's prosperity after being defeated in World War II.

None of Jong Un's reported utterances to Fujimoto indicate a questioning of the fundamentals of the North Korean model or criticism of the personality cults and regime ideologies. Jong Un was already thoroughly indoctrinated with the belief that he was destined to lead, so he was unlikely to conceive of a path for North Korea without a Kim at the helm. Nevertheless, these statements offer a glimpse into the young prince's naïveté about the roots of North Korea's problems: a centralized command economy and a caste system that stifled innovation and market activity, a gulag system that punished not only the accused but also their families, and the diversion of scarce resources to fund its military and nuclear weapons program at the expense of its citizens' lives.

Fujimoto claims that Jong Il had chosen his youngest son to succeed him as early as 1992. He cited as evidence the scene at Jong Un's eighth birthday banquet where Jong Il instructed the band to play "Footsteps" and dedicated the song to his son: *Following our General Kim's footsteps; Spreading the spirit of February* [a reference to Kim Jong Il, who was born in February]; *We, the people, march forward to a bright future.* Not just the lyrics, but the deliberateness with which the proud father timed and presented the song suggested to the attendees that the Dear Leader was signaling that Jong Un would lead North Korea into the future, guided by his spirit and legacy. In fact, Kim Jong Il was circumspect about who would succeed him, maintaining ambiguity to limit palace intrigue, to stifle the emergence of coalitions around any particular son or family branch, and to protect himself from other challengers while he consolidated and reinforced his own power.

In any case, whether by the process of elimination or because young Jong Un began to show positive signs for leadership, by 2009, it was becoming clear that the third son had been tapped to lead.

FIVE

THE EDUCATION OF KIM JONG UN

OCTOBER 10, 2010: an auspicious date for a country that loves numerology, 10-10-10. It was the sixty-fifth anniversary of the establishment of the Korean Workers' Party and the day that Kim Jong Un made his debut at a massive military parade, standing next to his father, who had taken his usual spot on the observation platform high above Kim Il Sung Plaza. The elder Kim was walking a bit tentatively, holding on to the rail for stability, suggesting that he was still feeling the effects of the stroke in August 2008 that had kept him out of the public eye for several months. He appeared more fit than when he'd shown up at a parliamentary meeting in April 2009, looking wizened and weak. Next to his then twenty-six-year-old son, who was robust and portly and sporting a simple, dark Mao suit like his grandfather used to wear, Jong Il looked old and frail.

Side by side, the two watched the spectacular event, the largest military parade in the country's history. Waves of goose-stepping male and female soldiers marching to the music of brass bands, long-range missiles, and tanks carrying rocket-propelled grenades paid tribute to the Dear Leader and his heir apparent. Military officials bedecked with an impossible number of medals saluted as they marched or rode by. Banners about defeating the United States festooned the parade. The streets were lined with cheering crowds who were yelling with full-throated fervor—as they were supposed to do—"Kim Jong Il! Protect him to the death!" "Kim Jong Il, let's unite to support him!" The military vice marshal Ri Yong Ho spoke at the event with a blustery call to arms: "If the U.S. imperialists and their followers infringe on our sovereignty and dignity even slightly, we will blow up the stronghold of their aggression with a merciless and righteous retaliatory strike by mobilizing all physical means, including self-defensive nuclear deterrent force, and achieve the historic task of unification!"

Eager to promote the display, the regime took the unprecedented step of inviting scores of foreign journalists, even providing them with Internet access to ensure that the coverage of Jong Un's debut reverberated beyond the physical location to the virtual world. The message? To show the world that Kim Jong Un had the full support of both the party and the North's mighty military, plus the nuclear weapons to ensure yet another hereditary succession within the Kim family. Following the parade, a senior party official gave an interview to the Associated Press. "Our people are honored to serve the great president Kim Il Sung and the great leader Kim Jong Il," he said. "Now we also have the honor of serving young general Kim Jong Un."

For Jong Un, the parade capped a series of events aimed at bolstering his new status. A few weeks earlier at a rare party conference—the first in thirty years—Jong Un was appointed the vice chairman of the Central Military Commission and to the party's Central Committee, putting him at the epicenter of power. And despite never having held a previous military rank, he was made a four-star general, highlighting not only the absurdity of North Korea's system but also the importance of stamping the heir with bureaucratic titles to reinforce his position in the existing hierarchies.

The successor clapped and saluted appropriately and stood at attention on a platform alongside officials three or four times his age. But some of his movements indicated a level of uncertainty and nervousness. His salutes and clapping sometimes started a split second after his father and the others began. He glanced backward at one point as if slightly startled by an unexpected movement behind him, significant only because North Korean events are so highly orchestrated and ritualized. Nevertheless, the enormous display of revolutionary fervor, the impressive, though aging, military arsenal—much of it was refurbished from the Soviet era—and the thunderous chants of the mass of people beneath him must have made his heart pound in excitement. It was quite a meteoric rise for someone who, just ten years earlier, had been playing basketball in Switzerland.

But in fact, Kim was made for this moment, having been nurtured into his elite status. The generals had been bowing to him since he was a young boy; now they were doing it publicly for all the world to see. As the journalist Mark Bowden wrote in a 2015 profile, "At age five, we are all the center of the universe. Everything—our parents, family, home, neighborhood, school, country—revolves around us. For most people, what follows is a long process of dethronement, as His Majesty the Child confronts the ever more obvious and humbling truth. Not so for Kim. His world at age 5 has turned out to be his world at age 30. . . . Everyone *does* exist to serve him."

Yet confidence and genetics alone cannot make up for experience, and Kim Jong Il almost certainly was concerned about how his son would fare. Compared with Jong Il, who had nearly three decades of experience working his way through the regime infrastructure, manipulating and mastering the art of repression, accompanying his father on international trips to woo, cajole, and bolster ties to other leaders, Jong Un had had an extremely compressed grooming period of less than a handful of years. Kim Jong Il's stroke in 2008 must have made him realize that he needed to speed up his son's succession because soon after, Jong Un began to accompany his father on publicized inspections of military units, had his birthplace designated a historical site, and collected a slew of leadership titles and roles in the military, party, and security apparatus.

Though Jong Un had about three years as the designated successor to learn from his father, his most formative experiences were in the early 2000s, when he returned to North Korea from Switzerland and entered college at Kim Il Sung Military University, where he was in a position to see his father in action. It is unclear quite when Kim Jong Il started to choose his successor in a definitive way or when he privately decided on his youngest son to be his heir. Perhaps it was when he turned sixty in 2002—an important birthday for Koreans, who believe it signifies the next chapter in a person's life. Or he could have started thinking about it as early as 1971, when his first son was born. Or he might have become aware of Ko Yong Hui's ambition to place one of her sons in power. In any case, the first decade of the twenty-first century was a good laboratory for educating his sons in the ways of statecraft and nuclear diplomacy.

PAVING THE NUCLEAR PATH

To survive as his revered father's successor, Jong Il had to hustle, carefully nurturing and building the cult of the Kim family dynasty while managing an economy that was precipitously declining, coping with abandonment by the Soviet Union, charting the unfaltering rise of South Korea as an economic powerhouse, and steeling the nation against the West's embrace of Seoul's liberal democracy. South Korea's growing wealth was also making even more distant North Korea's dreams of unification on Pyongyang's terms. The vibrant South offered a stark contrast to the famine-hobbled North, with its decaying infrastructure, human rights violations, and nuclear program that was under increasing international scrutiny while the post–Cold War world was moving in the opposite direction.

While confronting these threatening circumstances as the leader of North Korea, Jong Il was also a father who was thinking about the future of his family. And possession of nuclear weapons seemed to be precisely the wild card that could ensure that his country's relative decline did not necessarily mean irrelevance and eventual absorption by South Korea. Kim Il Sung had started the nuclear program as a guarantee for regime survival amid a hostile neighborhood, but Kim Jong Il improved, expanded, and showed off North Korea's nuclear capabilities, a legacy that he bestowed on Jong Un.

For Kim Jong Un, the arc of his education regarding the nuclear weapons program began in 2002, when he was eighteen and a student at Kim Il Sung Military University. In January of that year, his country's fraught relationship with the United States over nuclear weapons was encapsulated in President George W. Bush's State of the Union address, in which he spoke of "an axis of evil," comprising North Korea, Iran, and Iraq. In the aftermath of the terrorist attacks on the United States on September 11, 2001, the subsequent invasion of Afghanistan, and the drumbeat of war that eventually led to the invasion of Iraq, Washington was in no mood for Pyongyang's pursuit of nuclear weapons. Bush described North Korea as "a regime arming with missiles and weapons of mass destruction, while starving its citizens," and warned, "America will do what is necessary to ensure our nation's security."

Ties between Washington and Pyongyang were tense, as the Bush administration in 2001 sought ways to squeeze North Korea. At the time, the two countries were parties to the 1994 Agreed Framework, which emerged after a nuclear crisis prompted by North Korea's threats to withdraw from the international Treaty on the Non-Proliferation of Nuclear Weapons (NPT), which was designed to promote global efforts to prevent the spread of nuclear weapons and technologies. For two decades prior to Bush's election, the United States had been wary about the possibility of North Korea's pursuit of a covert nuclear weapons program, and experts began to sound alarms about Pyongyang's progress throughout the 1980s. In the 1990s, the Clinton administration seriously considered military options as Pyongyang refused inspections of its facilities and kicked out International Atomic Energy Agency inspectors from the country.

The threat of war was palpable. Secretary of Defense William Perry publicly warned North Korea that the United States was determined to stop its nuclear weapons development, even if it meant "facing up to them in a way that could cause a catastrophic war." In fact, the Pentagon had stepped up military buildup in and around the Koreas, and gone as far as to draw up plans to send cruise missiles and F-117 stealth fighters to strike at Yongbyon, then North Korea's only reactor that could produce weapons-grade plutonium. Combined with the fact that around 65 percent of North Korea's armed forces, as well as 8,400 artillery pieces and 2,400 multiple rocket launchers, had been stationed just sixty miles away from the Demilitarized Zone, as Don Oberdorfer of *The Washington Post* noted, there were real fears that the stage was set for a military conflict.

The seemingly inexorable march toward war began to dissipate when North Korea invited former president Jimmy Carter to meet with Kim Il Sung, and Carter flew to Pyongyang in June 1994, despite the Clinton administration's unease. Kim agreed to a temporary freeze of his nuclear weapons program and allowed for inspectors to remain. Subsequently, the United States and North Korea agreed to start negotiations, defusing the first North Korea nuclear crisis. As part of the Agreed Framework, North Korea would freeze its plutonium production program in exchange for economic assistance, the provision of two proliferation-resistant light-water reactors (LWRs), and annual deliveries of five hundred thousand tons of fuel oil (worth about $50 million per year) to meet their heating and electrical needs while the reactors were being built by an American-led international consortium. The agreement also included a pathway for dismantlement of the North Korean nuclear program, eventual normalization of ties, and security assurances. For North Korea, the deal was worth more than $4 billion. The North Korea analyst B. R. Myers observed that the regime characterized this resolution as the result of Kim Jong Il's firmness and determination, and "thus endowed the heir to the throne with his own myth of national rescue." For the United States, the deal succeeded in preventing North Korea's production of potentially scores of nuclear weapons.

The implementation of the Agreed Framework was far from smooth, however, as it was beset with bureaucratic wrangling, budgeting issues, and delays in the construction of the LWRs and delivery of the heavy fuel oil. A frustrated North Korea occasionally threatened to restart its nuclear program even as it continued to work on other aspects of its arms strategy. The regime tested its first long-range ballistic missile over Japan in 1998 and built a massive underground covert nuclear weapons site—in part to extract additional concessions from the Clinton administration.

The Agreed Framework slowed down North Korea's nuclear program, but it did not eliminate it. The agreement's death throes and the second nuclear crisis began when Assistant Secretary of State James Kelly confronted North Korean leaders about their covert uranium enrichment program during his visit there in October 2002. Things went from bad to worse, and the threat of a U.S. attack against North Korea grew, following revelations of both its uranium enrichment program and its ability to produce fissile materials for nuclear weapons. That was when North Korea doubled down and became the first country to leave the NPT, in 2003. A few weeks later, North Korean fighter jets intercepted a U.S. Air Force spy plane that was conducting a mission over the Sea of Japan. Global tensions spiked again when the United States invaded Iraq in March 2003, on the ultimately false premise that Baghdad was producing nuclear weapons, generating fears that Washington was serious about punishing the countries in the axis of evil.

But at the same time, Washington was exploring diplomatic options and initiated what eventually became the Six-Party Talks—to include the United States, North and South Korea, China, Russia, and Japan—to try to defuse tensions and provide a forum for nuclear negotiations. The group first met in August 2003 and convened for five more rounds of talks. When North Korea announced that it possessed nuclear weapons "for self-defense" in February 2005, experts at the time estimated that the country had around six plutonium bombs. There was a brief moment of hope in September 2005, when the six parties reached a breakthrough with the historic Joint Statement in which the countries pledged to work toward verifiable denuclearization of the Korean Peninsula, cooperate on regional security, and promote economic collaboration. Washington and Pyongyang also endorsed taking steps to normalize ties. Most important, Pyongyang committed to "abandoning all nuclear weapons and existing nuclear programs."

The optimism engendered by the Joint Statement eroded quickly, however. Almost concurrent with the nuclear negotiations, the Bush administration had placed restrictions on U.S. financial transactions with Banco Delta Asia (BDA), a bank in Macau, which it accused of laundering money for the Kim regime and other financial crimes. BDA responded by seizing more than fifty North Korea–related accounts, totaling $25 million, and began an extensive audit to stem the run on the bank and repair its reputation. An angry North Korea refused to continue nuclear negotiations and proceeded to test the Taepodong 2—a long-range ballistic missile—on July 4, 2006. The missile failed about forty seconds into the launch but was theoretically able to carry a nuclear warhead to the western United States. A few months later, in October, the regime tested its first nuclear weapon. These actions elicited quick condemnation from the international community and U.N. sanctions, but President Bush ultimately authorized the return of those funds to try to wrest some progress on denuclearization.

Despite the overwhelming military power of the United States, sanctions, international opprobrium, and isolation, Kim Jong Il faced down Washington and relentlessly pursued his nuclear weapons program. He used dialogue to buy time and extract political and economic concessions. In the meantime, he conducted tests to experiment with and improve the weapons and to reinforce his military-first grand strategy that drove Pyongyang's internal and external relations.

It's not clear if Jong Un was aware of the tortuous background of negotiations, if he appreciated how close North Korea and the

United States came to a military conflict, or if he knew what factored into his father's courses of action. But as a student living in the age of his father's military-first policy, and studying at the Kim Il Sung Military University, where he wrote a thesis entitled "A Simulation for the Improvement of Accuracy in the Operational Map by the Global Positioning System," Jong Un was no doubt keenly interested in North Korea's nuclear development. His father would later laud his son's thesis for its incorporation of "the great military strategy theories" of Kim Il Sung and Kim Jong Il, laying the groundwork for publicly highlighting Jong Un's education and commitment to the revolutionary ideals based on self-reliance.

If Jong Un began his formative years in the thick of the United States' implied and explicit threats in 2002, by the time he was just two months away from graduation, on October 9, 2006, North Korea had defied all odds and conducted its first nuclear test. The Foreign Ministry declared, "Our strong revolutionary might [has] put in place all measures to counter a possible U.S. pre-emptive strike. . . . [A] pre-emptive strike is not the monopoly of the United States. . . . We made nuclear weapons because of a nuclear threat from the United States." After the test, regime media proudly proclaimed this major milestone as "an historic event that brought happiness to our military people" and called it a "great leap forward in the building of a great prosperous, powerful socialist nation."

The aggressive rhetoric of the first term of the George W. Bush administration probably reinforced the regime's decision to pursue nuclear weaponry, to continue its self-imposed isolation, and to engage the West on its own terms. Jong Il's style of coupling defiance with selective engagement throughout the decade was primarily driven by a fundamental defensive need. The Congressional Research Service suggested a range of motivations for the nuclear test in 2006 that could be broadened to cover his general commitment to the nuclear weapons program as a whole, including a desire to increase North Korea's leverage in potential bilateral negotiations with Washington, to ensure security of the regime against a U.S. attack, and to test technical capabilities. Ultimately, the George W.

Bush administration ended up in the same place that the Clinton administration had landed. It eased sanctions and removed North Korea from the State Sponsors of Terrorism list as it negotiated another nuclear agreement in February 2007 and resumed food aid. From Kim Jong Il's perspective, it seemed that the United States could be managed if North Korea remained steadfast in its commitment to nuclear weapons development.

For Kim Jong Un, possession of nuclear weapons was more than just national strategy. That brazen nuclear test, along with the ideological and existential justification wrapped up in the concepts of *juche* and *suryong,* provided him with multiple layers of protection. It steeped the nation in the Kim family mythology of supreme power and further warped the coddled young Jong Un's sense of reality and expectations. But that October 2006 test, and his grandfather's and father's decisions to commit to advancing nuclear weapons, would also narrow his choices once Jong Un took power, boxing him into the conviction that the fate of his nation and its twenty-five million people rested on the survival of this nuclear legacy. Kim and his classmates at the military university—the future military elite—no doubt celebrated that nuclear milestone, which probably also fortified their optimism about their country's future and reinforced their belief in their role as defenders and heroes.

TRAINING A MILLENNIAL GUERRILLA

In the two years after Kim Jong Il's stroke, North Korea undertook a series of actions driven by a combination of a desire to look strong for both domestic and international audiences, despite the leader's obvious health problems, and to provide some opportunities for Kim Jong Un to learn the art of North Korea's coercive diplomacy. The regime also undoubtedly intended to assert its position vis-à-vis the incoming Obama administration to be able to better dictate the terms on which it would engage—or not—with the United States. In a statement released immediately before Obama's inauguration, the North Korean Foreign Ministry proclaimed that the country's "status as a nuclear weapons state will remain unchanged," signaling its resistance to negotiating away its nuclear weapons. In April 2009, Pyongyang conducted a satellite launch, claiming its right to the peaceful use of space, but in reality it was most likely a test of the technology for its intercontinental ballistic missile systems. Using the ensuing sanctions and international condemnation of its space launch as justification, the regime withdrew from the Six-Party Talks, said it would not follow through on its obligations under the agreements reached in that framework, and conducted a nuclear test in May, claiming, "The results of the test helped satisfactorily settle the scientific and technological problems arising in further increasing the power of nuclear weapons and steadily developing nuclear technology."

Meanwhile, the regime continued to manufacture crises and take opportunistic advantage in other ways, events that served as important training moments for the rising Kim Jong Un. Just two months after President Obama was inaugurated, North Korea apprehended two American journalists, Laura Ling and Euna Lee, who were covering a story about North Korean defectors near the Chinese border in March 2009. Three months later, the regime sentenced them to twelve years of hard labor for intending to produce a documentary to "slander" North Korea. Tensions were high as reports indicated that they were beaten and dragged across the border to North Korea by zealous border security guards. The two journalists were released only when former president Bill Clinton went to Pyongyang to retrieve them, and the photos of Kim Jong Il beaming as he sat across the table from Clinton dominated the headlines. The regime did not waste the opportunity for a propaganda moment, stating, "Clinton expressed words of sincere apology to Kim Jong Il for the hostile acts committed by the two American journalists . . . [and] courteously conveyed to Kim Jong Il an earnest request of the U.S. government to leniently pardon them." The Clinton visit succeeded in its obvious intention of optimizing the perception of North Korea's status among equals, while also conveying that Kim, despite his stroke, was lucid and firmly in charge.

When the conservative politician Lee Myung-bak assumed the South Korean presidency in 2008, a decade of the previous government's engagement-focused Sunshine Policy, which had poured an estimated $3 billion into the North's coffers, came to an end. He took a new hard line, eliciting harsh responses and name-calling from Pyongyang. Tensions continued in March 2010 with North Korea's sinking of the South Korean navy ship *Cheonan* and, later that year, the shelling of an island near the disputed maritime border, under the pretext of responding to South Korean military drills nearby. One resident described the result: "Houses and mountains are on fire and people are evacuating." The South Korean air force scrambled their F-16 fighter jets and fired artillery; the prospect of a military conflict on the Korean Peninsula seemed inevitable. The United Nations and alarmed leaders from Washington and Beijing cautioned restraint on both sides. Yet at nearly the same time as the island-shelling incident, North Korea revealed a large uranium enrichment plant to visiting U.S. former officials and academics, who were amazed by the modern, advanced facility, which triggered suspicion about the regime's intention to make highly enriched uranium bomb fuel.

As an insurance policy against regime-ending retaliatory acts by the United States or South Korea, and to be better positioned to extract political and economic concessions, Kim Jong Il engaged in a flurry of diplomatic activity with North Korea's biggest patron, Beijing. He visited China multiple times after his stroke, sent and received high-level delegations, and pledged undying friendship and cooperation. His effort paid off, as Chinese leaders publicly welcomed the transfer of power to young Jong Un.

In the meantime, the Obama administration, working in concert with the conservative Lee government in South Korea, adopted and maintained a policy often derogatorily called "strategic patience." This meant a refusal to engage without a sincere effort by Kim Jong Il to move toward denuclearization and improve inter-Korean relations, while tightening sanctions, expanding missile defense systems in the region, bolstering U.S. alliances, and prodding Beijing to alter its strategic approach to North Korea. Strategic patience led to charges that President Obama was simply responding to North Korea's provocative actions and providing space for the continued advancement of Pyongyang's nuclear weapons program. But North Korea's commitment to bolstering Kim Jong Un's bona fides, its unwillingness to negotiate, and the regime's apparent desire to complete its strategic weapons program regardless of the consequences constrained U.S. and South Korean options. At the same time, Kim's belligerence provided an opportunity for the Obama administration to deepen alliance coordination and motivate Beijing to take a tougher stance to rein in Pyongyang's recklessness.

These were the first major lessons Kim senior tried to convey to his son. Jong Un almost certainly began to appreciate the mechanics and the art of coercive diplomacy—maintain the initiative, manufacture tension, sow fear, freeze out and then mend fences with China, the United States, and South Korea, all the while steadily making progress on the nuclear weapons program.

Two generations removed from the devastation of the Korean War, distanced physically and psychologically from the horrors of the famine, and inheriting an advanced nuclear weapons program that put North Korea in the center of the region's geopolitics, Jong Un had reason to be optimistic about his country's future. There was much to learn still, but no one, perhaps not even Kim Jong Il himself, could have predicted that his son would be such an apt student.

SIX

BIGGER, BADDER, BOLDER

T MAY HAVE BEEN the final gift for Kim Jong Un from his cinephile father. On January 8, 2012, on the younger Kim's twenty-eighth birthday and just a couple of weeks after the elder Kim's death, North Korea released a documentary chronicling the successor's military exploits. It was part of a frenzied effort to build Jong Un's leadership credentials and martial excellence in order to bulk up his thin résumé. In the first scene, Jong Un is shown galloping on a black-and-white dappled horse, a hero leading his country forward. He is then seen driving a tank, observing firing exercises, speaking with pilots, and smiling and shaking the hands of grateful soldiers and commanders. Then he is pictured as a decisive leader at a satellite control center after the April 2009 launch, boldly declaring, "I had decided to wage a real war if the enemies shot down" the rocket, indicating that the regime sought to tie Jong Un's bona fides to the burgeoning ballistic missile program. The documentary quotes Kim Jong Il saying that his son, "our general, resembles me" and that he has "outstanding [military] strategies and is well versed in military tactics. . . . He is a man of many abilities and the genius among geniuses."

Just a week earlier, on January 1, 2012, in a joint New Year's editorial, North Korea's three main state newspapers asserted Jong Un's legitimacy, stating, "Kim Jong-un, the supreme leader of our Party and our people, is the banner of victory and glory of Songun . . . Korea and eternal center of its unity." And it exhorted "the whole Party, the entire army and all the people" to "become human bulwarks and human shields in defending Kim Jong-un unto death."

The birthday documentary had a decidedly optimistic tone, and a sense that its youthful protagonist would, by the sheer force of his confidence and masculine vigor, propel the country toward a socialist—and nuclear— paradise. This confidence was his natural right, given that the blood of Kim Il Sung coursed through his veins. Rooted in the ideological and institutional structures of the regime, it was advanced by the propaganda machinery that created a hero and lauded his every move. Unburdened by the historical experience of colonization, war, and famine, or any sense of affinity with Beijing and Moscow, which had figured so prominently in the consciousnesses of his grandfather and his father, Kim Jong Un was positioned to believe that he could create history himself.

SWAGGER

Elder brother and erstwhile successor Kim Jong Nam told a Japanese journalist soon after his father died that dynastic succession is "a joke to the outside world" and that his half-brother would be "just a nominal figure, [and] the members of the power elite will be the ones in actual power." He prognosticated that North Korea would collapse without reforms. "The Kim Jong Un regime will not last long," he added ominously, claiming that China did not in fact welcome the hereditary succession but merely acknowledged it for the sake of maintaining stability. Jong Nam was openly voicing what most outside observers thought and some insiders probably suspected. How could a twentysomething with no known experience in governing a country, much less a nuclear-armed nation with a moribund economy under the tightening noose of sanctions, possibly survive?

Instead of timidity, there was swagger. Right out of the gate, Jong Un started to poke and prod, test and push the bounds of international tolerance, calculating that he could withstand almost any punishment. Perhaps he felt he had no choice but to push. The East Asia specialist Kongdan Oh Hassig points to "an inferiority complex": "He is trying to show that he has a strategic mind, that the military stands behind him and that no one stands against him." He chose to double down on his nuclear weapons program, despite the financial consequences and international isolation. For the first six years of his rule, Kim kept the world on edge with his belligerent rhetoric while accelerating the demonstration of his nuclear and missile capabilities. To a large extent, he has maintained his initiative, to the frustration of the United States and his neighbors. At the CIA, where I was a lead political analyst at the time, that meant providing the analysis for a seemingly never-ending series of National Security Council policy meetings, producing President's Daily Briefs—our signature product designed to support the president, the cabinet, and other senior officials—and spending lots of late nights at the office.

On leap day in 2012, after two years of bilateral negotiations, North Korea agreed to a deal with the United States that called for a suspension of uranium enrichment, international inspections, and a moratorium on nuclear and missile tests in exchange for 240,000 tons of food aid. A mere two weeks later, the new Kim regime announced its intention to conduct a space launch banned by U.N. sanctions. North Korea had long insisted on its right to peaceful use of outer space and claimed that it wanted to send satellites into orbit to better predict the weather and harvest yields, but international voices argued that this was simply a cover and that the regime intended to test ballistic missile technology. The April 13 launch failed and earned a fresh round of U.N. sanctions. Washington called the test a violation of the leap day agreement and suspended its plans to deliver the food aid. But surprisingly the regime admitted its failure rather than push out propaganda that it had succeeded, as it had done for the previous failed launch in 2009. It was the first sign for many of us in Langley that Jong Un might be a different kind of leader, more transparent and more willing to take risks and see failure as an opportunity to improve and learn. Within hours of the launch, regime media reported, "Scientists, technicians and experts are now looking into the cause of the failure."

The admission of failure was also striking given the fact that the most important day in North Korea—the hundredth anniversary of Kim Il Sung's birthday, April 15, 2012—was just a couple of days away. One would have thought that the new leader would want to use the occasion to highlight his success. On that day, Kim presided over his first military parade and again, departing from received practice, delivered a twenty-minute speech, unlike his father, who had avoided public speaking during his entire seventeen years of rule. As six road-mobile intercontinental ballistic missiles—some or all of which might have been mock-ups rather than the real thing—rolled by, provoking concern about North Korea's increasing capabilities and intentions, Kim saluted, clapped, and waved.

The speech itself wasn't special, but the event was still captivating. Kim swallowed hard before he uttered his first words, shuffled his feet as he spoke, and had his eyes glued to his notes, revealing considerable nervousness. In that first public address, he was at once affirming the legacy of his grandfather and his father and upholding his father's military-first policy. But with the first nuclear test in 2006 and improved development of ballistic missiles notched in his belt—as the road-mobile ICBMs showed—he proclaimed that "the days are gone forever when our enemies could blackmail us with nuclear bombs." In veering away from his father's customary practice of avoiding public speaking, Kim Jong Un's decision to address the people in this massive plaza on the most important day of the year also reflected his different approach to leadership. As longtime

North Korea expert Cheong Seong-chang from South Korea's Sejong Institute put it, "Kim Jong Il was behind mysterious curtains, refrained from making public speeches and gave orders through the party." As a result, Cheong added, "the public feared him. . . . But Kim Jong Il was never loved by the public." Jong Un, on the other hand, seems intent on creating that personal bond with the people and linking the regime's powerful rhetoric to himself. The young general was undoubtedly claiming ownership of North Korea's security and showing off his full control of the military to an outside world that was still snickering and taking bets on how long he would last, and to the home audience he wanted to assure and warn that he was here to stay.

Eight months later, in December 2012, North Korea announced its intention to launch another "satellite," despite Washington's admonition that it would view the launch as "a highly provocative act." And launch they did, on December 12, 2012—12-12-12—and earned another set of U.N. sanctions. In television coverage, the regime portrayed Kim Jong Un as a hands-on leader who personally ordered the launch from a satellite command center, smoking a cigarette while looking at the data and results, in an attempt to frame the young man as bold and action-oriented in the face of widespread international censure. Two months later, in February 2013, just a little over a year into Kim's rule, North Korea conducted its third nuclear test, and Kim's first. Director of National Intelligence James Clapper testified in his annual threat assessment for the Senate Committee on Armed Services that the satellite launch of December 2012, the ballistic missiles previewed at the parade, and the February 2013 nuclear test "demonstrate North Korea's commitment to develop long-range missile technology that could pose a direct threat to the United States, and its efforts to produce and market ballistic missiles raise broader regional and global security concerns." His statements reflected the growing uneasiness in Washington about the North Korean threat.

Under Kim, North Korea codified its status as a nuclear-armed state by inscribing that description into the constitution it revised in

2012, seemingly drawing strength from the growing list of sanctions and U.S. and regional warnings. Posted on its Web portal, the document's preamble credited Kim Jong Il for "turn[ing] our fatherland into an invincible state of political ideology, a nuclear-armed state and an indomitable military power, paving the ground for the construction of a strong and prosperous nation." It also reinforced Kim Jong Un's role in advancing these nuclear capabilities, further solidifying his authority over their use. But while Pyongyang in a 2013 law declared North Korea a "full-fledged nuclear weapons state," it asserted all the while that its weapons program was intended for deterrence to underscore that it would be a responsible nuclear power.

Regime propaganda kept pace with the developments in North Korea's strategic arsenal, further linking Kim Jong Un to the growing size and sophistication of the nuclear weapons program. There is Kim smiling broadly as the regime conducts a ballistic missile test from a submarine, his hair blowing in the wind, a cigarette held casually in his hand against the backdrop of an azure sea. There is Kim with scientists and technicians observing what appears to be a miniaturized nuclear warhead that if successfully put atop a ballistic missile would be a serious threat to the United States and North Korea's neighbors. There is Kim observing a long-range rocket launch, his back to the camera, the plumes floating majestically against the mountainous landscape. All of these photos sent experts scurrying to ascertain North Korea's latest nuclear capabilities. Within the first six years of his rule, Kim Jong Un tested three times more missiles than his father and grandfather combined—including new ballistic missiles of various ranges from multiple locations and a submarine-launched version—and conducted four of the North's six nuclear tests, all before he turned thirty-five years old.

MAKING "MILITARY FIRST" GREAT AGAIN

Not satisfied with just advancing North Korea's strategic weapons program, Kim Jong Un also sought to selectively modernize its conventional armed forces, which at more than a million soldiers makes it the world's fourth-largest military. Nearly three-quarters of its armed forces are positioned just thirty-five miles away from the Demilitarized Zone that divides the Koreas, making the peninsula one of the most dangerous places in the world. For context, thirty-five miles is roughly the distance between Washington, D.C., and Baltimore, or New York City and Greenwich, Connecticut, the distance of a commute to work that millions of Americans do every day. The North has thousands of forward-deployed and fortified artillery pieces aimed at the South, thirteen hundred aircraft, around seventy submarines, and naval vessels able to support amphibious operations and the insertion of special operations forces, all detailed in "Military and Security Developments Involving the Democratic People's Republic of Korea," a 2017 Defense Department report to Congress.

On paper, the North Korean military is formidable, and given its location, the threats that the regime has made, and the potential for any minor incident to spark a military conflict, it cannot be discounted. Nevertheless, as the Pentagon's report to Congress noted, the military is operating with aging equipment that was given or produced based on Soviet and Chinese designs from the 1950s, '60s, and '70s, a painful reminder of North Korea's best days of support from its friends in Moscow and Beijing. Moreover, many of the soldiers fare not much better than the general population in terms of diet and nutrition, and the regime has had to occasionally reduce the minimum height requirement for conscription because of stunted growth that has resulted from the 1990s famine. Around the time of Kim's ascension, the minimum height was reduced to four feet nine inches. The regime also regularly uses conscripts for nonmilitary activities, including construction projects and agricultural duties.

Kim almost certainly understands the limitations of the military, given that his grooming during the succession process and his personal interest were in this field. And although he probably understands that he is unlikely to win a conventional war against the United States and South Korea, he has not abandoned living up to his father's ideological legacy of "military first." Kim has placed a high priority on modernizing some aspects of North Korea's conventional capabilities, presiding over artillery firepower exercises, fighter pilot competitions, and artillery drills that simulate striking military targets in South Korea. Kim watched a night-combat flight drill and ordered training to be done as if North Korea were in a state of war. The regime has also demonstrated new surface-to-air missile launchers and accompanying radar, debuted missile capabilities that could improve its reach into South Korea, upgraded selected naval ships, and produced missile-armed patrol boats and corvettes. In 2013, the regime also used a drone in a live-fire military drill, suggesting that the Korean People's Army was trying to incorporate new technologies. Kim could also rely on his 180,000 commandos, the elite special operations forces, who are well-fed, highly motivated, and "designed for rapid offensive operations, internal defense against foreign attacks, or limited attacks against vulnerable targets in [South Korea]," according to the Defense Department's 2017 report to Congress. In 2016, the regime publicized a simulated special operations forces battalion assault on the Blue House, including helicopter insertions and a mock abduction of the South Korean president.

The regime matched these displays of muscular defiance with its rhetoric. Within Kim's first year and a half of rule, the regime threatened to attack South Korea "by unprecedented peculiar means and methods of our own style," the first of many menacing statements. Pyongyang also threatened preemptive nuclear attack against the United States, warned foreign diplomats in Pyongyang that their safety could not be guaranteed, urged foreigners in South Korea to leave the country, declared the Korean War armistice null and void, and restarted the plutonium reactor at Yongbyon, which had been shuttered in 2007. Pyongyang also released a photo of Kim sitting at a massive table, surrounded by three military officials, possibly reviewing martial plans. The most important aspect of this room was a large map titled "U.S. mainland strike plan," depicting four lines—intercontinental ballistic missile trajectories—coming from Asia and hitting four targets in the United States, including Washington, D.C. The purpose of this propaganda was to showcase Kim's defiance to the world at the outset of his takeover.

It didn't seem to matter to the regime that its actions and bluster were undermining its ability to make money. To protest annual U.S.–South Korean military drills and U.N. sanctions that were piling up as a result of North Korea's nuclear and missile tests, the regime pulled fifty thousand North Korean workers from the lucrative inter-Korean Kaesong Industrial Complex, which was earning the North around $100 million per year. The tension also had an impact on North Korea's tourism industry, another source of hard currency. Kim's actions during these first months suggested that he was keenly focused on boosting his military credentials for domestic and international audiences, particularly the much older and more experienced leaders in Washington, Beijing, Seoul, and Tokyo, ensuring that he was not to be taken lightly. Indeed, he deliberately deepened North Korea's isolation. Having rebuffed U.S., South Korean, and Chinese attempts to reengage, preferring instead to use bluster and bullying to try to get his way, Kim refused to meet with any foreign head of state for the first six years of his rule. He limited his significant foreign contacts to Kenji Fujimoto, the Japanese sushi chef whom he knew in his youth and whom he invited to Pyongyang in 2012, and Dennis Rodman, an American basketball player, who has visited North Korea four times since 2013.

Kim Jong Un was intent on doing things his way.

THE NEW NORMAL

In the intelligence community during these tense years, we started to talk about the "new normal"—in which we saw ballistic missile tests almost every two weeks and heard sustained, alarming rhetoric that most veteran watchers of North Korea agreed was the worst observed in twenty years. The United States and regional allies responded with sanctions and robust shows of force, including sending fighter jets, warships, and bombers to the region, and deploying missile interceptors. U.S. leaders sought to reassure allies about their commitment to the defense of the region and show North Korea that they would not be cowed into engaging on its terms or offering concessions without seeing significant progress on denuclearization, while urging Pyongyang to abide by its international obligations. Chinese leaders continued to make excuses for the regime's behavior—for example, by refusing to put the blame on Pyongyang for the attack on the South Korean naval vessel *Cheonan* in 2010—prioritizing regional stability over denuclearization. But China's new leader, Xi Jinping, elevated to power in November 2012, was not a fan of Jong Un's impetuous behavior, which triggered unprecedentedly public hints that Chinese leaders were questioning the value of the relationship with North Korea. President Lee Myung-bak of South Korea and his successor Park Geun-hye—whose mother had been assassinated by North Korean commandos in 1974 during an attempt to kill her husband, the South Korean president—were also in no mood to appease Pyongyang and chose to tighten their alliance with Washington, while trying to obtain Beijing's cooperation to rein in North Korea.

While the overt demonstrations and public pronouncements from Pyongyang were dominating the headlines, eliciting a response precisely as they were designed to do, Kim adjusted his behavior. About a year and a half into his rule, he began showing an ability to calibrate his actions to avoid triggering an unmanageable response from the United States and the region. For example, in April 2013, U.S. and South Korean troops increased alert levels based on signs that North Korea was planning to conduct the first test of its road-mobile, intermediate-range ballistic missile, the Musudan. With a range of between 1,550 and 2,500 miles, the weapon, if operational, would have put all of South Korea, Japan, and the U.S. military base in Guam within range. Washington, Seoul, and Tokyo believed that a test was highly likely and would have taken regional tensions to a new level. China, claiming prescheduled military exercises, conducted live-fire drills along its border with North Korea, while putting the squeeze on North Korean banks doing business with Chinese entities.

Whether the result of Chinese pressure or technical difficulties, or because the regime was spooked by the ability of U.S. and South Korean intelligence to locate these untested missiles, North Korea removed the Musudans from their launch locations—it wouldn't attempt to test this missile again until 2016, which it did eight times that year. In 2014, North Korea threatened a "new form" of nuclear test, which some took to be a thermonuclear detonation, but Kim then backed off from this threat, possibly because of the tightening noose of sanctions, his sensitivity to Chinese tolerance, or South Korea's testing of its own ballistic missile capable of hitting all of North Korea. Kim's calculus might have been informed by all of these factors, suggesting that he was learning to read his environment and assessing the risks and benefits of his actions, even as he showed every indication of making rapid progress toward the ability to threaten the United States and its allies while developing an arsenal for survivable second-strike options in the event of a conflict.

Meanwhile, we in the intelligence community were also learning to adapt and adjust ourselves to the new reality. We had seen belligerent North Korean actions and behavior before, but the combination of the uncertainty of Kim's intentions and the escalation of the intensity of his regime's maneuvers and rhetoric, without an apparent exit strategy, kept the world on edge. Indeed, the world had inadvertently become comfortable with Kim Jong Il's relatively predictable pattern of provocation followed by a charm offensive to extract political and economic benefits. As the commander of the U.S. forces at Pacific Command Admiral Samuel Locklear told Congress in April 2013, "His father and his grandfather always figured into their provocation cycle an off-ramp of how to get out of it. . . . It's not clear to me that [Kim Jong Un] has thought through how to get out of it." Even amid the threats, we in the national security bureaucracy didn't see signs that North Korea was preparing for war—for example, Pyongyang residents were going about their normal business.

But because the CIA had a duty to warn and prepare for the worst, we maintained vigilance while forecasting to the best of our ability Kim's intentions in those early days. We were all too aware that the furious pace of the missile tests and the regime's military modernization efforts had the potential to spiral quickly into an armed confrontation. At the time, one of our biggest questions was who or what served to constrain Kim's behavior. How likely was Kim to veer toward a serious miscalculation? What—or who—were the brakes or enablers of his actions?

What we were confident about was that Kim's risk tolerance was high and his confidence was growing.

DESPITE ALL THE CHEST-THUMPING and bad behavior, Kim is not looking for a military confrontation with the United States. He is rational, not suicidal, and given his involvement in his country's military affairs and almost certain knowledge of its deficiencies, he is aware that North Korea would not be able to sustain a prolonged conflict with either South Korea or the United States. Although Kim is aggressive, he is neither reckless nor a madman. In fact, he has been learning how and when to recalibrate. And it is his ability to change course and shift tactics that requires us to heed former CIA officer Richards Heuer's warnings about the "weaknesses and biases inherent in human thinking processes" and continually challenge our assumptions and perceptions about "patterns of expectations" in North Korea analysis. The intelligence community has to learn how to incorporate new information about what is driving Kim Jong Un and how we might counter this profound—and ever evolving—national security threat. So while he has stopped short of actions that might lead to U.S. or allied military responses that would threaten the regime, Kim has also made it clear that he will not give up North Korea's nuclear weapons, regardless of threats of military

attacks or engagement, and that he sees the program as vital to regime security and his legitimacy as the leader of North Korea.

The North Korean regime has often made reference to the fates
of Iraq and Libya—the invasion and overthrow of their leaders—as
key examples of what happens to states that give up their nuclear
weapons. Director of National Intelligence Dan Coats, at the 2017
Aspen Security Forum, said that Kim "has watched . . . what has
happened around the world relative to nations that possess nuclear
capabilities and the leverage they have" and added that the lesson
from Libya for North Korea is: "If you had nukes, never give them
up. If you don't have them, get them."

If we unpack this comparison, we can envision how much Kim
Jong Un might have been affected by the death of Muammar al-
Qaddafi. The once "king of kings in Africa," who ruled Libya for
four decades, was captured by rebels in October 2011, well into Jong
Un's grooming process and just two months before Kim Jong Il's
death. Graphic images of the bloodied Qaddafi ricocheted around
the world, and one can imagine how the pictures might have been
seared into Kim's brain as he adopted his relatively new public status as the anointed leader of North Korea. As one contemporary
account described:

> A dazed and confused Gaddafi is led from the drain where he was
> captured, bleeding heavily from a deep wound on the left side of
> his head, from his arm, and, apparently, from other injuries to his
> neck and torso, staining his tunic red with blood. He is next seen on
> the ground, surrounded by men with weapons shouting "God is
> great" and firing in the air.

As the angry mob pummeled Qaddafi's body, the once powerful
man begged for mercy before he drifted out of consciousness. Befit-
ting his gruesome and humiliating end, "the body of the former dictator once so feared by his Libyan opponents was facing a final
indignity—being stored on the floor of a room-sized freezer in Mis-
rata usually used by restaurants and shops to keep perishable goods."

Washington's promises of a better future if North Korea denuclearized probably sounded hollow to the regime in Pyongyang. The North's Foreign Ministry said at the time that Qaddafi's overthrow showed that the U.S.-led effort to coax Libya to give up its weapons of mass destruction had been "an invasion tactic to disarm the country."

And for Jong Un and his generation, who had come of age in a nuclear North Korea, denuclearization is most likely a foreign concept, an artifact of a distant "pre-modern" time. Furthermore, Qaddafi's death occurred in the context of the so-called Arab Spring, during a wave of popular protests against authoritarian regimes in the Middle East and North Africa, which must have highlighted for Kim the consequences of exercising insufficient suppression over a potentially powerful populace fueled by discontent and unfulfilled dreams. While nurturing the nuclear weapons program, Kim sought to fulfill those dreams of a socialist utopia, as *he himself* defined it.

SEVEN

A TWENTY-FIRST-CENTURY DICTATORSHIP

KIM JONG UN COULD not have asked for a better year to emerge as North Korea's leader, just in time to celebrate the centenary of his grandfather's birth, April 15, 2012—the day that Jong Un chose to give his first public address. The regime, under his father, had long been preparing for this date, which for North Koreans is like Christmas and the Fourth of July rolled into one. It was a sad occasion, to be sure, coming just five months after Kim Jong Il died, but it presented an ideal opportunity for his son to harness sympathy, filial piety, and nationalism to his advantage.

So when North Koreans listened to Kim Jong Un deliver his speech that day, it was the first time that they had heard their leader's voice since the days of Kim Il Sung. Adopting the mantle of the mythical, godlike leadership role that his grandfather and his father assumed and continued to hold even in death, Kim played up his likeness to his grandfather in appearance and demeanor to emphasize continuity and the bloodline, as if to proclaim himself the reincarnation of Kim Il Sung, whose policies were imprinted in his genes. Playing that role gave the new leader an aura of inevitability and predestination, while the centennial year imparted a sense of time being a flat circle.

But Kim Jong Un hasn't been one to rest on his predecessors' laurels. And while he has invoked the legacy of his grandfather and his father, he seems determined to chart his own path.

THE GUERRILLA'S GRANDSON

North Korea's fashioning of Kim Jong Un to resemble his grandfather is most likely a deliberate attempt to brush away the inconvenience of his real background and experience. If Kim Jong Il's propagandists had little to work with, given his own privileged upbringing and lack of guerrilla credentials when he succeeded his father, Jong Un was even more problematic. His mother was a dancer born in Japan, his martial experience was nonexistent in a society that glorified "military first" and perpetuated a war mentality, and he had spent several years in Europe, where he played video games while hundreds of thousands of people back home ate rats and tree bark to survive. Moreover, the temporal distance from the war and Kim's young age made it impossible to place him at the center of the narrative of the North Korean state.

Therefore, Kim's April 15 speech was heavy on history, especially that of the Korean People's Army, to show his mastery of the subject. Subsequently, the regime began "with . . . new urgency" to commemorate the Korean War, as Adam Cathcart, an astute observer of North Korean propaganda, and several other experts have pointed out. Suzy Kim, a professor of Korean history, noted that Kim renovated the Victorious Fatherland Liberation War Museum in 2013, in time for the sixtieth anniversary of the armistice. The regime declared that it was intended to serve "as a base for anti-U.S. education as it equips service personnel, working people and youth and students with the Juche idea, the anti-imperialist revolutionary ideas, outstanding commanding art, and military strategies and war tactics of President Kim Il Sung."

Jean Lee, who was the Associated Press Korea bureau chief based in Pyongyang from 2011 to 2013, visited another Korean War museum in Sinchon—where North Korea claims U.S. troops massacred civilians during the war—that Kim enlarged and refurbished in 2014. What had once been "a simple building on a grassy knoll was replaced by a palatial museum that is a veritable house of horrors, with room after room graphically bringing to life the gruesome atrocities attributed to the Americans." Lee observed, "A visit there is like walking through the set of a horror movie; visitors can walk right up to the tableaus and can practically smell the blood and hear the screams. In one tableau . . . a life-sized American soldier yanks the hair of a young Korean woman tied to a tree as another American sinks a knife into her heart. In another room, suffused in red light as though drenched with blood, American soldiers drive nails into a Korean woman's head. Rabid glee distorts their faces." As Suzy Kim pointed out, "In North Korea, the Korean War is relived continually, not just through museums and memorial sites, but also through the constant reminder of continued conflict with the United States."

For Jong Un, the invocation of Korean War history, including the documented and imagined American atrocities and the North Korean triumph over the U.S. imperialists, as well as his own heredity, of course, all serve to connect him to his guerrilla ancestry. He has harnessed the nostalgia for the era before the 1990s. "This is a man comfortable within the folds of this history," Cathcart has observed, "to the extent that he does not appear to mind imitating his grandfather's stately strolling pose or that the central massive statue in the Korean War Museum appears to look more like Kim Jong-un than the man who began the Korean War." During his frequent public appearances, Kim can be seen giving guidance at various economic, military, and social and cultural venues, as his grandfather and his father did, but he is more like the former than the latter in the way that he has allowed himself to be relatively transparent and accessible. He hugs, holds hands, and links arms with men, women, and children, seeming comfortable with young and old.

Yet while basking in the glow of his grandfather's omnipresence among his people, Kim doesn't seem content with just reliving history—though it serves to legitimize him—but wants to propel the country forward toward a new modernity.

A "SOCIALIST FAIRYLAND"

While the outside world looks askance at the young dictator, Kim Jong Un appears determined to make his youth a virtue as he reinforces the impression that he is young, vigorous, and on the move—qualities that he attributes to his country as well. Rather than giving static guidances or merely standing in stately observance while his entourage dutifully takes notes, Kim is yanking weeds, riding roller coasters, pulling the lever at the lubricant factory, navigating a tank, and galloping on a horse. The pictures of Kim during his routine visits to various locations seem almost spontaneous, with children at a nursery falling over him, tugging at his sleeve, or with women aviators who are holding on to his arm as they walk forward together toward the camera. Speaking directly to the people at that April 2012 celebration was a way of creating intimacy and conveying his confident promise that North Koreans would no longer have to tighten their belts, a striking contrast to the "two meals a day" famine years. He announced his *byungjin* (parallel development) policy the following year: that North Korea can have both nuclear weapons *and* prosperity. Animated by the optimism of one whose privilege makes him believe anything is possible, he has prioritized both of these issues and personally taken ownership of them—all part of creating and nurturing his brand.

If the architecture of the military component of *byungjin* is displayed in Korean War museums and military-inspired statues and memorials, the structures devoted to the other half of *byungjin* are represented by the monuments to leisure. Kim has built ski resorts, a riding club, skating and amusement parks, a new airport, and a dolphinarium, perhaps because he considers these to be markers of a modern state. Or in his naïveté he may simply want his people to enjoy the things to which he has had privileged access. (The sushi chef Fujimoto claimed that Kim once said, "We are here, playing basketball, riding horses, riding Jet Skis, having fun together. But what [about] the lives of the average people?") Though his father had begun the trend shortly before he died, it was under Kim Jong Un that North Korea undertook a massive building boom and promoted tourism—let's create a "socialist fairyland," the regime proclaimed—even as it was volleying threats and missiles, apparently oblivious or indifferent to the incongruity of it all.

The colorful frivolity of the water parks and roller coasters provides a stark contrast to the imposing landscape of war memorials, breathtaking in their size and smothering the country with the weight of North Korea's real and imagined martial history. North Koreans, young and old, can be seen gleefully frolicking in the massive pools of the Rungra People's Pleasure Ground. Women wearing stylish but modest swimsuits clutch at each other joyfully as they meet the machine-made waves; in the background is a labyrinth of candy-colored water slides. Boys playfully aim giant water guns at one another. Kim waves as he walks with his entourage on one of his visits, and a big group of people wearing swim trunks and swim caps cheers and waves back. At the Mirim Riding Club, opened in October 2013, visitors can "ride the horses, view equestrian shows, and relax at the beer and snacks stand," according to one of the Western-based tour companies that operate in North Korea. There are 120 horses to rent—for $8 outdoors or $10 indoors—including the prestigious Orlov Trotters that Russian president Vladimir Putin gifted to North Korea. Another tour company touted that the riding club also features "a pavilion, restaurants, sauna and more!" If horse riding or water slides are not to one's taste, pleasure seekers can go to a high-tech shooting range, play miniature golf, watch a movie in a 4-D cinema, or see dolphins do tricks. The Masikryong ski resort has nine slopes and a nine-floor chalet with a swimming pool, sauna, and spa, and its shop sells European goods like cheese and chocolate, according to the journalist Kim Wall, who visited there in 2014.

One of the new regime's strangest early moments was in the summer of 2012 when state media released a photograph of Kim Jong Un and some foreign diplomats riding a roller coaster in the new Rungra People's Pleasure Ground at its official opening on July 26. Kim is buckled in, grinning widely as his legs dangle in the air against the pale blue sky. Senior North Korean officials are also on the ride, some enjoying it, others looking terrified. The impossible juxtaposition of the leader of the world's most closed society, the nuclear-armed serial violator of human rights, on a roller coaster enjoying himself with boyish abandon was jarring and grotesque.

The epicenter of this socialist fairyland is Pyongyang, the locus of power where the elite live, work, and play, and where we now see a glimpse of an emerging material and consumer culture. The fevered construction boom under Kim's rule has created what foreign diplomats there call "Pyonghattan." The Changjon Street Apartments, for example, consist of an eighteen-tower complex, some up to forty-seven stories tall, creating a skyline that one would expect to see in New York City or Seoul. Indeed, visitors to North Korea over the years have returned with reports of new construction, streets crowded with imported cars and taxis, and new restaurants serving a dozen varieties of pizza and pasta accompanied by wine or beer.

Consumerism has been entrenched, embraced, and encouraged. Since Kim came to power, more North Koreans enjoy smartphones, taxis, flat-screen televisions, and home appliances made in Japan and South Korea. A wide range of these and similar goods are available in hundreds of markets and state-run shops. Wall described what she called "mundane life and everyday happiness: uniformed military couples holding hands at Pyongyang's funfair; roller-skating girls in pink sweats buying ice cream; bored parents waiting on benches in the shade." A year later, Oliver Wainwright, the architecture and design critic for *The Guardian,* also noted signs of an emerging prosperity, at least in Pyongyang. "Kids zoom around the public spaces on rollerblades," he wrote, "while women sport brightly coloured fitted jackets and high heels, shading their faces from the sun with glittery lace parasols and oversized sunglasses— fashion accessories that were unheard of just a few years ago."

Outside Pyongyang, starting in 2014, Kim has also sought to develop the east coast area of Wonsan, roughly 150 square miles of it, aiming to attract millions of tourists. It is one of the few North Korean economic ventures not under international or U.S. sanctions, even though he has conducted scores of missile tests from the area. The Korea Maritime Institute, a South Korean think tank, estimated that tourism pumps the equivalent of around $44 million into the North Korean economy, with 80 percent of the visitors coming from China. According to a North Korean brochure seeking foreign investors that was analyzed by Reuters, Kim sought backers to help build a $7.3 million department store and a $123 million golf course, and had sent a delegation to Spain to study several successful tourist attractions there. The regime had already constructed a new airport and a ski resort in the area to spur Wonsan's development.

The images that the regime chooses to disseminate and weave into Kim's hagiography say a lot about how he envisions North Korea's future and his place in it. The master builder of Pyongyang, who chose to juxtapose war monuments and nuclear weapons and ballistic missiles with his country's newly available luxuries and resorts, might be trying to educate the people about how they have this prosperity *because* of the nuclear weapons program that keeps them safe from the hostile outside world and provides them with status.

Kim may also be using the imagery of these amenities as a corrective, a way to undermine the dominant external narrative of a decaying, starving, economically hobbled North Korea. And the reality is that outside Pyongyang, a city of around three million where only the elite have the privilege of living and working, roughly twenty-two million North Koreans live in a bleak, denuded landscape, where they eke out a living from what remains of the public distribution system, engaging in market activity and receiving urgently needed goods and services from international aid groups, with little hope of ever visiting the glitzy capital, much less dining at one of the high-end restaurants.

More important, Kim may be deploying these signs of affluence not as mere window dressing but to show the world the success of North Korea's self-reliance and to craft an internal narrative about North Korea's well-being at a time when his people are being exposed to more and more information about South Korea's wealth. DVDs and flash drives of the South's soap operas and K-pop have been smuggled into the North in ever greater numbers, infiltrating its previously sealed mental and cultural landscape and presenting a danger to the regime. As a result, Kim has engaged in border crackdowns, as in the spring of 2014, and strengthened punishment for crimes including illegal contact with foreigners, viewing South Korean shows and listening to foreign radio broadcasts, and aiding defectors, among a slew of other acts. The international advocacy organization Human Rights Watch noted in a 2019 report that Kim has not relented on his desire to maintain control over North Koreans' movement and access to information and goods. He has upped the number of CCTV cameras, barbed wire fences, and border guards along the 880-mile border with China. This has led to a dramatic decrease in the number of North Koreans successfully defecting to South Korea, from 2,706 in 2011 to only around 800 in 2018.

Kim's focus on leisure and entertainment suggests that he is concentrating on the younger generations whose minds are more pliable and susceptible to fantastical claims by the regime that Kim has supernatural powers. Certainly recognizing that as the young come of age they become even more removed from the war and the need for North Korea's continued isolation, he is systematically creating an education infrastructure that seeks to shape their minds. As several North Korea watchers have found, the regime has directed its propaganda and education efforts toward creating a new generation of loyalists by reviving children's and youth organizations and intensifying indoctrination. A North Korean high school syllabus shows that the regime has instituted a three-year course on Kim Jong Un's early life, totaling eighty-one classroom hours. In 2014, the regime released childhood photos of Kim wearing a general's uniform, pointing out that he was an expert marksman with a pistol at the age of three and had learned seven languages, and that as a teenager "discovered new geographical features" of North Korea and was an erudite scholar of military leaders.

Christopher Richardson, a researcher who focuses on how childhood is experienced in North Korea, points out that the regime is seeking to paint Kim as a child genius with "messianic destiny" and the natural heir to the revolution. In addition to extolling Kim's brilliance, the aim is to show the youth how they can be like him, in the way that Christians, for example, exhort their believers to walk in the way of their god. They, too, can help advance the revolution by following their leader. They, too, with their youthful vigor, idealism, and purity, can drive the country forward, safe in the knowledge that their leader has provided the ultimate protection through his possession of nuclear weapons.

In 2015, Oliver Wainwright booked a trip to Pyongyang with a Beijing-based tour company and traveled through the city for ten days, along with three North Koreans who were there to make sure he would not do anything subversive. Despite the surveillance of his minders, he was able to photograph the capital in rich detail, offering poignant observations from his perspective as an expert in architecture and the arts. He wrote that in every new building "there is a peculiarly consistent style of preschool colour schemes and shiny synthetic surfaces, the pastel palettes and axial symmetry giving an eerie feeling of walking into a Wes Anderson film set"—quirky, escapist, and saturated with color. Wainwright described it as "architecture as anaesthetic, a powerful tool for the state to infantilise its people." He's right. For Kim and his generation, people who came of age in a nuclear North Korea, combining images of a nation in a perpetual state of war—posters, statues, military parades—with the pastel wonderland of leisure and consumption makes complete sense. Infantilization of the North Korean people is intentional, and a logical outgrowth of extreme repression, in which the regime has the power to dictate where one lives, marries, works, and plays, subsuming their individual desires to those of their leader.

But as Kim peddles upscale apartments and appliances to the elite, he can't help but create hope and generate more desire for luxury and leisure that must be satisfied. Kim has linked his legitimacy to improving people's lives, so he has to keep delivering on his promises. Hope is powerful—not only can it help people adapt to their surroundings and deal with inefficiencies and obstacles, but it can also lead to discontent, with the potential to send the entire construct crumbling, physically and metaphorically, slowly or spectacularly. Rüdiger Frank, a German expert on North Korea, has pondered whether North Korea will go the way of the Soviet Union or East Germany:

> North Koreans are now as materialistic, greedy and unsatisfied as their comrades in the Soviet Union and East Germany once were. . . . North Korea has begun playing the capitalists' game, and it has gone much further than most European socialist countries ever went. Shortages are not the dominant issue anymore, and access to almost anything is guaranteed—as long as one has enough money.

Defector interviews reveal some of that dissatisfaction, including the frustration born of being unable to advance. One defector who left in 2014 said in a *Washington Post* interview, "I wanted to progress in life, I wanted to go to university, but because my mother had defected to China, it looked like I wouldn't be able to go any further." A twenty-five-year-old who was thwarted from pursuing his dream as a result of having family living in China said, "I was ambitious. I wanted to be a party member and enjoy all the opportunities that come with that. My dream was to make lots of money and be a high-ranking government official. Family background means so much in North Korea." Another young adult decried the contradictions: "We were told in school that we could be anybody. But after graduation, I realized that this wasn't true."

It remains to be seen whether Kim Jong Un will be able to satisfy people's aspirations more swiftly than the growing level of frustration, and whether repression can continue to sufficiently contain and shape hope in tandem with the regime rather than against it.

THE *JANGMADANG* GENERATION

While Kim Jong Un lived a frictionless life of ease, enjoying luxuries during the famine of the 1990s, eating his favorite foods, playing his favorite games, surrounded by servants and family members eager to please the son of the dictator, his fellow millennials—the *jangmadang,* or "market," generation—eked out a living, depending on their status, by begging, stealing, smuggling, or engaging in micro-entrepreneurial activities. Kim Jong Un was populating the North Korean landscape with amusement parks, restaurants, and department stores carrying luxury items, and its people were walking around carrying lace parasols, in sharp contrast to his grandfather's North Korea, which had been "as anticonsumerist a culture as could exist in the twentieth century," according to the author Barbara Demick. Anticonsumerism made sense when the regime provided everything from food to employment, healthcare, and clothing (one set for summer and one for winter), and when North Korea could rely on its friends in the Soviet bloc and China for subsidized food, oil, military hardware, and industrial equipment. But after the Cold War ended, North Koreans could no longer depend on the state, as rations diminished or disappeared altogether, forcing even the true believers to turn to the black market to survive.

The inability of the government to feed its people and the all too real imminence of death by starvation gave birth to market activities, even though, being antithetical to Communism, they were technically illegal. In 2007, Kim Jong Il directly addressed the growth of market activity, decrying it as "eating away at the socialism of our own style . . . and a birthplace of all sorts of nonsocialist practices." But this was a trend he could not stop, as a generation grew up watching their parents sell tofu and cookies, rent out rooms for romantic trysts or prostitution, or smuggle goods from South Korea and China, and they in turn engaged in these activities themselves.

Yeonmi Park wrote in her memoir that her father ran a smuggling business in Pyongyang, while she and the rest of the family lived far from there, and that he was not alone. "Capitalism was . . . alive and well," she wrote, adding that "if you knew where to look, you could also find things like digital watches and DVD players from vendors who operated in the gray area between legal and illegal trade in the new North Korea." Teenager Kim Hyuck, whose account Demick described in her award winning book *Nothing to Envy,* made repeated trips across the Tumen River, which separates China from North Korea. He bought irons and other household goods in North Korea and would sell them in China wherever there was a demand. As Demick described, he would spend the proceeds on more goods from North Korea, buying them for a pittance from people desperate to help their families survive, and resell those goods in China for a big profit.

Ha-Young, a defector who came from Musan, on North Korea's border with China, recounted how she helped her mother's wholesale business thrive during and after the worst of the famine. According to Jieun Baek, who cataloged these defectors' stories, Ha-Young's mother would acquire around one thousand pounds of used clothing at a time from China, paying everyone involved in the transaction to ensure the safe transport of the items across the border, as well as to protect herself. Ha-Young would help her mother categorize the goods based on quality and then price them, after which the items would be fanned out to other women who sold them in their own businesses. She recalled that as a result of her mother's success, her family had a refrigerator, a washing machine, a television, and plentiful and varied food. How did they manage to circumvent the laws? "Since her family was consistently profitable for the police, there was a patrol officer dedicated to protecting Ha-Young's mother in case she got into any trouble," Baek explained.

The regime tolerated these activities, turning a blind eye and even encouraging them, probably because it realized that it could not provide for its people as in the past, and because of the impossibility of shutting them all down. Many of North Korea's elite and senior members of the Korean Workers' Party leveraged their positions to engage in this same sort of private trade, though usually on a much larger scale. "The Kim regime has survived, and in some ways prospered," noted William Brown, a former senior official at the Office of the Director of National Intelligence and an expert on North Korea's economy, "by allowing continuous growth in market activity often at the expense of state enterprises and state control." The government started legalizing markets as early as 2003, according to South Korea's Korean Development Institute, and by 2017 the institute estimated that there were more than 400 state-sanctioned markets in the country, and if they counted the informal markets carrying on business in the alleyways, the number could be as high as 750.

Recognizing the need to assert the government's role in economic activities and to generate goodwill for Kim Jong Un, the regime has tried to replicate in the provinces what it was doing in the capital. For example, in Sinuiju, a midsize provincial city with a population of around 350,000 people, according to the 2008 North Korean census, the most recent one we have access to, the regime built a new stadium and a theater, renovated schools, and began construction on a new park, to demonstrate, it was made clear, their leader's love for the people. Kim also expanded and renovated facilities for market activities, providing a tax boon for the central government as well as for North Korean entrepreneurs. Data on whether this type of project has succeeded in generating goodwill toward Kim is hard to come by, given the difficulty of eliciting honest responses from North Koreans, who are afraid of expressing anything resembling criticism of their government.

As for the countless, smaller unofficial markets, the regime has been unable to tame them. For example, John Everard, a former British ambassador to North Korea, witnessed a police raid on one that consisted of just a handful of women. When approached, the women ignored the police at first but then packed up their bundles and just moved to another street. As soon as the police left, they set up their stalls again at the original spot.

North Korea's economy, as the political scientist Robert Kelly has described, "is an incredibly inefficient, byzantine arrangement of bribes, cronyism and favours that make for a near-impenetrable business atmosphere in which no one is sure where the state ends and private economy begins." The moneyed elites, known as the *donju,* "the masters of money," have generated their wealth by taking advantage of the ambiguous spaces created by Kim Jong Un's tolerance for market activity.

Indeed, the rise of the *donju* has been one of the most profound changes in North Korean society over the past two decades, according to defectors and as reported by the tourists and journalists who have witnessed it in their travels. "There are great and unexpected changes taking place within North Korea," the elite defector Thae Yong Ho explained in testimony before the U.S. House of Representatives. "Contrary to the official policy and wish of the regime, the free markets are flourishing." Of course, national policy is one thing, but actually implementing it is another, and given the web of relationships and money flows between North Korea's small entrepreneurs and the local officials, it would be difficult to make big changes in these now entrenched practices without massive disruption and potential unrest. Some estimates indicate that 1.6 million North Koreans are working in informal markets, producing, on average, 70 to 80 percent of a North Korean's income.

As numerous experts and North Korea watchers have pointed out, the country's urban elites are making money, and lots of it. They are wearing colorful designer clothing, driving Audis, carrying leather bags, and using cell phones from China. They spend their money on the new amusements dispensed by the regime and provide their children with goods unfathomable a generation ago. They are hailing taxis to get to their destinations, often buying snacks from one of the many stalls as they wait. Even as early as the aughts, money was shaping the lives of children born to the *donju*. Yeonmi Park recalled that in 2000 her father, who was a smuggler, brought back "loads of gifts": perfume, new clothes, books, makeup, and a 1980s-era Nintendo console. Those with regime ties—high-ranking military and party officials—have reaped the most benefits. Using those connections, they have amassed fortunes by overseeing Kim Jong Un's numerous infrastructure and building projects, often exploiting foreign contacts that they cultivated when working overseas. Aspiring entrepreneurs rely on proximity to the regime's inner circles, where kickbacks are the name of the game. In the words of the journalists Daniel Tudor and James Pearson, "In a sense . . . the top leadership of North Korea is operating a protection racket."

The visibility of the wealth generated by the *donju* and the *jangmadang* generation is probably reinforcing the view among his people and the outside world that Kim Jong Un is living up to his own rhetoric of improving the quality of life for North Koreans. Indeed, Kim seems to be encouraging people to improve their condition through their own grit to overcome the realities of frequent electrical outages and lack of public goods and services.

Jean Lee, the former Associated Press bureau chief in Pyongyang, has articulated how the regime has been using soap operas and films to help disseminate the regime's priorities. In her fascinating study of North Korean soap operas produced under Kim Jong Un, she comments on how these television shows reflect changes in the regime's vision of North Korean life—from the dreary, battlefield dreams of the days of Kim Il Sung and Kim Jong Il, to the uplifting ideals of a happy middle-class proletariat. Episodes show scenes of homes in newly built apartment complexes, "fussily decorated with curtains, clocks, wallpaper, table lamps, flowers and plants. . . . Tables overflow with food." The men wear fancy gold watches and the women wear smart blouses and skirts; students learn in classrooms filled with technology such as computers, microphones, speakers, telescopes, and recording devices. The characters' days are filled with schoolroom hijinks, women gossiping, and neighbors plotting to play matchmaker and helping one another out by lugging water up the stairs when an electrical outage causes the elevator to stop functioning. The North Koreans, from Kim's perspective, are "young, bright, clever, loyal and sometimes mischievous—innocuous versions of the leader himself." They celebrate when the December 2012 rocket launch succeeds and neighborhood rivals "forget momentarily that they despise one another and dance in a circle."

But even as the regime tacitly allows formal and informal markets to flourish, there are risks both for the entrepreneurs and for Kim. North Korean citizens have to walk a fine line between the acceptable and unacceptable and pay a premium in bribes and fees for the privilege of carrying out their businesses. They also face the constant threat of running into trouble, of inadvertently crossing officials or fellow citizens who could make gains at their expense, not unusual occurrences in a system that rewards corruption and extortion. For the regime, the messy hybrid world of private-public enterprise allows for interlocking webs of elites and moneymakers who are invested in the survival of the current system, even as the cult of personality and the revolutionary ideology might be weakening. But that market activity inherently involves access to outside sources of information, whether in the form of DVDs or USBs smuggled into North Korea, as part of the travels and conversations with foreigners that are a necessary aspect of many entrepreneurs' businesses.

The seepage of information into the country began during the famine years and has deepened skepticism about the regime over the past two decades. One doctor who started a business selling Chinese goods described how, in 1999, he went to China with a Chinese businessman, bribing border guards along the way. "The first, most shocking thing I saw in China was a market in a tiny, rural town. It was filled with poor people, but they weren't that thin. And this market had everything! Rice, oil, bananas, meat—anyone could just buy and eat these. . . . I realized that something was very wrong." One defector said that he was amazed when he watched a popular South Korean movie with a friend. Regime propaganda had indoctrinated people into thinking that South Koreans lived in abject poverty, while North Koreans lived in paradise. Instead of the South Koreans who "seduce people and abduct them . . . kidnap foreigners and take their blood," he saw in the movie how in South Korea "there were nice cars on the street. . . . People were so well off, and the Seoul-ites' way of speaking Korean was so interesting, so elegant. . . . I couldn't stop thinking about it."

In November 2017, *The Washington Post* compiled a report, "Life under Kim Jong Un," cataloging defector accounts that further illustrate the effects of marketization and information penetration. A twenty-five-year-old is described as watching DVDs of Chinese, Russian, Indian, and South Korean soap operas. A thirty-seven-year-old contemporary of Jong Un's recalled ninety minutes of ideological training every day in which "they would tell us that we needed to make sacrifices in our daily lives so they could build these weapons and protect our country, keep the nation safe. I was so sick and tired of hearing about all this revolutionary history." A forty-year-old said, "We would hear about how Kim Jong Un had done this and this and that [he] was working so hard for the party and for the nation and for the people . . . but this exaggeration was just too much. It just didn't make sense." There were fissures in the alleged socialist paradise. Ha-Young, whose story is told by Jieun Baek, said, "I hung out with the popular girls at school and ignored other people who didn't have as much money as us, or didn't dress as well."

The reality for the vast majority of North Koreans is a shocking contradiction of this image of paradise that the regime has been trying to advance. The country is still poor, even as Kim and the elites spend hundreds of millions of dollars on showy monuments and luxury items. The United Nations in 2019 reported that of the 25 million citizens, nearly 11 million are undernourished, 140,000 children under the age of five suffer from acute malnutrition or wasting, and nearly 20 percent of children are stunted, making these citizens more vulnerable to diseases such as tuberculosis. The situation is exacerbated by the fact that millions do not have access to basic sanitation facilities or clean water.

Kim's recognition of the cognitive dissonance between government propaganda and lived realities might be driving his efforts to create "Pyonghattan," a way to combat fraying ties between the *jangmadang* generation and the regime, and keep the state relevant despite the decimation of the public distribution system. But if people are not convinced by soft power, Kim has all of the tools of repression built by his grandfather and his father to enforce compliance. Against the backdrop of his pastel wonderland, he rules through terror and repression, and the terrorized and the repressed will have little choice but to feed Kim's illusions and expectations, his grandiose visions of himself, and of North Korea's destiny.

EIGHT

PRUNING THE FAMILY TREE

ENTERING HIS THIRD YEAR in power in 2014, Kim Jong Un delivered his annual New Year's address. He paid his obligatory respect to the revolutionary martyrs and extolled his father and his grandfather. Kim also lauded the party, the military, and the people for advancing the policy of *byungjin* that he had laid out the previous year, and celebrated the ideological fervor of the people whose "blood-sealed ties . . . have reached a new, higher stage." But he also called for intensified ideological training, stamping out anything that might "infringe on the unity of the Party and revolutionary ranks and undermine their single-hearted unity." Kim's focus on the "mental strength of the masses" reflected on an event that had happened just a few days before, during which, as he triumphantly claimed, "our Party detected and purged the anti-Party, counter-revolutionary factionalists."

That cancer on the body politic was none other than Kim's uncle Jang Song Thaek, the husband of his father's beloved and trusted sister Kim Kyong Hui. Just two years into his reign, Kim had his uncle executed, reportedly by antiaircraft guns, a shocking public humiliation that reverberated across the globe, as Washington, Seoul, Beijing, and Tokyo wondered what this would mean for whatever constraints existed to tame Jong Un's behavior. Even by the standards of North Korean brutality, it was unprecedented that a family member would be treated in this way. The execution of Jang so early in Kim's rule was a defining moment. It hinted at the young leader's boldness, confidence, brutality, and high tolerance for risk.

THE FALL

When Jong Un took over in 2011, Jang Song Thaek's prospects looked secure and indeed quite promising. After all, he was married to the new leader's aunt, Kim Kyong Hui, Kim Jong Il's trusted confidante, who had faithfully supported her brother throughout his rise and nearly twenty years of rule. Jang had become part of the family despite the wishes of Kim Il Sung, who opposed the match. Kyong Hui was besotted with Jang, who was funny and charismatic, from the moment they'd met at Kim Il Sung University in the 1960s. Tall, masculine, and popular, Jang was a natural-born leader whose singing ability and prowess with the accordion made him even more endearing. Kim Jong Il had elevated Jang to the inner circle right around the same time that he was grooming Jong Un, suggesting that the elder Kim intended for Jang to help his son navigate the bureaucracy along with Kyong Hui. In 2013, Jang was in his late sixties, a seasoned and savvy bureaucrat who probably had at least another decade or so left in a regime that was dominated by septuagenarians and octogenarians. The international media touted him as the second-most-important individual behind Kim Jong Un, and his experience and vast network of contacts, especially with Chinese leaders, stimulated speculation about how Jang might be a key player in North Korea's potential reform and opening.

Jang had survived purges before—he had been demoted and "reeducated" at least twice, standard practice for the Kim regime— but this was different. On December 8, 2013, Kim Jong Un's regime accused Jang of a litany of charges during an enlarged meeting of the Political Bureau of the Central Committee of the Korean Workers' Party. A few days later, a military tribunal found that Jang and his followers committed the "hideous crime [of] attempting to overthrow the state." Not only had he violated the trust and benevolence of Kim Il Sung and Kim Jong Il, but the "despicable human scum Jang, who was worse than a dog," also had perpetrated "acts of treachery" in his attempts to create an alternative power structure to counter the unitary and supreme leadership of Kim Jong Un.

His greed and arrogance knew no bounds, according to the charges levied against him. Jang "rallied ex-convicts" around him and worked to consolidate power under his offices, his "little kingdom." With his band of conspirators, he plundered the nation's resources for his own benefit, putting his "stooges" at the head of the most lucrative coal and metals industries and selling off land to foreign powers—specifically, to China. The list of his economic crimes against the state and people spanned decades, and the tribunal charged that he had taken more than four million euros into his coffers. His avarice extended beyond political and economic crimes, for he "worked to stretch his tentacles even to the People's Army with a foolish calculation that he would succeed in staging a coup." In his "confession," Jang stated that his intention was to lead the country toward bankruptcy, increase the people's discontent, and use his accumulated funds to buy loyalty and cement his power when he took over.

The once powerful and imperious Jang was escorted out of the courtroom following the tribunal; hunched over, he looked older than his age and defeated. Two of his deputies had already been executed days before by antiaircraft guns. Whatever remained of their bodies was burned by a flamethrower, as Jang was forced to watch; he reportedly collapsed after having witnessed their gruesome deaths. After his sentencing, Jang was reportedly taken to the Kanggon Military Training Area, on the outskirts of Pyongyang, and executed in the same way as his deputies. Jang's highly publicized downfall and humiliation and the grisly and disproportionate execution method with machinery designed for warfare made one thing clear: Kim Jong Un would not tolerate any dissent, not even from members of his own family. The new leader had easily accomplished what he'd likely wanted to do: extinguish any nascent and existing dissent and instill fear through a spectacular act of intimidation.

Even by the standards of North Korea's bloody past, the Jang purge was shocking. "The spectacle of public humiliation—and liquidation of a royal marks a radical departure from business as usual," observed longtime North Korea watcher Nicholas Eberstadt. Kim Il Sung and Kim Jong Il had carried out purges in secret—leaders simply disappeared without explanation. As Andrei Lankov and others have noted, such high-ranking officials were usually exiled and had a good chance of being remediated and brought back into the fold after a sufficient period of atonement. But this time was different. Kim Jong Un's methods—publishing in full Jang's crimes and the lengthy indictment and releasing photographs of him stooped over in complete submission—seemed to suggest that he was far more brutal than his predecessors and even savored the drama and the theatrical flair of the whole affair.

Fear gripped North Korean officialdom. With methodical and systematic discipline, the Kim regime began to root out close associates of Jang and in the process revealed the extent to which North Korean officials depended not only on access to regime insiders to make money but also on the entrenchment of nepotism to obtain plum official assignments or government contracts. Jang's nephew, the ambassador to Malaysia, was recalled soon after the execution, as were the deputy ambassador to UNESCO in Paris and the ambassadors to Cuba and Sweden. Sources inside North Korea reported that security forces had also targeted Jang's blood relatives, who were transferred to political prison camps. The regime also replaced the heads of the coal and metal industries, lucrative businesses that could yield a bonanza for the new leaders and their sycophants, given the hundreds of millions of dollars that the North's abundant natural resources have generated for the regime over the years. Jang's competitors eagerly accepted the new government posts and state enterprises, filling the spots left vacant by the purge of Jang and his associates.

Since the Jang incident, Kim Jong Un has continued with waves of purges—more than 340 senior officials, according to South Korea's Institute for National Security Strategy, a government think tank. Even before the Jang episode, Kim had already purged his defense minister Ri Yong Ho, who was relieved of his duties due to "illness." Given the dangerous atmosphere of those early years, with all the uncertainty about the new leader's preferences and approach, it was much easier and safer for everyone, from the rank and file to the highest officials, to not make waves, doubling down on their loyalty to Kim Jong Un rather than offering resistance or criticism. And one can imagine the intense competition among these well-connected men and women to demonstrate their unwavering devotion as they jockeyed for position to exploit the vacuum in order to enrich themselves and their families.

KIM'S MOTIVATIONS

The purge of his uncle was consistent with Kim Jong Un's bold approach to external relations, the internal changes occurring concurrently with his belligerent and muscular attitude toward the United States and South Korea, as he conducted several provocative actions and issued threats that raised concerns about a military conflict. Kim's decision to lop off the top layers of his government so early in his rule was probably driven by a number of factors.

First, Kim seemed intent on creating his own base of support rather than relying on his father's loyalists, who had been installed to ease the grooming process and the transition. Both the surprising dismissal of Ri Yong Ho in July 2012 and Jang's execution suggested that Kim "is eager to prove that he is no longer the puppet controlled by some senior minister reigning behind the curtain," according to Zhu Feng, a noted Chinese expert on North Korea, and that "he's able to establish his absolute authority in the system and has capacity to govern the country directly." Kim Jong Il elevated Jang's position to assist with his son's succession probably to ensure that Jong Un had at his side a family member who was deeply knowledgeable about the bureaucracy and possessed administrative skills, strong ties to China, and a proven ability to raise funds and manage the regime's financial infrastructure.

But it was those same qualities that made Jang a threat to Jong Un, particularly given the rumors and speculation that Jang was really the one pulling the levers behind the scenes, plus global media commentary about the potential for Jang—whom observers considered more of a reformer—to emerge as the real leader of North Korea. The intense international criticism of Kim's youth and inexperience, as well as conjecture about North Korea's collapse under his leadership, was likely also an irritant. Furthermore, as reflected in the criminal charges against him, Jang's decades of experience and position as a power broker and member of the royal family meant that he had a deep and broad patronage network that was loyal and invested in him rather than his nephew.

Second, Jang's hubris and the confidence that it engendered in his underlings regarding their control of the regime's natural resources probably played a role in his ultimate fall. The list of Jang's crimes included his exploitation of the coal and metal industries, exposing how corruption and patronage reinforce and sustain the power and privilege of the most elite in the North Korean system. Consistent with the charges of economic malfeasance laid out in accusations against Jang, reports surfaced that he and his followers had engaged in a struggle for control of North Korea's state-run natural resources businesses. According to various South Korean and American reports, the battle for the profits among senior officials came to the fore in the Jang case.

The New York Times reported that the military tried to reclaim a prosperous crab and clam fishing ground appropriated by Jang and his loyalists; the poorly trained and poorly fed North Korean soldiers were defeated in battle by armed forces that were close to Jang or his confidants. The incident apparently enraged Kim Jong Un,

who undoubtedly was egged on by the military and anti-Jang officials, both of whom had much to gain from Jang's comeuppance. As
The New York Times wrote, the "open warfare" among these groups
"revealed a huge fracture inside the country's elite over who pockets
the foreign currency." Ra Jong-yil, a former senior South Korean
intelligence official, recounted several other incidents of Jang's perceived or real acts of misconduct against Kim that might have led to
his execution, but he observed that Kim was also to blame for
"lack[ing] the leadership to act as mediator" and perpetuating an
environment in which discord and deadly competition prevailed.

Since the 1970s and '80s, the North Korean regime has directed
its overseas diplomatic and military officials to generate hard currency through licit and illicit means, while state entities have received the go-ahead to engage in foreign trade. The famine and the
new geopolitical circumstances of the 1990s and the early 2000s required the state entities to be even more entrepreneurial and creative, since they had to provide for both themselves and the regime,
often blurring the lines between official and unofficial, private and
public, state and non-state, licit and illicit. Over the past several decades, diplomatic, trade, and military officials overseas have been
charged with generating funds through the drug trade, insurance
fraud, and counterfeiting U.S. hundred-dollar bills (the last scheme
alone earned the regime between $15 million and $25 million per
annum over several years). North Korean entities or their foreign
partners have been caught smuggling endangered species products—
such as ivory and rhinoceros horns—and counterfeit international
brands of cigarettes and drugs like Viagra. At Jang's level, the highest echelons of the regime's military and party apparatus controlled
the importation of luxury items—one of Jang's particular skills;
buying the elite generous gifts was a key way for the regime to
maintain their support—and trade involving weapons and the
country's natural resources.

According to Justin Hastings, an academic who has studied
North Korea's economy, the country's ability to make money to
fund the state and its priority programs, despite the burden of sanc-

tions and international isolation, points to the efficiency and adaptability of its trade networks. Like a criminal syndicate or a mafia, as numerous experts have called North Korea, the state and state-affiliated trading companies use their government prerogatives and protections and their relationships with foreign and North Korean private brokers to facilitate transactions with anyone who will do business with them. In effect, as the Asia specialist Sheena Chestnut Greitens argues, a "symbiosis" has developed "between state-run companies and essentially private enterprises, with political connections required for business to flourish and political actors benefitting from the activities of businesspeople."

But proceeds from the sale of fake Viagra, methamphetamines, fake hair, and rhino horns, or the smuggling of gold and luxury items through the diplomatic pouch, or even arms deals, pale in comparison to what the state and its affiliates earn from selling coal, iron and iron ore, seafood, and lead and lead ore. Coal is the single largest export; in 2016 alone, coal exports to China earned North Korea $1 billion. But it is just one part of North Korea's wealth in natural resources. The country reportedly has an estimated total value of between $6 trillion and $10 trillion worth of mineral wealth. It has about two hundred kinds of metals and minerals, including gold, iron, zinc, magnesium, and graphite, and rare earth elements that are critical components of smartphones, digital cameras, computer monitors, flat-screen televisions, and electronic displays. Seafood, one of the reasons for Jang's trouble, is worth around $300 million per year, according to U.S. estimates. The government also dispatches up to one hundred thousand North Korean laborers to work overseas, mostly in China and Russia, in mining, logging, textiles, and construction, among other occupations, earning the regime hundreds of millions of dollars per year—about $500 million, according to recent U.N. estimates—while the workers themselves get to keep only a small fraction of their wages.

The income generated by individuals and private entities is spent in part to make loyalty payments to satisfy the regime. But it is also used to personally enrich individuals. While the elite buy expensive

Western luxury brands, including Chanel and Dior, dine at high-end restaurants, and reside in high-rises, people outside the capital live very different lives. Suki Kim, a journalist who went undercover as a teacher at the Pyongyang University of Science and Technology, witnessed this stark contrast firsthand. During a rare excursion outside the city, she recalled seeing men at a construction site "with hollowed eyes and sunken cheeks, clothing tattered, heads shaved, looking like Nazi concentration camp victims." Despite U.N. Security Council Resolution 1718 (2006), which prohibited the sale of luxury goods to North Korea, Italy in 2010 confiscated cognac and whiskey worth around $17,000 and equipment for a thousand-person theater valued at nearly $200,000. In 2013, North Korea imported around $650 million worth of luxury goods, more than twice the annual amount that Kim Jong Il imported during his rule. That number soared to $800 million in 2014 and dropped to $640 million in 2017. The 2014 U.N. report also showed how North Korea over the years tried to procure a dozen Mercedes-Benz vehicles, music recording equipment, cosmetics, and a dozen pianos no doubt intended for the upper crust in Pyongyang. Subsequent investigations revealed the continuous flow of luxury items, including ski equipment and vodka. And in 2019, Pyongyang showed off in its state media a newly renovated department store that sold Swiss watches, Dyson and Bosch appliances, and other consumer electronics.

Given the amount of money at stake, even as U.S. and international sanctions put pressure on the North Koreans' ability to make money through licit and illicit means, it's not surprising that Kim would try to ensure that he alone controls who has access to power and privilege. These purges create new bases of support and prevent networks from ossifying, keep everyone guessing and on their toes, and demonstrate that the elites' political, economic, and social benefits are directly linked to their loyalty to the regime, thereby tethering their livelihoods to Kim's success. The lesson for those living in the Kim Jong Un regime is that it's okay to make money, but don't forget who you work for and who is in control.

Another benefit of Kim's systematic purges is the way they replace older officials with younger leaders, perhaps to match his new, modern outlook and to inject fresh blood into a system dominated by men in their seventies and eighties. The current leadership is younger—South Korean reports indicate that Kim's generational shift had reduced the average age of the inner circle from seventy-six to sixty-two—and in his first two years, Kim replaced half of the 218 party heads, ministers, and military officials. But a reservoir of even younger officials is poised to serve Kim Jong Un in the decades to come. These "princes" and "princesses" wield influence as a result of their familial and financial networks and form Kim's own base of support as he cultivates a new generation that is beholden to him and not his predecessors. Perhaps he sees them as less wedded to the old ways of conducting business—literally and figuratively—and more pliable and risk tolerant.

There have been signs of Kim's disdain for the older generations and their corresponding attitude toward governance. His sushi chef and childhood playmate, Fujimoto, saw a teenage Kim kick and taunt an elderly former aide to his grandfather; the aide had no choice but to take the abuse. And Kim's viciousness extended well into his adulthood. An official from South Korea's Institute for National Security Strategy said in 2014 that "when analyzing Kim's lip movements during his chats with elderly party members on television, it is not rare to find him insulting them with foul language." Just months after the Jang execution, Kim made a speech of more than six thousand words decrying the lack of ideological fervor, stating that "even a rolling stone may gather moss," probably referring to elite officials who have become too complacent in their positions. In a rebuke to his officials, Kim denounced the "ideologically degenerate" who had become "inwardly contaminated with bourgeois ideology and culture" and allowed themselves to be "overcome with fear [of] the imperialists." They cowered and wavered, he implied, even as Kim was facing down the United States with a successful satellite launch in December 2012 and a nuclear test in February 2013 and refusing to back down in spite of increasing sanctions pressure and isolation. In the context of the Jang aftermath and the ensuing anticorruption drive to root out the ideologically weak, the speech was a powerful reminder to all officialdom of how important it was to maintain vigor, purity of purpose, and momentum toward a Kim-led nuclear North Korea.

They were also expected to be physically fit and ready for war. In July 2014, as Kim smoked cigarettes, with his prominent belly jutting out, he ordered commanding officers of the North Korean navy to strip and swim in the ocean. "The commanding officers are not qualified if they lack physical ability," he said, "no matter what good ideological and moral qualities they have and no matter how high military and technological qualifications they are possessed of as they should stand in the [vanguard] of the combat ranks." Regime media indicated that Kim was pleased with the swimming drill, but one can imagine how some of the older officers might have worried about how they would perform and feared for their future if they were not up to Kim's exacting standards. Earlier that year, Kim had also commanded a sixty-seven-year-old senior army official to fly a fighter jet. Kim observed scores of other such drills, whether they were artillery firings, archery contests, or air force units mobilizing night infiltration capabilities, not only to demonstrate his hands-on approach to military readiness but also to show these senior military leaders—and their underlings—who was really in control.

Kim has frequently called out ineffectiveness and publicized it, in contrast to his father, who kept regime deficiencies mostly under wraps. Kim has not held back from private and open criticism. During an inspection of an amusement park in 2012, he berated officials for the poor state of the facilities and said that their attitude toward the park's physical state was a reflection of their attitude toward the people and their lack of ideological vigor and presumably loyalty to him. Describing the incident, regime media reported, "Spotting weeds sprouting between pavement blocks . . . Kim Jong Un personally plucked them one by one with a frustrated look and said in an enraged tone: how could functionaries not see this; if the functionaries in charge of managing the funfair had a master-like attitude, affection for their work sites, and a conscience for serving the people, how could they work like this?" One can imagine the horror and fear of those standing around their leader as he bent down to weed the ground himself, wondering what their fate might be as he spit out, "I had no idea the park could be so pitiful."

In a much more serious incident, possibly hundreds of people died in 2014 when a twenty-three-story apartment building—one of the structures built to fulfill Kim's desire to turn the capital into a modern metropolis—collapsed in Pyongyang. Kim grieved intensely, according to the regime media that publicized the tragedy, yet another unprecedented move by the regime to be "transparent." Kim "sat up all night, feeling pained after being told about the accident," a senior official said. An undoubtedly livid Kim forced his uniformed senior officials, including his seventy-year-old minister of public security and others more than twice his age, to bow in contrition in front of the residents of the building and the district.

No official, high or low, was safe from Kim's inspections. During a 2015 tour through a terrapin farm, an angry and frustrated Kim chastised the managers for the facility's "serious shortcomings" and for not paying enough attention to the teachings of Kim Jong Il, who had intended terrapin farms to "provide the people with tasty and nutritious terrapin widely known as a precious tonic from olden times." Their fault lay not just in their technical incompetence but in their "outmoded way of thinking," suggesting that they had not yet adopted Kim's innovative and modern style of improving the lives of the people. Shortly after his visit, Kim reportedly had the manager of the farm executed, spurring fear in lower-level officials that they, too, are in the crosshairs of Kim's wrath if they do not perform to his satisfaction and do not show sufficient loyalty.

The leaders of the older generation were convenient scapegoats for insufficient progress in advancing Kim's priorities, never mind the inadequacies of resources, the rampant corruption that encouraged faulty construction, or Kim's unrealistic expectations. But Jang's execution and Kim's desire to humiliate the leadership, almost all of whom are more than twice his age, may also point to a thin-skinned young man with an outsize view of himself, who during his entire life was coddled and heard nothing but sycophantic praise from those around him. After all, did they not bow deeply to him at his childhood birthday parties? One of Jang's crimes was clapping "halfheartedly" when Kim was elected vice chairman of the country's Central Military Commission in 2010, suggesting that the future ruler's wrath was driven by deep insecurity about the strength of the senior leadership's support. The incident also shows that Kim has patience: He waited three years to conduct the purge until he had time to build a case against Jang. The most proximate reason for the downfall of Defense Minister Hyon Yong Chol, who was reportedly executed in 2015, might have been that he fell asleep during one of Kim's speeches as the new leader, but Hyon also might have offended Kim by questioning his early decisions to adopt a belligerent approach to external relations.

In fact, Kim's scorn and disregard for the older generation extended outside of his country's borders. He wasn't just a young head of state in North Korea; he was also the youngest by decades among the constellation of leaders in the region. Lee Myung-bak, South Korea's president until 2013, was born in 1941; his successor, Park Geun-hye, was born in 1952. Park, China's president Xi Jinping (born 1953), and Japanese prime minister Abe Shinzo (born 1954) were children of former leaders or senior officials of their respective countries. President Obama was the youngest in this group, in his early fifties when his presidency and Kim's ascendance coincided. Kim has used vitriolic rhetoric against these regional and world leaders in the same way he used execution to deal with internal offenders. The regime spewed unashamedly racist language against the African-American president, calling him "a monkey in a tropical forest." Park Geun-hye, South Korea's first female president, was a "bitch" and a "cold-blooded animal," who was like a "despicable prostitute" whose "fancy man [pimp]" was Obama, referencing the close coordination between Washington and Seoul and their alliance against North Korea's provocative actions.

Kim's regime would take a more circumspect tone in its criticism of Chinese leadership, undoubtedly because North Korea depends on Chinese political and economic aid. Ties between Pyongyang and Beijing had suffered since Kim came to power, with the numbers of high-level and working-level exchanges and visits plummeting as Kim kept China at arm's length, probably because he had little appetite for heeding what were sure to be Chinese leaders' admonitions about continuing to sow tension in the region. Indeed, in November 2012, when President Xi Jinping dispatched an envoy— the first visit by a Chinese official to Pyongyang since Kim took the reins—he reportedly sent along a letter that advised the new leader to refrain from launching a ballistic missile. Yet not even two weeks later, Kim successfully launched a rocket, in defiance of Xi's warning. Kim would occasionally send an envoy to Beijing in a halfhearted effort to at least pay lip service to the relationship. But when Kim felt jilted or disrespected by Xi's government, he would retaliate to show that he would not be cowed, that he was the master of his decisions.

For example, in what was touted at the time as a thaw in relations, Kim dispatched the Moranbong Band—an all-female group of musicians made up of women Kim reportedly handpicked—to Beijing for a weeklong tour. Kim then abruptly recalled them to Pyongyang, apparently because Beijing decided to send lower-level officials to the planned concert. Irked by the provocative declaration Kim had made in Pyongyang that North Korea had developed and deployed a hydrogen bomb, senior Chinese leaders apparently wanted to show their disapproval. Kim's decision to bring the band back home, in response to the Chinese snub, reflects his strong will and lack of interest in mitigating the consequences of his actions. Did he think that issuing an inflammatory statement about thermonuclear weapons would go unnoticed by Beijing? The incident ultimately laid bare the clash of wills between the senior Xi and the young North Korean leader. For Kim's part, he was not going to yield to Chinese preferences or let his personal girl band suffer the indignity of Chinese aspersions. Negotiating and compromise were not part of his vocabulary.

Kim was cold and aloof to political leaders and even business moguls like Google's chairman Eric Schmidt, who went to Pyongyang in early 2013 with a delegation led by Bill Richardson, the former governor of New Mexico and a frequent visitor to Pyongyang. But he met with Dennis Rodman, a flamboyant U.S. basketball player with a colorful background who sports multiple piercings and tattoos. In February 2013, Rodman and three Harlem Globetrotters were recruited by Vice Media to play an exhibition game in North Korea. Kim made a surprise visit and sat next to Rodman—making him the first American to meet Kim. Rodman told him, "You have a friend for life." Afterward, Kim and Rodman partied together at one of his villas and Kim reportedly invited the player back to North Korea; Rodman would subsequently make three more trips. Photos of the two of them laughing and joking together were splashed across multiple news media, an incredible juxtaposition of a dictator threatening nuclear war with an iconoclastic U.S. basketball player, who at six foot seven towered over the pudgy, five-foot-seven Kim.

Rodman's second trip took place in September 2013, sponsored this time by an Irish bookmaking firm, as if the whole situation required an additional element of absurdity. He spent time with Kim and his family at their private resort in Wonsan and met Kim's daughter, Ju Ae, then an infant, confirming for the first time that Kim had at least one child with his wife Ri Sol Ju. The men partied for seven days, drinking and smoking cigars and spending time on Kim's two-hundred-foot yacht, a "cross between a ferry and a Disney Boat," according to Rodman. "It's like going to Hawaii or Ibiza, but [Kim's] the only one that lives there," he added. His was a rare firsthand glimpse of the full extent of Kim's lavish lifestyle and wealth.

Kim's very public camaraderie with Rodman created an international stir, reinforcing the growing perception of the young leader as the erratic, eccentric, and immature head of a nuclear-armed country. This series of events reminded me of Heuer's warning: "Too frequently, foreign behavior appears 'irrational' or 'not in their own best interest'" because we project American values onto foreign leaders rather than try to understand the thinking behind their actions. If we view it from Kim's perspective, his surprising friendship can be seen as a way to show his senior leadership and external audiences that he will do as he pleases, poking a thumb in the eye of those who might criticize his behavior. But it also likely reflected his desire to connect with someone who was decidedly apolitical, who didn't care about the North's belligerent approach or judge Kim for his pursuit of nuclear weapons or his country's human rights violations. He might have been eager to show a more approachable side of his personality and to demonstrate that he was more than a despot who was only interested in punishing rather than having fun. After all, Kim had been a U.S. basketball fan since he was a carefree child—and showcasing the country's modernity using Rodman as a vehicle was a clever way to broadcast those desired optics.

Kim was also eager to show off his magnanimity toward the only other foreigner who had significant personal interaction with him in those first six years of his rule. Kenji Fujimoto, who was Kim Jong Il's sushi chef and Jong Un's playmate when he was a child, defected in 2001, escaping during a trip to Tokyo to procure sea urchin for Jong Il's insatiable appetite. Fujimoto had been supplementing his living by selling his remembrances about his time spent in North Korea's inner circle, but he also lived in fear of North Korean agents who were known to track down and intimidate or kill defectors. But instead of a hit squad, Kim Jong Un sent an invitation, wrapped in red velvet, for Fujimoto to visit Pyongyang. As he recounted to *The Washington Post,* Kim Jong Un welcomed him with open arms, as Fujimoto wept and bowed, apologetically telling Kim, "I, Fujimoto the betrayer, have now come back." To his relief and gratitude, Kim said, "It's okay, it's okay," as they hugged and the older man cried on Kim's shoulder.

Kim Jong Un's warmth toward both Rodman and Fujimoto—individuals he'd admired during his childhood—and the fact that he chose to have his closest interactions with only these two foreigners on his home turf in the entirety of his first six years in power suggest that he was not ready or comfortable to engage with the outside world as he crafted his persona as North Korea's new leader. Kim came from a line of dictators who were expert in theater. But while he made an effort to show a kinder, gentler Kim, he was superficially glossing over the systematic cruelty of his regime. The vicious purge of his uncle and other senior leaders was only the tip of the iceberg when it came to the lengths that the regime would go to squelch any dissent on a mass scale, with barbarity rivaling that of Nazi Germany.

KIM'S GULAGS

If the backdrop of amusement parks, department stores, and high-end restaurants is intended to serve as a manifestation of Kim's generosity and love for his people, a sprawling network of known prison camps stands as a terrifying reminder of what happens to ordinary North Koreans who display insufficient loyalty to the regime. As many as 120,000 North Koreans are held in a half dozen of the country's worst prisons—the gulags—which the regime has used for decades to suppress dissent and ensure Kim family rule; and there are untold numbers in the two dozen detention and hard labor camps. After conducting scores of interviews with defectors, among whom were former prison guards, the United Nations Commission of Inquiry on Human Rights in the Democratic People's Republic of Korea concluded in its pathbreaking report that the North Korean regime has been practicing "systematic, widespread and gross human rights violations . . . committed by its institutions and officials." The nearly four-hundred-page document confirmed what human rights advocates and North Korean defectors had been saying for years, and shed light on the depth and breadth of the regime's cruelty and disregard for human life and dignity. While Kim has promoted the pastel socialist paradise to represent North Korea to the world, the prison camps are the regime's dirty secret kept as a hidden but necessary part of control over the entire population. Kim did not create the camps—his grandfather did in the 1950s and modeled them after Stalin's gulags—but despite his efforts to establish a narrative of modernity and prosperity, his perpetuation of these coercive institutions reflects their importance as a pillar of regime survival and security.

North Korea has two types of prison camps: the *kyohwaso,* which are prisons for criminal and political offenders, usually with fixed terms and some established judicial mechanisms in place, and the *kwanliso,* or political prison camps, for major political offenders who have committed crimes deemed "anti-state" or "anti-people," vague offenses that can be interpreted in myriad ways to justify the detention of individual "criminals" as well as three generations of their families for guilt by association. The U.N. report indicated that more than a third of all inmates—nearly 36 percent—were imprisoned because of their assumed associative guilt. The difference between the two kinds of prisons can be seen in the intensity of their punishments rather than qualitative distinctions, such as torture, rape, and sexual violence, forced starvation and labor, and summary executions, which are standard practices in both. Both crime and punishment often seem arbitrary, and the severity of each depends on one's *songbun,* which determines the ability to bribe one's way out of trouble or obtain the help of powerful sponsors.

The father of the defector Hyeonseo Lee was accused of bribery and was beaten during his interrogations—he subsequently died from his injuries—but Lee surmised that the more likely reason for his arrest was that "he had fallen out of political favour, or had put some senior cadre's nose out of joint," suggesting that prisoners could use their connections or money to escape punishment and that their fate could be negatively decided by someone with a vendetta. Lee also recalled the fate of one family deported to a prison camp because the father had rolled a cigarette using a piece of newspaper that happened to have Kim Il Sung's picture on the other side. The U.N. Commission of Inquiry reported one case in which security forces tortured a seventeen-year-old caught watching South Korean movies, shattering his ankle and disfiguring his face. They released him after his family paid a bribe, but the boy subsequently died from a brain hemorrhage resulting from the torture.

The Kim regime does not acknowledge the existence of the *kwanliso,* the political prison camps, either domestically or internationally, since to admit the existence of dissent would be anathema to a regime that espouses the total devotion of its populace. The U.N. Commission of Inquiry described the *kwanliso* as camps that "serve to permanently remove from society those groups, families, and individuals that may politically, ideologically, or economically challenge the current political system and leadership." In effect, the prison camps serve to identify and isolate perceived challengers to the regime. Kim Il Sung himself said that intergenerational imprisonment and punishment were required especially for "class enemies"—those who were born in South Korea, collaborators with the Japanese colonial government, and former landowners— because "their seed must be eliminated through three generations." Former camp guards who testified to the U.N. Commission of Inquiry confirmed that their training included this instruction, leading the commission to conclude that this practice was intended to "re-engineer the social fabric" of North Korea to "conform to the ideology of the *suryong* system by purging entire groups and individuals from general society." In other words, they should not exist.

The regime considered the worst "crimes" to be watching South Korean movies, attempting to escape to China, engaging in proscribed economic activity, or having had contact with Christian missionaries or being in possession of a Bible. Often the prisoners did not know why they were there, and children especially had no idea why they and their families were uprooted and taken by security officers to the isolated camps. One defector told the U.N. Commission of Inquiry that she was thirteen years old when she was arrested while on her way home from school and driven to a prison camp where her family had already been taken. For the nearly three decades of her incarceration, she never found out why her family had been punished, only later to discover that her grandfather had fled to South Korea during the Korean War, thereby tainting her family as being among the "hostile" classes and vulnerable to the most extreme treatment from the regime.

The memoirs and testimonies of the defectors, both young and old, are difficult to read because of the horrific violence perpetrated on their bodies and minds. When Kang Chol-hwan entered the infamous Yodok gulag for the first time, he "cringed at getting too close to the other detainees. Their faces were ugly, they had missing teeth, their hair was caked together and overgrown, and they were all filthy as animals. Yet more striking than their physical appearance was the aura of weakness that oozed from their every pore." Kim's camps are meant to dehumanize the individual and facilitate death. Inmates, including children, are forced to work in grueling jobs—mining, farming, construction—with insufficient rations, requiring them to supplement their diets by eating rodents, frogs, snakes, and insects or by informing on other inmates to curry favor or additional rations.

Physical and psychological torture is common. Prisoners' heads are covered with a plastic bag and submerged in water. They are deprived of sleep or mobility by being forced inside a small cage or suspended from the wall by their wrists. Rape and sexual torture are rampant, according to a report from the International Bar Association War Crimes Committee. Prison guards take advantage of their position to assault female inmates, and women also use sex to try to survive. Those women who become pregnant are forced to abort, often in a brutal manner, such as "an abortion induced by three men standing on a plank placed on pregnant prisoner's stomach," or pushing a stick into the vagina or beating a woman to trigger premature labor. Fetuses and newborns are thrown into the garbage, fed to guard dogs, or suffocated with a wet towel while the mother watches. A former North Korean army nurse said she witnessed abortions being conducted through the injection of motor oil into the wombs, while other rape victims she saw tried to induce abortion themselves by inserting a rubber tube in their vaginas.

The United States and the United Nations have declared that

these human rights violations are sanctioned by the top leadership in North Korea. For the first time, in July 2016, the United States called out Kim Jong Un, his sister, Kim Yo Jong, and other senior officials for their human rights violations, as part of Washington's overall efforts to squeeze the regime. Adam Szubin, the acting undersecretary for terrorism and financial intelligence, stated in a press release that "under Kim Jong Un, North Korea continues to inflict intolerable cruelty and hardship on millions of its own people, including extrajudicial killings, forced labor, and torture. . . . The actions taken today by the [Obama] Administration . . . highlight the U.S. Government's condemnation of this regime's abuses and our determination to see them stopped." Six months later, in January 2017, Washington sanctioned additional regime officials, including Kim Yo Jong for her role as the vice director of the party's Propaganda and Agitation Department, as well as heads of the key party and security organizations responsible for "severe human rights abuses," "rigid censorship policies," and activities that conceal the regime's crimes against humanity.

Like his father and his grandfather, Kim relies on and has cultivated tight, overlapping security organizations whose leaders are rewarded for their suppression of human rights and their loyalty. "The more zeal they demonstrate in support of the regime's policies, including human rights denial," North Korea researcher Robert Collins writes, "the greater the privileges they receive." The hundreds of thousands of bureaucrats employed in North Korea's half-dozen party and security organizations are in charge of surveillance and monitoring of every individual, including high-ranking officials, and ensuring the personal security of Kim Jong Un and senior leadership, in addition to running the political prisons and other apparatuses of repression. These repressive institutions—from the Organization and Guidance Department, which controls the appointment of senior functionaries and the surveillance of them, to the ministries in charge of the secret police, counterintelligence, local policing for criminality, and the protection of senior officials in Pyongyang—are organized to not only protect Kim from internal threats but also prevent these same organizations from turning against the leadership. The goal of coup-proofing, Sheena Chestnut Greitens argues, requires that the autocrat "increase the degree of fragmentation within the internal security apparatus" with "overlapping or competing responsibilities and limited lines of interorganizational communication and coordination." Kim and his father have done this well by elevating their family and chosen descendants of the guerrilla generation to emphasize that the livelihood of their senior leadership depends on the regime's survival and by demonstrating that Kim has the sole authority to control personnel appointments.

Surveillance is a state-wide affair that involves every individual down to the neighborhood level. Vigilantes roam the streets looking for violations of social mores—a woman's hair is too long or a man forgot to put his Kim Il Sung button on his lapel as he rushed to get to work. White-gloved inspectors barge into homes unannounced to make sure that the framed photos of Kim Il Sung and Kim Jong Il that are displayed in every household are spotless. And the heads of the *inminban,* a neighborhood watch system in which every citizen is enrolled, make sure that each small fact about every household under their jurisdiction is recorded, including what each family has in its possession, who stays overnight, and other intimate details of daily life. Everyone is an informer or a potential informer, and everyone is vulnerable to punishment for real and perceived crimes. Under this system, Hyeonseo Lee said, "the state made accusers and informers of us all."

The infrastructure of repression that Kim Jong Un inherited and strengthened through the unprecedented execution of his uncle and ongoing purges has inevitably resulted in groupthink among his closest advisers, who are unlikely to veer too far from what they perceive to be his preferences. In fact, their very survival and their families' futures depend on demonstrations of loyalty to Kim and only Kim. His unpredictability and boldness—and his advisers' fear about what he might do next and who might be in his crosshairs— have minimized any potential negative consequences for his actions, while at the same time reinforcing his confidence about the correctness of his decisions. Kim's determination to establish his supremacy in the domestic sphere through a combination of violence and promises of prosperity reflects his acknowledgment of the importance of elite loyalty and the necessity of repression.

Repression and the nuclear weapons program thus form the two pillars of his regime's survival; the denial of human rights and the country's status as a nuclear weapons power are mutually reinforcing. The regime's narrative of a "hostile" United States bent on North Korea's destruction justifies the aggressive weapons program, the diversion of scarce resources to support these strategic armaments, and even the regime's crimes against humanity. The crushing of any potential dissent coupled with the leadership purges create an echo chamber in which Kim is surrounding himself with yes-men, even as he wants to be seen as a modern leader. As much as Kim might want to break from the old ways of thinking and create a twenty-first-century, amenities-filled country, he relies on the inherited infrastructure of terror for regime survival.

The regime's decades-long practice of extreme repression and Kim's efforts to bolster it through the bold purge of his uncle and other senior leaders has no doubt fueled his belief that he can manage the consequences of his actions, interpreting the absence of blowback—whether domestically or internationally—as validation. It has surely also increased his confidence that he can manipulate individuals and situations to yield to his will. Fear of the leader's wrath may have minimized any consequences, for now, but the dependence on repression has boxed Kim into the existing paradigm of North Korean isolation. Whether he knows it or not, the building blocks of fear, the earliest of which were laid by his grandfather and built upon by his father, now constrain his vision and his ability to see beyond the walls.

It wasn't too long after executing his uncle that Kim applied his tools of coercion outside his country's borders to punish an American company, in an effort to shape the outside world with the considerable means at his disposal.

NINE

KIM'S HACKERS

KIM JONG UN STROLLS into the studio for his interview, wearing his usual dark Mao jacket and matching trousers. He settles into his chair and smiles broadly to show the world his sincerity in this live international broadcast. In addition to telling the interviewer that he loves karaoke and that he is an accomplished painter—in his effort to show the world that he's just a normal person—he veers into politics, condemning the United States both for starting the Korean War and for incarcerating more people per capita than any other country, including his own. The atmosphere gets more tense as the interviewer challenges him about his gulags and how he spends hundreds of millions of dollars on his nuclear weapons program even as he starves his people. Glaring at the interviewer, who is ignoring the approved questions, Kim seethes, "Dave, you are incapable of conducting a real interview. You're a joke!," pulls out a gun, and shoots Dave Skylark, the hapless American television journalist. Millions of viewers across the globe gasp in horror and disbelief, and at least some in North Korea begin to doubt whether their leader is in fact the god they were taught to believe in.

Still furious, Kim orders his commanders to prepare their nuclear weapons for launch, as Skylark and his producer, Aaron Rapaport, attempt to escape in Kim's private tank. Kim chases them in a helicopter, shooting at the tank, but the Americans dodge the bullets. Skylark and Rapaport fire from the tank, hitting Kim's helicopter and turning it into a ball of flames. Kim is dead.

In the last decade, North Korea has inspired an array of tacky humor in the "stoner comedy" genre, including *The Interview,* from Sony Pictures Entertainment. The film is based on an improbable scenario: The Central Intelligence Agency sends a hard-drinking, pot-smoking, and fun-loving television personality and his ambitious producer into North Korea with nothing more than a couple of strips of ricin to assassinate Kim Jong Un. Once inside the reclusive country—where they stay at Kim's personal residence, another element that requires viewers to suspend their disbelief, given the leader's well-known paranoia—Skylark strikes up a friendship with Kim. The camaraderie is understandable, perhaps, given Dennis Rodman's visits to Pyongyang and his relationship with Kim. The film is replete with gratuitous violence, scantily clad women, heavy drinking, and even a basketball game between Kim and Skylark as the two bond over their mutual insecurity about not living up to their fathers' standards. Skylark learns that Kim likes margaritas—even though his father thought they were "gay"—and loves Katy Perry's song "Firework." Kim admits, "I am thirty-one years old. . . . The fact that I am running a country is batshit crazy."

Before *The Interview,* there were dozens of documentaries and films that ridiculed and criticized North Korea's tyrants, including the successful movie *Team America: World Police* about Kim Jong Il from the creators of the irreverent show *South Park.* The difference was that *The Interview,* an action-comedy depicting a CIA plot to assassinate Kim Jong Un by enlisting the bumbling duo of Skylark (played by James Franco) and Rapaport (Seth Rogen), elicited a serious response and highlighted the extent to which Kim would go to defend his name and honor. Clearly, *The Interview* had hit a nerve with Kim, and true to form, he took action. In November 2014, North Korean hackers broke into the systems of Sony Pictures Entertainment, stole confidential information from the company, and posted it online. The regime then announced that the release of the movie would constitute an "act of war" and threatened 9/11-type attacks against theaters that showed the film.

What drove Kim to respond in the way that he did? Was it because the movie depicted the luxurious and frivolous lifestyle of Kim and his loyalists? Perhaps exposing the regime's propaganda of Kim's godlike status and its farcical claims that North Korea was a land of prosperity hit too close to home. Maybe the insinuations that Kim was effete were too insulting, or acknowledging that there were factions within North Korea that were intent on unmasking the hypocrisy of the existing regime and determined to foment a coup was too dangerous. Beyond the personal insult to Kim, the film had the potential to reach millions of North Koreans who were already smuggling in banned DVDs of South Korean TV dramas and films, given the increasingly porous borders and the people's insatiable appetite for these types of entertainment.

Paul Fischer, the author of *A Kim Jong-Il Production,* noted that the 2013 movie *Olympus Has Fallen* had not elicited Kim's fury, probably because it was about North Korean commandos attacking the White House—Kim "had no problem being portrayed as rogue, dangerous, or aggressive. But funny . . . that's taking it too far." However, a story about the removal of Kim and the potential for a new government led by the North Korean people probably gave the regime good reason to worry. Perhaps they even read about the South Korean activist who wanted to use balloons to carry one hundred thousand copies of the movie on DVDs and USBs across the border in the belief that "North Korea's absolute leadership will crumble if the idolization of leader Kim breaks down." Jang Jin-sung, one of the North's most prominent propagandists and a member of Kim Jong Il's inner circle, due in part to his skill in nurturing the cult of personality, and who defected in 2004, said that "from the North Korean's point of view, [the movie is] as explosive as if a real bomb were dropped on Kim Jong-un. It's a cultural bomb. . . . It's so shocking. It's beyond-the-pale blasphemous."

The Sony attack demonstrated the twenty-first-century capability of a twenty-first-century millennial dictator who also happens to be thin-skinned. Not only is Kim comfortable with technology in the form of cell phones and laptops, but in the media he is also shown speaking earnestly with nuclear scientists and overseeing scores of missile tests, flying his own plane, providing guidance to the crew as he boards a submarine, and driving a tank. During their visit to Beijing in March 2018, Kim and his wife reportedly experienced a virtual reality demonstration and admired the latest technology shown to them by their Chinese hosts. Kim is a "digital native," the term coined by the author Marc Prensky to describe the generation that is defined by the technological culture in which they grew up. And it's apparent that Kim has fully embraced science and technology as part of his brand and a key component of his tool kit of coercion. Cyberattacks have the added benefit of ambiguity, since attribution takes a great deal of forensic work, creating plausible deniability for the regime that perpetrates these strikes.

It appears that Kim is determined to move beyond the development of nuclear weapons and ballistic missiles by using North Korea's cyber capabilities to advance his goals. He is also looking to further establish his brand as a modern warrior by cultivating a generation of cyber guerrillas, to manipulate the environment through coercive means, regardless of geographic borders.

THE SONY HACK

Around Thanksgiving 2014, about two weeks before *The Interview*'s red-carpet December 11 U.S. premiere, Sony Pictures Entertainment employees logged in to their computers to find this message:

> We've already warned you, and this is just a beginning. We continue till our request be met. . . . We've obtained all your internal

data including your secrets and top secrets. If you don't obey us, we'll release data shown below to the world.

It was accompanied by a glowing red skeleton and signed "Hacked by #GOP," or Guardians of Peace. At first, Sony employees were nonplussed. One person said, "It felt like getting hacked in the early '90s. . . . The message looked like something out of *Hackers,* the movie. . . . It was a throwback. Almost cute." In the days that followed, speculation about who was behind the Sony hack ranged from Russia to hacktivists to disgruntled Sony insiders. North Korea as the culprit was at the bottom of the list, even though in June of that year, when the movie trailer was shown, its Foreign Ministry spokesman threatened "merciless" retaliation if the film about an assassination attempt against Kim Jong Un was released. The state media quoted the spokesman as saying, "Making and releasing a movie on a plot to hurt our top-level leadership is the most blatant act of terrorism and will absolutely not be tolerated." He added that the United States was using a "gangster filmmaker" to undermine the North Korean leadership. Seth Rogen joked on Twitter, "People don't usually wanna kill me for one of my movies until after they've paid 12 bucks for it." A little over a week after the hack, *Wired* magazine assessed it was "outlandish" to think that North Korea would be behind the Sony cyberattack. Among other reasons, *Wired* argued that "nation-state attacks don't usually announce themselves with a showy image of a blazing skeleton posted to infected machines or use a catchy nom-de-hack like Guardians of Peace to identify themselves."

Despite the North's formidable nuclear and ballistic missile programs, it is all too easy to underestimate the small country. Alexandra Alter of *The New York Times* noted that "North Korea is a long-running punch line in America pop culture." In the movie *Team America: World Police,* Kim Jong Il turns into a cockroach. On the television show *30 Rock,* Margaret Cho plays the cheese-loving, cognac-swilling leader Kim Jong Il, and late-night talk and variety shows like *Saturday Night Live* and *The Daily Show* have gotten laughs with endless Kim jokes. The Korea historian Charles Armstrong told Alter, "North Korea embodies all the stereotypes of imagery from the Cold War, but in an absurd way, so we can poke fun at it in a way that we couldn't poke fun at the Soviet Union or Communist China. . . . We don't take North Korea seriously enough." Michael Lynton, the chief executive of Sony Pictures Entertainment, said, "At that point in time, Kim Jong-un was relatively new in the job, and I don't think it was clear yet how he was different from his father. . . . Nobody ever mentioned anything about their cyber capabilities." After all, wasn't North Korea an isolated, backward country? How could they possibly have the technical prowess and the nerve to attack and threaten political coercion against a major movie studio?

The extent of the damage quickly became clear. An employee said, "It was like a bomb went off. . . . We looked around. We were still alive. So we started doing triage." An ex-employee remembered, "Everything was so completely destroyed. It was surreal. *Everything* was down." It wasn't just that the Sony employees had to handwrite everything, couldn't get paid on schedule, and had to work longer hours to complete tasks that normally took much less time. The Sony staff thought they could manage those problems.

But the hack did more than destroy the data of Sony Pictures Entertainment: Confidential information, including salary lists, nearly fifty thousand Social Security numbers, and five unreleased films, was dumped onto public file-sharing sites. The cyberattack exposed the movie industry's dirty laundry, sending a "ripple of dread across Hollywood to Washington." The hackers released massive amounts of emails and other documents revealing gossip, celebrities' online aliases, and battles about projects and actors, setting off a feeding frenzy by media hungry for salacious information about Hollywood stars, including Angelina Jolie, Natalie Portman, and Tom Hanks. But even the rank and file at Sony were hurt: Their identities were stolen, details about their medical procedures were exposed, and cybercriminals drained their personal bank accounts.

When the FBI investigated, a spokesman for the National Defense Commission—which at that time was North Korea's highest governing organization—denied their involvement in or knowledge of the hack, but gloated that the attack "might be a righteous deed of the supporters and sympathizers" of the regime. The NDC statement also said *The Interview* was a "film abetting a terrorist act while hurting the dignity of the supreme leadership" of North Korea. A little over a week later, the Guardians of Peace threatened 9/11-type attacks if Sony went ahead and released the film, warning in ungrammatical English, "We will clearly show it to you at the very time and places The Interview be shown, including the premiere, how bitter fate those who seek fun in terror should be doomed to. . . . The world will be full of fear. . . . Remember the 11th of September 2001."

No one could have anticipated that a raunchy bro-com movie could have led to a national security crisis. Sony and the multiplex operators—and the malls that housed them—took the threats of terrorism seriously. The film debuted in Los Angeles on December 11, but Sony canceled the wide release on December 17, and then reversed its decision two days later. But the major theater chains refused to show it over the holidays, fearful of another event like the 2012 massacre in Aurora, Colorado, in which a gunman murdered twelve people and injured scores of others during a screening of the film *The Dark Knight Rises*. The withdrawal of the movie by Sony and the refusal by major cinemas to show it led to soul-searching in the media and provoked a larger discussion about freedom of speech and artistic expression in the face of terroristic threats. Many Sony employees who had already suffered the brunt of the cyberattacks and were feeling vulnerable were in no mood to be in any further danger, especially for a product that wasn't by any measure an artistic achievement. "Why are we all paying the price for a movie that isn't even very good?" one employee asked. Others, like George Clooney, Steve Carell, and Michael Moore, felt compelled to advocate a firm stance against this type of coercion and criticized Sony for failing to protect artistic freedom.

Finally, on December 19, less than a month after the GOP threat appeared on Sony computers, the FBI announced that the North Korean government was responsible for the intrusion. Following an intensive investigation that involved multiple government agencies and the intelligence community, the FBI said that technical analysis revealed links to other known North Korean malicious cyberactivity. Director of National Intelligence James Clapper recalled in his memoir that "without a shadow of a doubt in my mind and those of our top cyber specialists . . . the Sony hacks had originated in North Korea." The FBI press release stated:

> We are deeply concerned about the destructive nature of this attack on a private sector entity and the ordinary citizens who worked there. . . . Though the FBI has seen a wide variety and increasing number of cyber intrusions, the destructive nature of this attack, coupled with its coercive nature, sets it apart. North Korea's actions were intended to inflict significant harm on a U.S. business and suppress the right of American citizens to express themselves. Such acts of intimidation fall outside the bounds of acceptable state behavior. The FBI takes seriously any attempt—whether through cyber-enabled means, threats of violence, or otherwise—to undermine the economic and social prosperity of our citizens.

The 9/11-type attack never happened, but the fear was real and the chaos and confusion it engendered shaped the decision-making of private U.S. entities and the exercise of their rights. President Obama criticized Sony's decision and cautioned, "We cannot have a society in which some dictator someplace can start imposing censorship here in the United States. . . . Imagine if producers and distributors and others start engaging in self-censorship because they don't want to offend the sensibilities of somebody whose sensibilities probably need to be offended." Peter Singer, a top U.S. expert on cyberwarfare, said, "The problem now is not the hack. It's how Sony responded to it. It's the cave-in. . . . They rewarded and incentivized attacks on the rest of us."

The over-the-top North Korean response to the release of the movie showed that the regime's tools of coercion go beyond missiles and nuclear weapons and that Kim Jong Un has the will and the capacity to punish perceived offenses outside his country's borders. "The movie offers an alternative that North Koreans aren't even given the leeway to think about. It offers an alternative imagination," said Jang Jin-sung, the propagandist-cum-defector. "It's not that people really believe all this propaganda about Kim Jong-un, that he's a God, and need someone to tell them otherwise or show them another way of thinking. North Koreans are people, and they aren't stupid. In the North Korean system, you have to praise Kim and sing hymns about him and take it seriously, even if you think it's only a shit narrative." And Kim Jong Un was making sure that no one challenges that narrative, even Americans. The Sony incident was the result of Kim's paranoia combined with his brazenness and high risk tolerance for testing his capabilities. The *New York Times* reporter David Sanger concluded, "Cyberweapons were tailor-made for North Korea's situation in the world: so isolated it had little to lose, so short of fuel it had no other way to sustain a conflict with greater powers, and so backward that its infrastructure was largely invulnerable to crippling counterattacks."

THE PREQUEL . . . AND THE SEQUEL

Sony was a wake-up call for Washington, dispelling any doubts about Pyongyang's cyber capabilities, though one could argue that the United States hardly needed one. For years, the regime's growing cyberattack prowess had been worrying experts. North Korean entities had already staged a number of intrusions into South Korean banks, the military intranet, and the email accounts of government officials and media organizations, reflecting the Kim family's goal of using these new tools to coerce, conduct espionage, and earn currency for the regime. Just a few months before the Sony hack, in April, General Curtis M. Scaparrotti, who was then commander of the U.S. forces in South Korea, told the House Committee on

Armed Services that "North Korea employs computer hackers capable of conducting open-source intelligence collection, cyber-espionage, and disruptive cyber-attacks." His assessment was that "cyber warfare is an important asymmetric dimension of conflict that North Korea will probably continue to emphasize—in part because of its deniability and low relative costs." His warnings about the cyberthreat were in line with what the U.S. intelligence community had been cautioning since 2013, when James Clapper said that "cyber" bumped "terrorism" off the top of the list of the major threats facing the United States.

While North Korea had been developing nuclear weapons and ballistic missiles over the decades, its interest in cyber is relatively recent, dating back to the early 2000s. Citing Kim Heung-kwang, who taught computer science at North Korea's Hamheung Computer Technology University, *The New York Times* reported that Kim Jong Il became interested in the Internet around 2003, when he told his military commanders that "if warfare was about bullets and oil until now, warfare in the 21st century is about information." Pyongyang's capabilities were rudimentary, but Kim Jong Un took them to another level, much like his approach to accelerating development of ballistic missiles and nuclear weapons.

In fact, for Kim Jong Un, the advancement of cyber capabilities seems to mesh well with his desire for quick results at relatively low cost and for burnishing his brand as a modern leader presiding over North Korea's technological improvements. As a digital native who has spent his entire life with video games, cell phones, video cameras, and other tools of our age, Kim is comfortable with incorporating cyber into the North's tool kit of provocative actions. "Cyberwarfare, along with nuclear weapons and missiles, is an 'all-purpose sword' that guarantees our military's capability to strike relentlessly," he reportedly explained. Kim has deployed approximately six thousand hackers and cyber support personnel to at least eight countries—China, Malaysia, New Zealand, India, Nepal, Indonesia, Mozambique, and Kenya—to avoid detection and to take advantage of their Internet infrastructures. Kim has also focused on cyberintelligence and cyberwarfare training programs, funneling the most talented students into Kim Il Sung University College of Computer Science, Kim Chaek University of Technology, Mirim University, and other institutions.

Kim's hackers see the South as an attractive target. South Korean officials have claimed that North Korea has conducted more than six thousand cyberattacks against it—relatively unsophisticated compared with the Sony hack and those that followed—since 2010, racking up around $650 billion in damages to South Korean private and government entities. In 2011, North Korea disrupted one bank's branches for ten days. North Korean malware directed against three South Korean media companies and three major banks in 2013 rendered computers unusable through a denial of service attack, leaving customers unable to access their accounts. It deleted credit card records and inflicted financial costs of around $800 million. North Korea's attacks against South Korea's financial and media sectors are an attempt to cripple the industries and openness that are at the heart of South Korea's prosperity. Pyongyang is likely aiming to make the point that the poorer Korea can inflict harm on its richer cousin south of the thirty-eighth parallel, while its own isolation and relative poverty make it invulnerable to proportionate punishment from Seoul or Washington. Pyongyang appears to be using its growing capabilities to generate money for the regime, in part to offset the slew of sanctions that hamper its more traditional methods of earning hard currency.

In 2016, Kim's attacks against Bangladesh Bank resulted in a theft of $81 million, demonstrating new, more sophisticated capabilities. The hackers breached the Society for Worldwide Interbank Financial Telecommunication's global messaging system—considered one of the most secure mechanisms for financial transfers—and fraudulently moved money from the bank's holdings in the Federal Reserve Bank of New York to their own accounts in the Philippines. The U.S. National Security Agency said in March 2017 that the 2016 attacks were "forensically" tied to the Sony attack.

In addition to the Bangladesh heist, North Korean hackers targeted Vietnam's TPBank in 2015, Far Eastern International Bank of Taiwan in 2017, and Bancomext of Mexico and Banco de Chile in 2018, among others, for a total of more than sixteen organizations in eleven countries at a minimum since at least 2014, highlighting the increasingly sophisticated and undeterred cyberactivities of North Korea since Kim Jong Un came to power.

But a study by the Foundation for Defense of Democracies in October 2018 struck a more worrisome note. It stated that North Korea has the potential to weaken and disrupt the national security infrastructure of the United States and South Korea, pointing to the U.S. Department of Homeland Security and FBI joint alert warning that North Korean entities were targeting the aerospace, telecommunications, and finance industries. Furthermore, in December 2017, the United States announced that North Korea was responsible for the WannaCry computer worm that affected 230,000 computers in more than 150 countries, costing billions of dollars. The White House homeland security adviser Thomas P. Bossert said the WannaCry attack was "a defining moment" and that "North Korea has demonstrated that they want to hold the entire world at risk, whether it be through its nuclear program or cyberattacks." Kim's hackers are undeterred. As detailed in an August 2019 U.N. report, they have become more sophisticated in their manipulation of cyberspace, successfully launching attacks on financial institutions and cryptocurrency exchanges to generate an estimated $2 billion to date.

The Interview was supposed to be funny at Kim Jong Un's expense. But, as it turned out, the joke was on us.

KIM'S SILICON VALLEY

Kim's cyberwarriors and their hit-and-run tactics are indicative of the regime's intent to wreak havoc and instill fear even outside North Korea, but Kim has been equally focused on developing technologies *within* the country, even at the risk of unsanctioned information penetrating the people's consciousness and laying bare the contradictions and falsehoods of state propaganda. Like a tech entrepreneur with all of the nation's wealth at his disposal, Kim has allowed his people, not just in Pyongyang but also in the provinces, broader access to the accoutrements of digital life that he can control, including laptops, tablets, and cell phones, but without access to what he can't control, namely the Internet. And as a dictator, he has also sought to nudge the populace onto digital networks to better limit how the North Korean people consume information—in effect, using technology and its access to strengthen his rule and amplify North Korean propaganda.

Kim has created an attractive environment for the tech elite, devoting regime resources to reward and incentivize scientists and engineers. One of the perks is the Mirae Scientists Street, a neighborhood for North Korea's Silicon Valley, located in a highly coveted area near the Pyongyang train station and adjacent to the Taedong River on a six-lane avenue. The residential project is punctuated by a fifty-three-story skyscraper topped with a "golden" orb as if to serve as a beacon for North Korea's aspiring techies and as a marker of their esteemed place in Kim's modern North Korea. It has a daycare center, school, stores, sports parks, and other amenities, not only to keep the workers and their families happy but also to inspire future generations to value their privilege in this society. Nat Kretchun, an expert on technology trends in North Korea, has argued that the regime's conscious cultivation of this population of scientists and engineers is designed to harness their skills in order to prevent the development of a domestic "hacker culture" in which they would have more incentive to undermine digital controls than to reinforce them.

In January 2016, just months after the regime celebrated the completion of Mirae Scientists Street, the North Korean government unveiled the Sci-Tech Complex to further demonstrate the high priority it places on scientific expertise. The complex is a high-tech park designed in the shape of an atom, perhaps as a poke in the eye to the United States, as it watches via satellite images of this brazen advertisement for North Korea's commitment to nuclear weapons and other technological developments. Inside, employees work diligently at computers connected to the North Korean intranet, as described by a CNN reporter who visited the facility. Enticed by inducements such as department store discounts, better housing, more food, exemptions from mandatory military service, and elevated status, parents are clamoring to get their children into the sciences, according to North Korean sources who were interviewed by Radio Free Asia in 2017. One source said that private tutors who teach math, physics, and science are earning the most money.

Kim's embrace of modern technology—and even American products—has filtered down to the elites, who can afford the luxury of digital connectedness. Regime propaganda regularly features Kim with cell phones, computers, and laptops, even an Apple MacBook Pro. Average North Koreans are also shown using cell phones. Kim Jong Il encouraged the development and use of technology, even though at first he feared the potential for outside information to seep in through it and threaten the status quo and regime propaganda. His son has no such fear of technology and its place in the modern world but demonstrably understands its opportunities and its power to amplify his control over his people. This attitude is certainly an acknowledgment that the regime recognizes the irreversible forces of the market economy, by using modern tools to allow horizontal connections among North Koreans rather than tamp them down. As InterMedia, a Washington-based research group, documented in its important 2017 study, "Expanding network connectivity to a broad swath of the population is arming the North Korean government with a new array of censorship and surveillance tools that go beyond what is observed even in other authoritarian states or closed media environments." In effect, Kim Jong Un's North Korea is "conducting more active strategic management of the information space," which is intended to "meet its surveillance and security needs, as well as spur economic growth, and create the appearance of development and modernization," according to the study.

North Koreans were no strangers to technology. After all, ownership of televisions, VCRs, and DVDs had begun to spread since around 2000. InterMedia found in 2012 that nearly three-quarters of surveyed North Koreans had watched television and about half personally owned one. According to a UNICEF study, nearly 100 percent of households owned a television by 2017. Based on his research of the borderland areas, the North Korea expert Andrei Lankov asserted that 70 to 80 percent of all households had DVD players by 2012. But as mentioned earlier, most North Koreans, not just the elites, now own or have access to advanced media devices, including computers, USB drives, and Chinese mobile phones. Lankov estimates that there are probably several hundred thousand computers in North Korea. Mobile devices are more common, with as many as four million subscriptions and growing.

The cell phones and tablets that North Koreans rely on for information, leisure, and conducting business activities are enabled with minimal 3G services, according to the research group Recorded Future, including voice, text messaging, and picture and video messaging capabilities. A *New York Times* reporter who visited Pyongyang in 2016 recounted a scene at a restaurant near Kim Il Sung University in which young couples used their North Korea–made smartphones, running a version of the Android operating system, to take photos of their hamburgers before eating, a scene that would be unremarkable in any other country. But it was remarkable in North Korea, even more so because of the casualness of the Pyongyangites' flaunting of their consumer goods and the accoutrements of modern, digital society, not to mention their appetite for a staple of American menus. These phones are not cheap—a cell phone and registration costs around $200, an exorbitant sum in North Korea— but their prevalence is another reminder of North Korea's marketization and wealth creation since the post-famine years. The journalists Daniel Tudor and James Pearson point out that for North Koreans a cell phone is both a necessity and a status symbol: Traders need it to get information on prices and connect with suppliers and potential customers; young people use it to impress friends and highlight their position in society. UNICEF found that more than 80 percent of North Koreans have used a mobile phone as of 2017.

Yet their experience with these devices is vastly different from ours. The conventional wisdom about the potential for the Internet and related technology to open new—and unfettered—spaces for communication simply does not apply. Suki Kim, who taught elite North Korean students in Pyongyang, observed that the teenagers did not know anything about the revolution in information and social networking as pioneered by the likes of Steve Jobs and Mark Zuckerberg. Martyn Williams, a technology specialist, explains how Kim's regime "is doing something that no other country has done: building a nationwide intranet that offers email and websites but is totally shut off from the rest of the world. It's an audacious attempt to usher in some of the benefits of electronic communications while maintaining complete control on an entire population."

North Korea doesn't just rely on censorship to block content; it has created an alternate virtual universe. The country's network, called Kwangmyong, allows its users to access domestic websites that are limited to content from the ruling party newspaper, the state news agency, a cooking site with recipes for Korean food, and online learning. In 2016, North Korea had approximately two dozen websites; by 2017, it claimed to have 168. The country also has a video-on-demand system to access state television programming. "It's no Netflix," says Williams. The regime in recent years has also introduced online shopping primarily aimed at smartphone users who might be interested in clothing, women's accessories, cosmetics, specialty food items, and furniture. Kretchun observes that "North Korea is systematically moving its people onto networks over which it has complete control," a command more extreme than that of other repressive states like China, which is also experimenting with similar information censorship and surveillance. An even smaller number of North Koreans—the elite of the elite—have permission to access the World Wide Web. That means only a tiny minority and top leadership are aware of world affairs, including perceptions of North Korea, the development of new technologies, and popular Western culture. Kim Jong Un almost certainly is one of these consumers of outside information. The government prohibits its general population from listening to or watching foreign media. Radios and televisions are preset to receive only domestic programming, with the threat of severe punishment to compel obedience.

Perhaps Kim's awareness of outside criticism of North Korea and his experience living in Switzerland, coupled with his political and tech savvy, have been driving his regime's efforts to project North Korean propaganda outside its geographical boundaries. The Korea Computer Center acts as a clearinghouse for the intranet and grants access only to regime-approved information. The regime has an official Twitter account and a number of websites devoted to making its propaganda and "news" accessible to outsiders. While the West has touted the Internet, social media, and virtual communities as a democratic leveler, where individual freedoms and potential are unleashed, the North Korea example shows how the Internet, as defense experts Peter Singer and Emerson Brooking argue, "has not loosened the grip of authoritarian regimes . . . [but] has become a new tool for maintaining their power."

In this context, North Korea's self-imposed isolation and use of repression to squelch dissent are not a deficit but a strategic advantage that provides the space for Kim to hone one of the newest methods of coercion toward cementing his power and constraining the ability of the United States and South Korea to punish his bad behavior. Kim already has the decades-old prison camps and the ideological infrastructure to disseminate regime propaganda. The new cyber tools provide another way to send that information, furnishing his bureaucrats with the implements to further police people's thoughts and behaviors.

From inviting foreign journalists to Pyongyang to amplify and lend legitimacy to the regime to using technology and cyberattacks to control the flow and consumption of information inside and outside North Korea, Kim has expanded the geographies of his control. Magnifying his power is the insidious way in which the regime's repressive measures seep into the consciousness of both the North Korean people and foreign visitors and journalists, who self-censor either to ensure that they do not run afoul of North Korean authorities or to maintain access.

For ordinary North Koreans, yielding to Kim's intimidation is a life-or-death decision, given their leader's mastery of his inherited art of repression to ensure his supremacy, updated to use modern technologies and accommodate the realities of a market economy. But for his older half-brother, who roamed outside the boundaries of North Korea, lobbing criticism from the safety of his perch in China, Kim had a different plan.

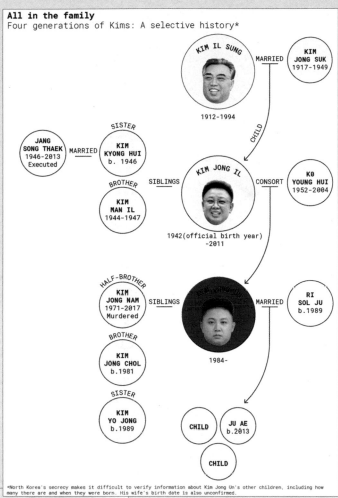

All in the family
Four generations of Kims: A selective history*

KIM IL SUNG
1912-1994

MARRIED

KIM
JONG SUK
1917-1949

CHILD

JANG
SONG THAEK
1946-2013
Executed

MARRIED

SISTER

KIM
KYONG HUI
b. 1946

BROTHER

KIM
MAN IL
1944-1947

SIBLINGS

KIM JONG IL
1942(official birth year)
-2011

CONSORT

KO
YOUNG HUI
1952-2004

HALF-BROTHER

KIM
JONG NAM
1971-2017
Murdered

SIBLINGS

BROTHER

KIM
JONG CHOL
b.1981

SISTER

KIM
YO JONG
b.1989

1984-

MARRIED

RI
SOL JU
b.1989

CHILD

JU AE
b.2013

CHILD

*North Korea's secrecy makes it difficult to verify information about Kim Jong Un's other children, including how many there are and when they were born. His wife's birth date is also unconfirmed.

THE BROOKINGS INSTITUTION

A young Kim Il Sung and his wife, Kim Jong Suk, during their guerrilla days.

Kim Il Sung, Kim Jong Suk, and their eldest son, Kim Jong Il, in an undated photo.

Kim Il Sung speaks with workers during one of his many trips criss-crossing the country, 1967.

Kim Jong Il with his son Kim Jong Nam in 1981. Jong Nam's maternal aunt Song Hye Rim, her daughter Li Nam Ok, and her son Li Il Nam stand behind them.

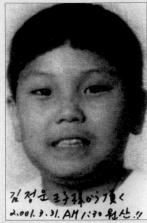

Kim Jong Un as a child.
REUTERS/COURTESY OF KENJI FUJIMOTO

김정은 포장까이기릇〈
2.00ㅅ 3. 31. AM 1:30 원산.!/

Kim Jong Il looks over at his son Kim Jong Un during the parade commemorating the sixty-fifth anniversary of the party on October 10, 2010. It was the young Kim's public debut. REUTERS/PETAR KUJUNDZIC

Pyongyang residents collapse and mourn upon hearing the news of Kim Jong Il's death.
REUTERS/KYODO

Kim Jong Un walks beside the hearse carrying his father's body during the funeral procession in Pyongyang on December 28, 2011. His uncle Jang Song Thaek, executed in 2013, is directly behind Kim. AP PHOTO/KOREAN CENTRAL NEWS AGENCY VIA KOREA NEWS SERVICE

Kim Il Sung greets Chinese leader Zhou Enlai in Pyongyang, 1958.

KEYSTONE-FRANCE/GAMMA-KEYSTONE VIA GETTY IMAGES

The regime has played up Kim Jong Un's likeness to his grandfather in looks and demeanor to emphasize continuity of the bloodline.

REUTERS/KOREAN CENTRAL NEWS AGENCY

Kim Jong Un and Ri Sol Ju wave to the crowd at the opening of the Rungra People's Pleasure Ground in July 2012.

REUTERS/KOREAN CENTRAL NEWS AGENCY

The pseudonymous Kenji Fujimoto, Kim Jong Il's personal sushi chef, speaks to a crowd about meeting with Kim Jong Un during his July 2012 trip to Pyongyang at Kim's invitation.

YOSHIKAZU TSUNO/AFP VIA GETTY IMAGES

Kim Jong Un engages in a conversation with former NBA player Dennis Rodman as they watch an exhibition game in Pyongyang in January 2014. Ri Sol Ju is sitting next to Kim.

KOREAN CENTRAL NEWS AGENCY/ KOREA NEWS SERVICE VIA AP

A poster for the movie *The Interview* hangs outside a movie theater in Nevada, December 2014. ETHAN MILLER/GETTY IMAGES

The cover of the January 18, 2016, issue of *The New Yorker*. Earlier that month, North Korea conducted its fourth nuclear test, Kim's second as leader.

ANITA KUNZ/*THE NEW YORKER* © CONDE NAST

Kim Jong Un has overseen four nuclear tests as of January 2020 and debuted ballistic missiles of various ranges, launched from multiple locations.

KOREAN CENTRAL NEWS AGENCY VIA REUTERS

Kim Jong Nam with his maternal grandmother in 1975.

AFP VIA GETTY IMAGES

Kim Jong Nam in 2001.

Kim Jong Nam died in February 2017 after two women applied the VX nerve agent to his face at Kuala Lumpur International Airport, Malaysia—an operation that was almost certainly ordered by his half-brother Kim Jong Un.

Shortly after President Trump's speech at the U.N. General Assembly in September 2017, during which he called Kim "Rocket Man" and threatened to "totally destroy" North Korea, Kim Jong Un issued an angry, defiant response. He said Trump was a "dotard," an old, senile person "unfit" to be the leader of a country.

U.S. vice president Mike Pence, seated next to Japanese prime minister Abe Shinzo, watches the opening ceremony of the 2018 Winter Olympics in Pyeongchang, South Korea. Kim Jong Un's sister, Kim Yo Jong, is second from top right. South Korean president Moon Jae-in and his wife, Kim Jung-sook, are on the far left, wearing white jackets.

Kim Jong Un, Ri Sol Ju, and Chinese president Xi Jinping and his wife, Peng Liyuan, walk together during the first North Korea–China summit in March 2018—Kim's first trip outside of North Korea as leader. Ri attracted much attention from Chinese social media for her physical appearance and fashion choices.

KOREAN CENTRAL NEWS AGENCY/VIA REUTERS

Kim Jong Un, Ri Sol Ju, and Kim's sister, Kim Yo Jong (foreground), at the first inter-Korean summit at Panmunjom, April 2018.

KOREA SUMMIT PRESS POOL/
POOL VIA REUTERS

President Trump meets Kim Jong Un for the third time on June 30, 2019, and briefly steps into North Korea, making him the first sitting U.S. president to do so.

REUTERS/KEVIN LAMARQUE

Kim Jong Un in October 2019, riding a white horse on snow-covered Mount Paektu—a significant location in Korean history and a key part of the Kim family propaganda—probably to imbue himself with a mystical heroism in his determination to stand firm against the United States.

KOREAN CENTRAL NEWS AGENCY VIA REUTERS

TEN

MURDER IN MALAYSIA

I T IS THE MORNING of February 13, 2017. Kim Jong Nam, Jong Un's older half-brother and his father's eldest son, enters the Kuala Lumpur International Airport in Malaysia. He is wearing a stylish light-colored blazer with jeans, designer loafers, and a backpack; what looks like a Louis Vuitton satchel he was known to carry is casually slung across his right shoulder. He appears to be just another middle-aged tourist or businessman, comfortably corpulent, waiting to catch his flight back to his home in Macau, known as the Las Vegas of China, an epicenter of gambling and glitz where he has been living in exile with his wife, son, and daughter. He walks purposefully into the airport, looks up at the departure screen—his fluid movements suggest he is familiar with this airport—and strolls toward the check-in kiosk.

Suddenly, a woman runs up to him and rubs his face with her hands. A second woman quickly follows and does the same. With these rapid, successive movements, they apply a chemical nerve agent called VX, one of the deadliest in the world. A single drop can be lethal. The women will not suffer from the toxins, perhaps because they will immediately wash their hands or because they handled compounds that became lethal only when mixed.

The video footage from the airport's security cameras is hard to watch. Kim asks for help and is escorted to a medical clinic at the airport. His gait is noticeably stiffer, and he writhes in pain as he waits for treatment inside the clinic. As the VX seeps into his body, Kim would have been experiencing blurred vision, trouble breathing, nausea, diarrhea, respiratory failure, and convulsions, which are the immediate signs of exposure, according to the U.S. Centers for Disease Control and Prevention. Just moments later, he is dead. The security footage shows people in the medical clinic bending down to help Jong Nam, as onlookers peer curiously through the window. The last few images are of officials wheeling him out on a stretcher, his T-shirt puckered up, exposing his bulging stomach. The Malaysian health minister said later that his final moments were painful.

Subsequent pathology reports indicated that VX was on Kim's face, eyes, clothing, and backpack, and in his blood and urine, doing lethal damage to his brain, lungs, liver, and spleen. One of the Malaysian doctors who conducted the autopsy testified in court that the large amount of feces in Kim's underwear and his pupil constriction led her to conclude that the death was the result of acute VX poisoning. Images of Kim Jong Nam's very public death ricocheted throughout the world and accusatory fingers pointed to his half-brother in Pyongyang, who was probably carrying on with mundane duties, such as touring a catfish factory, while Jong Nam lay dying among strangers. For a man who had been doted on by his father and pampered by armies of sycophants and servants, it was an ignominious end.

The whole incident seemed like a scene out of a bad movie. Of course, the airport authorities didn't know that the dead man was once considered the next leader of North Korea. But they could see that he was carrying a passport that identified him as "Kim Chol" and $120,000 in his designer backpack. And they certainly didn't know at the time that a chemical nerve agent had been applied or that the two women who had done it said they thought they were doing a prank for a reality show. One of the female culprits was wearing an almost mocking "LOL" sweatshirt.

The accused women, Doan Thi Huong and Siti Aisyah, both in their twenties, were terrified and shocked when they were arrested just a few days later. Huong and Aisyah, two young women from impoverished backgrounds, the former from a rural village in Vietnam and the latter from Indonesia, had pursued better lives for themselves only to descend into prostitution to make ends meet. But they had found themselves—probably inadvertently—at the center of international intrigue and facing the death penalty for their role in killing the half-brother of the world's most reclusive dictator, while their North Korean handlers and the regime they worked for escaped any consequences. (In March 2019, Aisyah was freed after the Indonesian government lobbied intensely for her release from the Malaysian prison. Two months later, Huong was also let go after similar lobbying from Hanoi.)

In response to South Korean officials' accusations that the incident was "an act of systematic terror ordered by Kim Jong Un," Pyongyang angrily and vehemently denied its role. To the horde of journalists camped outside the embassy, Pyongyang's diplomats in Kuala Lumpur proclaimed, "What others say about our diplomat are all lies and libelous slanders!" North Korea also maintained that the assassination was a conspiracy between Malaysia and South Korea, and denounced Washington and Seoul for "kicking up an anti-DPRK smear campaign," likening it to "the story of Iraq's possession of weapons of mass destruction." The United States and South Korea, however, concluded that the North Korean government was responsible for the murder.

It was not a secret that Kim Jong Un was not a fan of his older half-brother, once the favorite of their father. Kim almost certainly wanted to get rid of a potential rival, as he did with his uncle Jang Song Thaek. And the way he did it—in a public, painful, and humiliating way, widely disseminated through video and images to make it real and intimate—was a message to any challengers. Although Kim almost certainly ordered the assassination, it's unclear whether he micromanaged the event or if he left the planning and execution to his operatives. One can imagine that he was quite pleased with those who orchestrated the killing, for its sophistication, its deniability, and the drama that unfolded in its aftermath.

No dissenter or perceived dissenter is safe, whether he or she is in Pyongyang, like Uncle Jang, or, like Jong Nam, in a seemingly safe place—the bustling international hub of Kuala Lumpur—supposedly under the care of the Chinese government. The success of North Korean special operatives, who could conduct a sensitive, skilled attack in a public setting, and their use of a chemical weapon were a lesson to all who watched the videos and read about the killing. Plastered as it was all over the international and regional media, the assassination was proof that Kim's reach and revenge have no limits.

THE PLAYBOY AND THE PURIST

Kim Jong Nam knew he had a target on his back. One of his friends said, "He wasn't paranoid, but he was worried. . . . When he was out he was careful, and he avoided talking to Asians because he was worried they were spies." The head of South Korea's National Intelligence Service revealed in 2017 that Jong Nam, aware that Jong Un had been trying to assassinate him since 2011, had written to his brother in 2012, asking him to spare his life and that of his family. But he tried to lead a normal life in China, under Beijing's protection, getting married and having children there in the 1990s. He traveled regularly, to Southeast Asia and Europe, where his son was studying in France, and posted photos of himself at various locations on his Facebook page, under the pseudonym Kim Chol, which was also the name on his passport. His puffy face, bloated belly, and unshaven stubble were telling signs of a life of leisure, drink, and rich foods, while his Ferragamo loafers, fancy hats and sunglasses, and other designer clothes exuded a very un–North Korean aesthetic, a stark contrast to his younger brother's drab Mao jacket and matching slacks, severe haircut, and dark horn-rimmed glasses.

Kim Jong Nam reportedly never met the younger brother who had usurped their father's affections. Thirteen years Jong Un's senior, Jong Nam had become the face of what could have been in North Korea, as international media speculated about his real or perceived reformist tendencies and what changes he would bring to North Korea if he were named to lead the country. Jong Nam's occasional comments to the Japanese and South Korean press containing direct or oblique criticisms of the regime did not help endear him to his brother in Pyongyang. Although Jong Nam had refrained from openly criticizing North Korea in recent years, the fact that he was still in the public eye and posting his lifestyle on Facebook no doubt irritated Jong Un, who was demonstrably unable to completely control his brother. And for a regime that was obsessed and paranoid about stability and control, Jong Nam was an obvious outlier, not least because despite his stated desire to remove himself from politics, his very existence fostered as yet unrequited dreams about North Korean reform.

Perhaps Jong Un hated his brother—Westernized, gluttonous, corrupted—for what he represented. Jong Nam frequented brothels and reportedly had multiple girlfriends, while Jong Un portrays himself as a devoted husband to his wife, as evidenced by how often she accompanies him in public. While his brother indulged himself and gambled, Jong Un worked tirelessly to preserve the legacy of their grandfather and father and the country's sovereignty and strength. Jong Nam was effete and enslaved by his luxurious lifestyle, while Jong Un crisscrossed North Korea tending to his people's livelihood. Jong Nam was dependent on China for protection, while Jong Un was developing advanced nuclear and ballistic missile programs to preserve the North's dignity and independence. For Jong Un, his older brother might have been an alter ego, a degenerate who served as an example of what happens when one is not vigilant about hewing close to the regime's ideology, an entity at the extreme end of the spectrum from purity of thought and action as embodied in Kim Jong Un, the loyal son, father, husband, leader.

There was no possible redemption for Kim Jong Nam. And as for Uncle Jang, who also veered from the righteous path, elimination of the rot was the only option, according to the regime. The assassination itself was a mix of the old and the new—using a chemical warfare agent developed in the 1950s against the target in a public setting, the classic deployment of clandestine operatives to lure two probably unsuspecting young women looking to star in what they thought was a reality show, and having the entire attack and its aftermath recorded by surveillance cameras. It was a scene made for TV, as Kim surely intended.

The attack on Jong Nam was not about just one individual—it was meant to send a message to North Koreans about the deadly consequences of going against the grain. But a less obvious and more frightening reason for it was that it was a test: a test of the capabilities of a weapon of mass destruction, and the international reaction to it.

THE OTHER WEAPONS OF MASS DESTRUCTION

While most of the international attention on North Korea has been focused on the nuclear and ballistic missile programs, the Kim Jong Nam assassination put a spotlight on long-standing suspicions about North Korea's stockpile of biological and chemical weapons, further complicating the threat that the regime poses regionally and globally. Unlike the nuclear weapons program, which has been demonstrated through tests and celebrated in state media, other weapons of mass destruction at Pyongyang's disposal have not been flaunted. Furthermore, some of the components of biological and chemical weapons can also be used legitimately for agricultural and industrial purposes, which makes it even more difficult to assess North Korea's capabilities and intentions, let alone monitor them.

There have been various reports of North Korean acquisitions of biological and chemical weapons capabilities since as long ago as the

1960s. Two decades after initiating these programs, Kim Il Sung declared that the country had "succeeded in producing poisonous gas and bacterial weapons through our own efforts supported by Soviet scientists in the field." Various U.S. and South Korean government estimates and open-source information suggest that Pyongyang does have the infrastructure to weaponize biological and chemical agents. The Office of the Director of National Intelligence reported to Congress in 2006 that North Korean scientists and facilities have the "rudimentary biotechnology infrastructure" to produce infectious biological warfare agents or toxins.

Among North Korea's suspected inventory of potential biological weapons are anthrax, cholera, the plague, typhoid fever, and yellow fever, and its chemical weapons inventory includes nerve, blister, blood, and choking agents. The VX nerve agent that was used on Jong Nam is categorized as a Schedule 1 weapon of mass destruction under the 1993 Chemical Weapons Convention. Not a party to the CWC, which bans the use of chemical weapons in war and prohibits production and stockpiling, North Korea has an estimated reserve of 2,500 to 5,000 metric tons of chemical weapons, according to a 2012 assessment by the South Korean Ministry of National Defense, and an annual production capability of up to 12,000 tons. The North reportedly also has four military bases equipped with chemical weapons, eleven facilities for production and storage, and around a dozen research and development installations, according to a U.S. research organization. Information collected from defectors from the Korean People's Army by veteran analyst Joseph Bermudez indicates that North Korea has around twenty chemical agents for use in chemical weapons, with a focus on sulfur mustard, chlorine, phosgene, sarin, and the V agents. These weapons could be delivered through special operations forces or by missiles able to target South Korea and beyond.

Kim Jong Un in recent years has touted the potential for growth in the biological and chemical industries, further exacerbating existing concerns about how he might use them in a conflict scenario or sell them to other countries. He has been brazenly showing off the fact that Pyongyang is advancing its capabilities. In June 2015, regime media showcased Kim visiting the new Pyongyang Biotechnical Institute. Although state media said it was a factory for making biological pesticides to safeguard the cabbage crop, a close look at the video sparked fears about the pace and scope of these developments. Melissa Hanham, an expert on weapons of mass destruction, studied the equipment in the regime photographs and determined that the facility is likely being used to produce "military-sized batches of . . . anthrax." Pyongyang could have legally procured bio-insecticide at a low cost, but "instead, by choosing to illicitly import the dual-use equipment, North Korea is likely using the facility to maintain a latent [biological weapons] capability—or worse—actively producing anthrax," Hanham concluded. The United Nations in 2018 expressed concern about North Korea's pursuit of the production of sodium cyanide, which can be deadly on its own or developed into the nerve agent tabun, which is banned by the Security Council. It also called for Pyongyang to abide by the 2016 U.N. Security Council Resolution 2270, in which the international community called for North Korea to abandon all chemical and biological weapons and weapons-related programs.

In addition to the potential for deploying weapons of mass destruction in a conflict with the United States or South Korea, North Korea's latent or existing biological and chemical capabilities also pose proliferation risks. For at least two decades, the regime has been reportedly providing chemical weapons–related assistance and technology to Syria, Iran, Egypt, and Libya. In 2009, for example, the Greek government inspected a merchant vessel headed for Syria and seized four shipping containers with thirteen thousand chemical protective suits and other items that were made in North Korea.

Kim Jong Nam's assassination in 2017 and North Korea's flouting of international norms and sanctions in recent years in its development of multiple potential weapons of mass destruction underscore Kim Jong Un's brazenness and confidence about his ability to get away with murder, literally and figuratively. Although Washington redesignated North Korea as a State Sponsor of Terrorism in

November 2017 (Iran, Syria, and Sudan are also on the list), in part in response to the Malaysia assassination, and slapped on additional sanctions, Kim Jong Un almost certainly assesses that he can manage the fallout of his actions. Pyongyang had been a member of this ignominious club from 1988 to 2008 for its abductions of Japanese citizens, bombings and assassination attempts against South Korea, and commercial airline hijackings, but it was removed by the George W. Bush administration in an attempt to stimulate flagging negotiations on denuclearization and the regime's "authoritative and direct public statement affirming that it does not support international terrorism now and will not support international terrorism in the future."

But for Kim, this trade-off must be worth it, in that he assuredly sees the development of weapons of mass destruction as a way to strengthen his hand in his relationship with the United States, improve the North's defenses in a potential wartime situation, and add more luster to his desired image as a tough leader. After all, even Secretary of State Rex Tillerson admitted as much, stating that the State Sponsor of Terrorism designation was a symbolic move: "The practical effects may be limited but hopefully we're closing off a few loopholes with this." Meanwhile, two young women in Malaysia were for a time facing the possibility of the death penalty for their role in Kim Jong Nam's murder, while the regime suffered few, if any, real consequences. Given the fact that Huong and Aisyah were released from prison in early 2019, all involved in the killing have been absolved of responsibility.

The relisting of North Korea on the United States' State Sponsors of Terrorism list occurred as relations between the two countries reached a nadir in 2017, sparking fears about a nuclear conflagration. Kim's confidence, fueled by the apprehension of those around him and his evident success in extinguishing potential rivals, would give him the energy to confront his biggest adversary and his most powerful challenger: the president of the United States.

ELEVEN

TESTING TRUMP

A S KIM JONG UN entered his seventh year in power, he could count several successes. He had made significant headway in solidifying his power and installing loyalists. He had made progress in advancing the *byungjin* policy of advancing both the economy and the nuclear weapons program, building monuments of leisure and monuments for national defense, and seemingly ushering in a new and modern North Korea after decades of decline following the end of Soviet aid and the great famine of the 1990s. He had developed and advanced his nuclear and missile programs and tested new designs from multiple locations, fulfilling his goal of "diversifying" the nuclear weapons program. He had successfully demonstrated nonnuclear capabilities, wielding North Korea's cyber and chemical weapons expertise against his enemies. And not only had Kim poked and prodded the limits of international tolerance and challenged and defied global norms and gotten away with it—little more than a heap of sanctions were levied, which fell far short of posing a real threat to his regime—he'd outlasted his three main adversaries: Barack Obama, Park Geun-hye, and her predecessor, Lee Myung-bak. Unlike Kim, Presidents Obama, Park, and Lee were elected through a democratic process and left office—Obama and Lee after elections in their countries and Park after a yearlong series of peaceful protests and impeachment. For all the speculation about how Kim wouldn't last after he took the reins upon his father's death in 2011, it was Kim who could relish his endurance and longevity.

When Donald Trump was elected president in 2016, Kim, like everyone else, was surely trying to figure out this unconventional leader. He had reason to be suspicious of Trump and anticipate a hard-line policy approach on North Korea, based on what candidate Trump had said about the regime. In September 2015, during a Republican presidential debate, Trump called Kim a "maniac" who has nuclear weapons. In a February 2016 television interview, he blustered that if he were president, he would get China to make Kim "disappear in one form or another very quickly." There was a hint of respect for Kim, however: "I mean this guy's a bad dude— and don't underestimate him. . . . Any young guy that can take over from his father with all those generals and everybody else that probably wants the position, this is not somebody to be underestimated." Despite the harsh talk, Trump also said in May 2016 that he would have no problem speaking to Kim.

Amid uncertainties about altered regional dynamics, resulting from the new leadership in the United States and South Korea, Kim wasn't about to sit around. As the new government in Washington sought to get its footing in the aftermath of an unexpected win, Kim went about laying out the facts on the ground. In his New Year's speech, he set forth his successes and his intentions, fueling concerns and sparking speculation about how he might approach the era of Trump. Kim touted North Korea's purported first hydrogen bomb test in September 2016, its fifth and most powerful test, which the regime at the time alleged had been of a "nuclear warhead that has been standardised to be able to be mounted on strategic ballistic rockets." Ominously, Kim also declared that his country had "entered the final stage of preparation for the test launch of intercontinental ballistic missile[s]" that could potentially hit the continental

United States. And he promised to "continue to build up our self-defence capability, the pivot of which is the nuclear forces, and the capability for preemptive strike as long as the United States and its vassal forces keep on nuclear threat and blackmail." A day later, President-elect Trump dismissively tweeted, "North Korea just stated that it is in the final stages of developing a nuclear weapon capable of reaching parts of the U.S. It won't happen!"

So began a year of tweets, taunts, and threats between Trump and Kim; many Korea watchers and national security analysts were alarmed about how the new president's penchant for using social media to confront Kim might lead to a miscalculation toward a military conflict. Not one to cower in the face of threatening tweets, Kim continued to test Trump, lobbing new types of ballistic missiles most likely intended to provoke and show his mettle for domestic and external audiences and to demonstrate who was driving events on the Korean Peninsula. Less than a month after Trump's inauguration, and during a summit meeting at Mar-a-Lago with the Japanese prime minister, Abe Shinzo, Kim tested a new ballistic missile, a solid-fuel medium-range system that experts said could aid in the North's development of an ICBM. Kim, who was almost always front and center in the coverage of subsequent tests, would lob several others, ignoring Trump's tweets and threats, and then capped off the year with two tests of ICBMs in July and a third in November, and his sixth nuclear test in September.

If Kim felt apprehensive about the new president, he didn't show it. After all, didn't he have more political leadership and regional experience than Trump, who had been a businessman and a reality star? And hadn't Kim already gotten away with so much in the previous six years?

Kim was not backing down and neither was Trump.

PERSONALITY MATTERS

Although separated by almost forty years in age—Kim was in his early thirties and Trump into his eighth decade—Donald Trump and Kim Jong Un share many similar personal qualities. They were both in their twenties when they inherited wealth and an empire: Trump's was in real estate; Kim's was in nuclear weapons and a country of twenty-five million people. When Trump was growing up in Queens, New York, his family had worldly possessions that others could only dream about or aspire to obtain, though the Kim family's wealth—with their control over an entire country—was even greater. The Kims had scores of villas, resorts, armies of servants, a standing military, and the latest in consumer items. Trump boasted about challenging authority. He "punched" his music teacher when he was in the second grade because, as he described it, "I didn't think he knew anything about music, and I almost got expelled," according to the *Washington Post* journalists Michael Kranish and Marc Fisher, who wrote *Trump Revealed,* an authoritative biography of the forty-fifth U.S. president.

Although the extant information about Kim Jong Un suggests that he maintained a low-key profile, at least when he was in Europe, Trump acted the part of a brash, young, confident future heir to a real estate fortune. He was known for driving luxury cars around town and campus, cavorting with beautiful women, throwing parties, and bullying his peers and elders alike. Like Kim Jong Un, though, Trump was a mediocre student at best. *Trump Revealed* quoted a classmate at the University of Pennsylvania who said Trump "wasn't a dumb guy. . . . I don't think he ever studied for an exam. . . . He did what it took to get through the program." Athletic prowess and a competitive streak marked both men: Trump found success on the playing field, excelling at dodgeball, basketball, football, and soccer. His favorite sport was baseball. Kim's sport was basketball; his aggressiveness on the court was consistently noted by his classmates in Switzerland. And both were raised in masculine environments. Trump attended the New York Military Academy, where cadets were required to fire mortars and clean an M1 rifle, while Kim's entire world and identity were wrapped up in the military-first milieu in North Korea. Physical and verbal abuse and casual brutality were part of their respective worlds, and weakness was a dirty word.

They both had fathers who were larger than life, whom they revered and sought to emulate, but in their own way. Fred Trump, the patriarch, was less flamboyant and "stern, disciplined," according to Timothy O'Brien, who wrote another meticulously researched biography of Donald Trump. His critical look into the dark crevices of Donald Trump's life and his exposure of the truth hidden beneath layers of decades-old mythology provoked his subject into filing a $5 billion libel suit against him.

Unlike his father, the younger Trump was flashy and drawn to celebrity, with an insatiable appetite for praise and attention. In his dogged determination for self-aggrandizement, he harnessed the power of media, charming and browbeating reporters and image-makers, producing consumer goods from self-help books on business to vodka, ties, and suits in order to create a brand that embodied the ethos of luxurious excess, even though he was at times deeply in debt and a less than spectacular business success than he claimed. He placed his name on trophy real estate in Manhattan, which for the native of Queens, a less prestigious outer borough of New York City, represented his arrival in what he considered in *The Art of the Deal* to be "the center of the world." In dotting the landscape—and the skies and seas with his ill-fated airline and yacht—and penetrating American homes with his branded consumer items, Trump asserted in his 2000 book, *The America We Deserve,* that "it was no surprise to me that 97 percent of the American people knew who I was." Barbara Corcoran, one of New York City's most successful real estate brokers, said, "He bullshitted . . . but by bullshitting . . . he made it sell. I don't know of anyone who is a better marketer." Tony Schwartz, the ghostwriter for *The Art of the Deal,* told Jane Mayer of *The New Yorker,* "More than anyone else I have ever met, Trump has the ability to convince himself that whatever he is saying at any given moment is true, or sort of true, or at least *ought* to be true." Schwartz told Mayer that he regretted perpetuating the mythology.

Mythology, of course, was the Kim family business. Like Trump, who joined *his* family's business and became president of Trump

Management when he was twenty-five, Kim was just shy of twenty-eight when he took over North Korea upon his father's death. (In April 2017, Trump, as the newly elected U.S. president, expressed empathy for Kim, even as his regime was testing ballistic missiles and threatening the United States. Perhaps reflecting on his own experience, in an interview with Reuters he commented that Kim was young when he became North Korea's leader: "He's 27 years old. His father dies, took over a regime. So say what you want but that is not easy, especially at that age.") Of course, Kim had the cushion of an existing nuclear weapons program, a propaganda machine that had been humming along since the 1950s that extolled his bloodline and provided legitimacy, and a father who made the appropriate introductions to key officials and institutions in advance, to help his son solidify his power. If 97 percent of Americans knew who Trump was, 100 percent of North Koreans knew who held the power in their country.

Both Trump and Kim appealed directly to the masses, an incongruity given their pampered backgrounds and gilded mansions. Trump did it through massive rallies and by reaching millions more with his Twitter account. Kim did it through his propaganda apparatus but also via his constant on-the-spot guidances, traversing the country to hug schoolchildren and inspect water parks, zoos, farms, and factories while reminding his officials to think of the people first. Trump "fancied himself a man of the people, more interested in the praise of cabdrivers and construction workers than in accolades from the rich and the powerful," according to Kranish and Fisher. He won the admiration of middle- and lower-class Americans with his coarse language and insults against his opponents and the Washington "swamp." His supporters "saw him as a straight-shooting billionaire who had the bucks and the brass to stand up to anyone." For Kim, the execution of his uncle Jang and the steady drumbeat of purges were carried out not only to warn party and military officials to remember who they work for, but also to show the public that his crackdowns on the elite were on their behalf, to ensure that they knew they had an advocate in Kim.

As self-proclaimed champions of an idealized internal order, the two men have relied on rhetoric depicting a hostile outside world to reinforce that view of foreign relations. Pyongyang had long been inward-looking and suspicious of the outside world, while extolling the purity, optimism, and single-hearted unity and self-determination of the North Korean people and the state. North Korea requires a hostile outside world to legitimize the Kim dynasty, justify the military programs, and emphasize the belief in the populace that North Korea under Kim offers the only safe place, given the malevolent forces lurking outside. The United States is a constant, omnipresent threat, its big-nosed, rapacious soldiers ever ready to attack as soon as the North lets down its guard. The Chinese are untrustworthy, given Beijing's support for sanctions against North Korea: One party official allegedly told a conference, "Although Japan is a century-old enemy, China is a thousand-year-old enemy." Japan could not be trusted, of course, given the history of its colonization of the Korean Peninsula.

Donald Trump's message about the world is similarly dystopian—it is a dark, dangerous place, where evil people are constantly trying to hurt Americans, their values, and their way of life, as they try to pick their pockets. In addition to adversaries like Iran and threats like terrorism, traditional allies, partners, and international organizations are also part of the problem—and targets of Trump's transactional, zero-sum view of foreign relations and national security. After reviewing Trump's statements and actions since the 1980s, Thomas Wright of the Brookings Institution concluded that Trump is consistent in his thinking about foreign policy, which is mainly that America is overcommitted in the world. And to demonstrate his disgust at the overcommitment, he alienates his friends.

Take, for example, his attacks on the decades-old North Atlantic Treaty Organization, created amid the devastation of World War II to provide the United States, Canada, and Western Europe with collective security against the military threats posed by the Soviet Union. Trump bragged that "tens of billions of dollars more [are] pouring in because I would not allow member states to be delin-

quent in the payment while we guarantee their safety and are willing to fight wars for them. We have made [it] clear that countries
that are immensely wealthy should reimburse the United States for
the cost of defending them." Trump questions key U.S. alliances in
East Asia and repeatedly criticizes Seoul and Tokyo. Why do we
have to help out Japan if it's attacked (per the 1960 Treaty of Mutual
Cooperation and Security between Japan and the United States of
America)? That didn't seem fair to Trump. Of South Korea, he had
once asked in 2013, "We have 25,000 soldiers over there protecting
them. They don't pay us. Why don't they pay us?" He would return
to this theme again in 2015: "How long will we go on defending
South Korea from North Korea without payment?" And as president in 2017, he harped on this issue, insisting that Washington was
subsidizing South Korea and that "it doesn't make any sense" to
continue to have troops—now around 28,500—there.

Trump's calls for a ban on Muslims from entering the United
States and for a wall to prevent "illegals" from crossing the border
were demonstrative of his version of an idealized America and reminiscent of the ethnically pure Korea that the Kim family promoted
and on which it depended to marshal a vicious nationalism to rally
the people around Kim Jong Un. "Fear," candidate Trump told Bob
Woodward in March 2016, was where "real power" lay, and one
need not look too closely at North Korea to recognize that fear of
the outside and fear of the autocrat's power is where Kim stakes his
claim.

Both men had something to prove. And both were thin-skinned.
Trump the businessman, the candidate, and the president was obsessed with the perception that the world had long been laughing at
the United States. Kim, too, was hypersensitive to any real and perceived criticism. He purged senior officials who did not clap hard
enough, assassinated a half-brother who publicly questioned his
ability to lead, and attacked through cyber means a movie studio
that dared to produce a movie about a CIA plot to kill him. Amid
sneers, doubt, and condescending comments about their inexperience, unpredictability, and brashness, Trump and Kim defied the

critics and upended political and international norms. Their sense of competitiveness and confidence, born of their belief in their own headlines and their perceived victories, fueled their conviction that they can handle any challenge, including a potential nuclear confrontation in 2017. Hadn't Trump won the presidency, the ultimate prize, despite what all the haters said? Hadn't Kim become the youngest dictator with nuclear weapons and literally gotten away with murder, even amid predictions about regime collapse after his father died?

As Trump and Kim dug in their heels, used hyperbole to make their points, and challenged each other's manhood, the world braced for the possibility that these two unpredictable and aggressive leaders could bluster their way into a nuclear conflagration in their determination to prove their dominance.

TWELVE

TESTING KIM

WHEN DONALD TRUMP CAME into the White House, the outgoing
president, Barack Obama, warned him that North Korea
would be his biggest headache, and Kim quickly showed what a
pain he could be, launching medium-range (620–1,860 miles),
intermediate-range (1,860–3,400 miles), and intercontinental (over
3,400 miles) ballistic missiles, all in Trump's first year. After a two-
month policy review—a typical process for new administrations—
the Trump team announced a policy of "maximum pressure and
engagement." Although Trump declared that "the era of [Obama's]
strategic patience with the North Korea regime" was over, the strategy actually represented continuity with the previous administration's approach of increasing diplomatic, economic, and military
pressure on Pyongyang to punish it and try to force the Kim regime
to make a decision to come to the negotiating table in order to re-
lieve that pressure by taking credible measures to dismantle its nuclear weapons program.

In 2016, the Obama administration took actions to further
tighten the screws on North Korea, laying the foundation for the

Trump administration's maximum pressure policy. Obama's new measures had teeth—they constrained Kim's choices by shutting down his regime's efforts to generate funds through its exports of coal, seafood, and labor, expected to cost North Korea $1 billion annually, a not insignificant sum given the country's already stressed economy and the fact that the regime earns only $3 billion per year from export revenues. Maximum pressure also included targeting non–North Koreans who facilitate sanctions evasion and revenue generation, getting countries to limit or cut off trade and diplomatic ties to North Korea, and especially getting China—the country's biggest trading partner by far—to implement sanctions.

Things got personal as Pyongyang successfully tested its first intercontinental ballistic missile, the Hwasong-14, which achieved an altitude of approximately 1,700 miles before going down about 600 miles away, into the Sea of Japan. The regime tested it at a high angle to avoid overflying Japan, an act that would have been highly provocative, but if the missile had been launched at a typical trajectory, it could have traveled for 4,000 miles. Kim decided to test it on July 4, 2017, Independence Day, in a clear message that he was marking a milestone that brought North Korea closer to the ability to deliver a nuclear weapon to the continental United States. According to state media, Kim had "a broad smile on his face, [when he] told officials, scientists and technicians that the U.S. would be displeased to witness the DPRK's strategic option as it was given a 'package of gifts' . . . on its 'Independence Day.'" Kim also taunted the United States, directing North Korean scientists "to frequently send big and small 'gift packages' to the Yankees" and claiming that he would "not step back even one step from the path . . . to strengthen the nuclear-armed forces" unless the "U.S. hostile policy and nuclear threat to the DPRK are definitely terminated."

Alarmed and surprised at the test's success and the regime's blatantly hostile comments, leaders from both China and Russia condemned the test as "unacceptable" and cautioned against "any statements or actions that could lead to an increase in tensions." Their foreign ministries released a joint statement that said in part:

"The two sides propose that the DPRK (North Korea) as a voluntary political decision declares a moratorium on testing nuclear explosive devices and ballistic rocket launches." Anxious about U.S. and South Korean escalatory responses, Moscow and Beijing demanded that Seoul and Washington "refrain from carrying out large-scale joint exercises." Secretary of State Rex Tillerson said, "Testing an ICBM represents a new escalation of the threat to the United States, our allies and partners, the region, and the world." Tillerson's statement was appropriately condemnatory, a respectably strong comment that one would expect from a senior official from the United States. President Trump, however, had a decidedly Trumpian response. He tweeted, "North Korea has just launched another missile. Does this guy have anything better to do with his life? Hard to believe that South Korea and Japan will put up with this much longer. Perhaps China will put a heavy move on North Korea and end this nonsense once and for all!"

In response to these condemnations and to the U.S.–South Korean show of force, which included launching a "deep strike" missile drill, Kim Jong Un immediately declared that North Korea will "demonstrate its mettle to the U.S." and that he would never put his nuclear weapons program up for negotiation. Just a couple of weeks later, as if to put a punctuation mark on its Independence Day test, North Korea conducted a second test of the ICBM that went even higher, with a potential range of six thousand miles, which would put major U.S. cities such as Los Angeles, Denver, and Chicago at risk. And then in September, North Korea conducted its sixth nuclear test.

KIM DIGS IN HIS HEELS

The ensuing months of 2017 were a blur of additional ballistic missile tests, scrambles at the United Nations and in various capitals to issue statements and additional sanctions, and tweets and threats between Kim and Trump, creating a crisis atmosphere that was thick with tension and fearful anticipation. It was one thing for

North Korea to be behaving badly, but it was unprecedented for the U.S. president to be issuing inflammatory statements through his social media account, amplified by the highly influential platform from which he put out those tweets and the media that repeated and reported on every word.

Even as the Moon administration in South Korea sought to tame tensions and Secretary of State Tillerson stated Washington's willingness for dialogue, President Trump seemed to relish the war of words with Kim. In *The Art of the Deal,* first published in 1987, Trump had said, "When people treat me badly or unfairly or try to take advantage of me, my general attitude, all my life, has been to fight back very hard." A few years later, in 1990, he told *Playboy*: "When somebody tries to sucker-punch me, when they're after my ass, I push back a hell of a lot harder than I was pushed in the first place. If somebody tries to push me around, he's going to pay a price. Those people don't come back for seconds. I don't like being pushed around or taken advantage of." That tough, competitive approach held firm even on the campaign trail and in the White House, as Trump belittled those who disagreed with him, calling them names and issuing hyperbolic statements, at times with little regard for the facts. That willingness to engage in a showdown was on full display in Trump's response to Kim's highly provocative actions in the fall and winter of 2017.

Kim, for his part, wasn't falling for it. He has most likely read *The Art of the Deal* and studied other interviews and books by and about Trump. (During his June 2017 trip to North Korea, his fourth, Dennis Rodman had given his interlocutors a copy of the book to present to Kim.) Instead of backing down, Kim upped the ante, perhaps because he understood Trump's tactics based on his readings and on the president's tens of thousands of tweets. Or Kim might have been planning on demonstrating his capabilities in a highly provocative manner regardless of who was president of the United States. Or maybe he was acting out of his own emotions, a knee-jerk reaction to being challenged so publicly. His motivations for escalating tensions were probably driven by all of these factors. As stronger sanctions piled up and squeezed North Korea's ability to raise hard currency, the United States and South Korea conducted unprecedented military exercises to show how quickly the allies could respond with potentially devastating consequences for Kim if he dared to make real his threats to hit Japan, South Korea, the United States, and Guam with a nuclear-tipped ballistic missile.

Kim showed little inclination to concede, even amid Trump's tweets and taunts. In August 2017, after testing its second ICBM, North Korea threatened to "ruthlessly take strategic measures involving physical actions," and to punish the United States. The pair of incendiary comments President Trump made in response alarmed Korea watchers, national security experts, and the public from Washington to Los Angeles, to Seoul, Tokyo, and across European capitals. While at his golf club in Bedminster, New Jersey, Trump told reporters, "North Korea best not make any more threats," adding that they "will be met with fire and fury like the world has never seen," a statement that *The Washington Post* called "his harshest language yet." A few days later, Trump went further, hinting at the potential for a military strike against North Korea, when he tweeted, "Military solutions are now fully in place, locked and loaded, should North Korea act unwisely. Hopefully Kim Jong Un will find another path!"

Trump's comments sent a ripple of fear through the region and exacerbated an already precarious situation. Russia boosted its air defense system in its far east, Japan deployed its missile interception system, and South Korea's President Moon said, "There must be no more war on the Korean peninsula. Whatever ups and downs we face, the North Korean nuclear situation must be resolved peacefully." In China, an editorial in the state-run *Global Times* cautioned that "if North Korea launches missiles that threaten U.S. soil first and the U.S. retaliates, China will stay neutral," in a signal to Pyongyang that it would not come to its aid if it provoked a military conflict. But the editorial also warned that "if the U.S. and South Korea carry out strikes and try to overthrow the North Korean regime and change the political pattern of the Korean Peninsula, China will prevent them from doing so." Chinese president Xi also urged Trump to exercise restraint during a phone call that took place a day after the tweet.

Meanwhile, senior U.S. officials tried to calm the frayed nerves of the American public and East Asian allies. Tillerson and Secretary of Defense James Mattis affirmed the United States' commitment to peaceful resolution through the fall and winter of 2017, even as President Trump issued belligerent comments that focused on threats rather than dialogue. At the U.N. General Assembly on September 19, two weeks after North Korea had conducted its sixth, most powerful nuclear test, Trump introduced the mocking "Rocket Man" moniker. He stated that the United States will "totally destroy North Korea" if it is forced to defend itself and its allies. "Rocket Man" Kim "is on a suicide mission for himself," Trump said, as international leaders drew a sharp breath at the escalatory rhetoric. In October, he tweeted, "I told Rex Tillerson, our wonderful Secretary of State, that he is wasting his time trying to negotiate with Little Rocket Man. . . . Save your energy Rex, we'll do what has to be done!" Hours later he added, "Being nice to Rocket Man hasn't worked in 25 years, why would it work now?"

Yet the muddled messaging on U.S. intentions toward North Korea, with some officials highlighting peaceful diplomacy while the president was expressing his willingness to use military force, belied what was in fact a convergence of views within the administration on the threat that North Korea posed. The National Security Strategy (NSS) from December 2017, a document that the executive branch issues to present a comprehensive articulation of the country's national security threats and the goals of U.S. security policy, stated that "North Korea seeks the capability to kill millions of Americans with nuclear weapons," reflecting the growing concern in Washington following Pyongyang's testing of ICBMs and its recent nuclear test. The document also echoed the comments of National Security Adviser H. R. McMaster, who had said that the world is "running out of time" on North Korea. The potential for war with North Korea is growing with each passing day, he said: "We're in a race. We're in a race to be able to solve this problem." The NSS document emphasized the need to confront the threat:

> North Korea is ruled as a ruthless dictatorship without regard for human dignity. For more than 25 years, it has pursued nuclear weapons and ballistic missiles in defiance of every commitment it has made. Today, these missiles and weapons threaten the United States and our allies. The longer we ignore threats from countries determined to proliferate and develop weapons of mass destruction, the worse such threats become, and the fewer defensive options we have.

Such beliefs about Pyongyang's goals were driving the Trump administration's approach—to strangle North Korea's ability to earn hard currency to fund itself, through a steady course of sanctions, isolation, and military activity, including nuclear bomber deployments to the Korean Peninsula and U.S. Navy destroyers sent to patrol North Korea's east coast. Amid ongoing tweets from the president that "only one thing will work" in dealing with North Korea, senior administration officials continued to indicate that diplomacy is the preferred approach.

But they also repeated their refrain about U.S. "military options," suggesting that a real plan for military action against North Korea was in the works or at least being seriously considered. McMaster commented on the possibility of "preventive war," while Mattis told the Association of the United States Army that the army has "got to be ready to ensure that we have military options that our president can employ, if needed," and Tillerson told CNN that "diplomatic efforts will continue until the first bomb drops." On Capitol Hill, Senator Lindsey Graham, who became a close confidant of President Trump's, repeated comments about the possibility of war. He told CNN, "[Trump] is ready, if necessary, to destroy this regime to protect America, and I hope the regime understands that if President Trump has to pick between destroying the North Korean regime and the American homeland, he's going to destroy the regime. I hope China understands that also."

The murder of Kim Jong Nam in an international airport, the apparent torture and eventual death of American student Otto Warmbier, who was detained for seventeen months for an alleged "hostile act" against the regime, and Kim's reckless actions and statements also fed suspicions that Kim Jong Un was not "rational" and therefore could not be deterred from using nuclear weapons against the United States.

THE LOGIC AND ILLOGIC OF HITTING KIM JONG UN

Let's say that Washington decided to attack North Korea. There are three broad reasons why a limited military strike could have a positive payoff. First, a U.S. military offensive could shatter Kim's confidence in his ability to drive events on the Korean Peninsula. The strike would also invalidate Pyongyang's fundamental assumption about America's unwillingness to use military force, which has sustained Kim's perception that he is free to test the limits of international tolerance. Such a turn of events would force him to choose between his survival and his nuclear weapons. Pyongyang's future risk-taking might be curtailed by the fear of another attack. Second, Kim or his successor(s) might consider entering into negotiations with the United States on the nuclear weapons program to buy time and international goodwill, possibly driven by the voices of newly emboldened actors in the regime who might urge caution or apply a brake on Kim's ambitions. Third, Beijing and Moscow, fearing more assertive or follow-up U.S. military action or a U.S. president indifferent to their demand for restraint, could try to dramatically curb economic ties to get Kim or his successors to back down.

These hypothetical benefits are highly unlikely ever to materialize because Kim's interpretation of U.S. actions would be muddied by the unpredictability of actual war and by potential policy confusion and dysfunction as a result of the groupthink among his inner circle of advisers, given the silencing of dissent over the years. A

U.S. military offensive would probably be the first major challenge of Kim's reign and it is impossible to know how he would respond. Any military strike against North Korea, the first since the Korean War, even with clear signaling from the United States that it was not a prelude to a decapitation attempt, would present Kim with a use-or-lose dilemma, in which he would have to choose between using nuclear weapons first, or die knowing that his weapons failed at deterring an attack and ensuring regime survival.

Instead of denuclearization and a contrite Kim Jong Un, a preemptive military strike on North Korea would be counterproductive, with the potential to ignite a nuclear war and inflict high political and economic costs on the United States and trigger an unprecedented humanitarian crisis at a magnitude that the region and the international community would be ill-equipped to handle.

First, if Kim survived and North Korea continued to exist as a state, his commitment to maintaining his weapons would likely be reinforced by the U.S. attack, and he would use the offensive to rally the North Korean people around him. The pursuit of nuclear weapons and the existential war against the United States are in Kim's DNA; his grandfather became interested in a nuclear program in the devastating aftermath of the Korean War. A U.S. attack would be a fresh reminder of the need for nuclear weapons for younger generations of North Koreans who have only known a nuclear state and for whom their failed bid to take over the South by force in 1950 has been only a historical memory. An attack by the United States, limited or not, would validate decades-old regime propaganda about U.S. intentions toward their country and bolster Kim's status as a protector of the nation.

Second, Kim likely would respond to a limited strike with symmetrical military action, such as artillery strikes against South Korea's islands along the maritime border or shorter-range ballistic missile launches against South Korean and Japanese targets, in order to maintain the initiative and to show that he will not be intimidated. Kim's aggressive personality, his desire to project strength and demonstrate resolve to protect his domestic standing, coupled with his efforts over the years to improve North Korea's conventional military capabilities and diversify his nuclear arsenal and its launch locations, all suggest that Kim would be inclined to respond to strikes on North Korea, even at the risk of escalation.

Third, if a U.S. strike resulted in Kim's death or ouster, his removal would not provide a guarantee that North Korea will denuclearize. The new leadership could seek to develop nuclear weapons covertly and share the Kim family's view of a nuclear arsenal as a way to maintain leverage and protect itself in a hostile strategic environment. Our limited visibility into the full scope of North Korea's weapons program compounds the problem.

Fourth, a strike not premised on an imminent threat would draw widespread international condemnation from U.S. partners and allies as an illegal act of aggression, contravening the Charter of the United Nations and international law. It would damage the U.S. alliance with South Korea and prompt Moscow and Beijing to increase economic aid to North Korea and dial back U.N. sanctions to prevent regime collapse, claiming that Washington, not Pyongyang, is threatening regional stability. Beijing might also intervene militarily to assert its role and protect its interests in a quickly evolving situation.

Finally, if a U.S. first strike led to a conventional or nuclear war, the humanitarian and economic costs would be unacceptably high. The Seoul metropolitan area—located only thirty-five miles from the North Korean border, with about twenty-five million inhabitants, around two hundred thousand of whom are American citizens or soldiers stationed in nearby Pyeongtaek (and around a million Chinese tourists, students, and businesspeople at any given time)—would be difficult to defend against conventional strikes and virtually impossible to defend against strikes involving weapons of mass destruction. Tokyo, with a population of around thirty-eight million, would be similarly difficult to defend. The Congressional Research Service estimated that Pyongyang could blanket Seoul with ten thousand artillery rounds per minute and kill three hundred thousand South Koreans within a few days. North Korea's chemical weapons could potentially kill up to 2.5 million people in South Korea. An article on the website Vox grimly summed up the carnage: "Men, women, and children would very literally choke to death in the streets of one of the world's wealthiest and most vibrant cities. It would be mass murder on a scale rarely seen in human history."

If North Korea used a nuclear weapon—its September 2017 nuclear test indicated a bomb that, at around 150 kilotons, was about ten times bigger than the weapon that the United States dropped on Hiroshima in 1945—the devastation would be horrific. The bigger 20-kiloton bomb that hit Nagasaki generated a fireball that had an internal temperature of 540,000 degrees Fahrenheit, with portions of the ground below reaching 7,000 degrees. After spending a decade researching and interviewing survivors of Nagasaki, Susan Southard recounted in her masterful narrative, *Nagasaki: Life after Nuclear War,* what happened in the immediate aftermath. The heat and the blast force melted buildings, scorched bricks, and sent bullets of broken glass into people's already suffering bodies. One survivor told Southard that he saw people who were so badly burned that he couldn't tell whether they were men or women even though they were naked. He saw someone whose eyeballs were dangling from their empty sockets. The blast tore off heads and disintegrated internal organs. A woman who covered her face with her hands to protect against the blast found that when she removed her hand her face had melted into her palms.

Beyond the visible physical devastation inflicted by nuclear weapons, the victims and their progeny are vulnerable to the long-term effects of radiation on their genetic, mental, and physical makeup; in fact, the consequences for human beings, animals, and the environment are yet to be fully understood. Roberta Cohen, a leading expert on humanitarian and refugee issues, told an audience at a Brookings Institution event in March 2018 that "no amount of shelter, food, medicine, and gas masks could fully shield a civilian population under direct military attack." Kim would also deploy cyber tools to confuse, delay, and undermine military and aid efforts.

Even if the United States managed to stay out of it, a second Korean War—potentially involving China, Japan, and South Korea (respectively, the world's second-, third-, and eleventh-largest economies)—would have global economic ripple effects, impacting electronics, automobiles, and energy markets, while potentially pushing up federal debt in the United States and upending domestic economic priorities. At the March 2018 Brookings event, Scott Seaman, an expert on East Asia economics and trade, said that he would expect "to see massive trade disruptions and the collapse of major supply chains that will result in a significant recession around the world." Thus, a strike against North Korea is likely to have the unintended effect of sparking a series of events that would lead the United States toward a nuclear war.

The United States and North Korea flirted with disaster in 2017, and to the world's relief, a clash never happened. But those tense months exposed the disquieting truths that both sides have to reckon with at some point in the future. North Korea was facing a situation in which the regime's claimed reason for developing and advancing its nuclear and ballistic missile capabilities—deterring U.S. invasion and military actions—could backfire into actually *inviting* a military strike from the United States. At the same time, Kim's intransigence and aggressiveness, despite U.S. threats of military force, highlighted how a small, impoverished, and isolated country led by a risk-tolerant millennial dictator could undermine and constrain the most powerful country in the world.

KIM BEING KIM

Aware of the growing risk of a U.S. military strike, Kim—aggressive, antagonistic, and angry—reverted to his default style, a comfortable position that might be a demonstration of not only his confidence and arrogance but also his stubbornness. Just days after Trump's "Rocket Man" speech at the United Nations General Assembly in September 2017, Kim issued a rare, if not unprecedented, full-throated personal response. The statement, released by the regime's Korean Central News Agency, was accompanied by a picture of Kim looking straight at the camera, sitting at his desk; books are neatly arranged in dignified dark-wood bookshelves that one might find in a CEO's office in New York or Washington. He was holding a piece of paper, presumably his speech, with a microphone positioned in front of him. The relatively static visual belied the visceral passion and emotion of Kim's speech, his barely contained rage seeping out from his every word.

Kim condemned Trump's comments at the United Nations, speaking almost as if he were berating Trump for uttering a speech unbecoming a sitting U.S. president. Trump "made unprecedented rude nonsense no one has ever heard from any of his predecessors," he said, adding, as if he were the elder statesman in the relationship, "I'd like to advise Trump to exercise prudence in selecting words and be considerate of whom he speaks to when making a speech in front of the world." Consistent with the invective that he has directed against older North Korean officials, including his uncle Jang, Kim attacked Trump's age and intellect, calling him—as the regime media translated into English—"mentally deranged" and a "dotard," sending the world scrambling for the dictionary to find out that dotard is a synonym for an old, senile person. Trump's senility, weakness, and "hard of hearing" made him "unfit to hold the prerogative of supreme command of a country, and he is surely a rogue and a gangster fond of playing with fire, rather than a politician." Trump's threats of a military confrontation "have convinced me, rather than frightening or stopping me," Kim continued, "that the path I chose is correct and that it is the one I have to follow to the last." Trump didn't scare him because *he* was the one who was scared: "A frightened dog barks louder."

Kim reiterated his ownership of the nuclear weapons program four months later in his televised New Year's address in January 2018. Walking up to a massive podium, wearing a gray Western-style suit and his horn-rimmed glasses, he announced, "In no way would the United States dare to ignite a war against me and our country." The United States should know that "the whole of its mainland is within the range of our nuclear strike and the nuclear button is on my office desk all the time; the United States needs to be clearly aware that this is not merely a threat but a reality." He said that North Korea was a responsible nuclear power—for years another oft-repeated refrain from the Kim regime—and that he would not attack unless "hostile forces of aggression" infringed upon his country's sovereignty. But then he went on to promise that he would "mass-produce nuclear warheads and ballistic missiles." Once again, Kim's rhetoric emphasized that it was he alone who controlled the nuclear weapons, boasting about what North Korea had been able to achieve since he came to power. And once again, he was driving home the point to domestic audiences that only he could protect North Koreans from the United States.

Not one to sit around and let an opportunity to respond go by in the face of such a personal challenge to his manhood and leadership, Trump tweeted that same day, "North Korean Leader Kim Jong Un just stated that the 'Nuclear Button is on his desk at all times.' Will someone from his depleted and food starved regime please inform him that I too have a Nuclear Button, but it is a much bigger & more powerful one than his, and my Button works!"

The trading of barbs between Kim and Trump, attacking the size of each other's "nuclear button," heightened tensions and sent ripples of dread throughout the world. Senior U.S. officials had been echoing the president's threats, fueling fears that Trump was not acting on his own, but that there were credible plans afoot to use military strikes against North Korea. The U.S. ambassador to the United Nations, Nikki Haley, said at a meeting of the U.N. Security Council in late November 2017, after the North's ICBM test, "We are once again at a time of reckoning." Kim "made a choice . . . that brings the world closer to war, not farther from it." She said the United States did not seek war with North Korea, but "if war comes, make no mistake, the North Korean regime will be utterly destroyed." McMaster said in early December at an event in Washington that the North Korean threat is "increasing every day" and "there's not much time left."

Time seemed to be running out. The Bulletin of the Atomic Scientists announced in January that "it is now two minutes to midnight," the closest the world has been to midnight since 1953 at the height of the Cold War. In its statement about the Doomsday Clock, a symbol of concerns among scientists about the potential for nuclear annihilation, the Bulletin explained that its reason for moving the clock closer to midnight was the "hyperbolic rhetoric and provocative actions" by North Korea and the United States that "have increased the possibility of nuclear war by accident or miscalculation."

Fear dominated the news cycle at the end of 2017. Credible media reports from late December indicated that the Trump administration had "dramatically" increased preparations for a military strike—a "bloody nose" to show Kim that America was serious about its commitment to get him to relinquish his nuclear weapons program, even if that meant potentially igniting a military exchange. The threat of a conflict was so palpable that the situation made a false alarm in Hawaii about an incoming ballistic missile threat in mid-January entirely plausible. (For thirty-eight torturous minutes, the people of Hawaii thought that they were under attack. They sent text messages to say goodbye to their loved ones and some parents frantically tried to put their children into storm drains to protect them.) Moreover, the administration's withdrawal of its nomination of Victor Cha, an academic and former Asia adviser to President George W. Bush, as ambassador to South Korea—reportedly over a disagreement about the "bloody nose strike" and Trump's intention to withdraw from the free trade agreement with South Korea—inspired reams of newsprint devoted to arguing the illogic of a military strike and highlighting the immeasurable cost in lives.

As Trump and Kim, through their rhetoric and actions, boxed themselves into what seemed like an inexorable decline toward military conflict, no one—perhaps not even Kim or Trump—could have predicted the dramatic changes that would occur in 2018.

THIRTEEN

THE METAMORPHOSIS

O N A WARM SPRING day in late April 2018, the international media captured the dramatic presidential motorcade carrying South Korea's president Moon Jae-in to the first inter-Korean summit since 2007; he would be meeting for the first time with Kim Jong Un. Kim's father had attended the two previous summits; this would be Jong Un's first. The sirens announced the procession as it wove effortlessly through what on a typical day would be the congested streets of Seoul toward Panmunjom, a small border town that has served as a buffer zone between the divided Koreas since 1953, when an armistice ended the military operations of the Korean War. The sparse stillness of the facilities in the Demilitarized Zone, which extends 1.2 miles into North Korea and the same distance into South Korea, and is bisected by the Military Demarcation Line (MDL), belied its history as a locus of simmering tension, one of the most heavily fortified and tense 150 miles in the world.

Cameras positioned north and south of the MDL aimed their lenses at the two conference facilities that stand on either side of the MDL—the Tongilgak in the North and the Peace House in the

South. President Moon waited for Kim to appear from the Tongil-gak, the atmosphere taking on an almost matrimonial air, with dark-suited groomsmen flanking the South Korean president, the anticipation making hearts pound at the realization of this historic moment. The doors finally opened and Kim walked out, his face at times obscured by the tall, athletic-looking bodyguards who surrounded him.

When he broke away from the group and walked over toward Moon, he seemed almost vulnerable in a way that was only possible without the soft filters of North Korean media, the outlandish and blustery rhetoric, the missiles in the background, or the military generals at his side. As he strode purposefully toward Moon, his gait was confident, but his slight breathlessness and heaving at the end of his short walk betrayed his nervousness, his years of heavy smoking, and his considerable girth. With his plump features and his paunch, enshrouded in his signature, loose-fitting dark Mao suit, Kim looked paradoxically both younger and older than Moon, who was nearly twice Kim's age, but telegenic, trim, and dapper in his fitted suit, with his full head of salt-and-pepper hair and his angular, chiseled face.

If Kim was aiming for effect, he succeeded. That moment when he stepped over the MDL at Moon's invitation and set foot in South Korean territory—the first time for a leader of the North since the era of Kim Il Sung—was all about *him*. As cameras clicked furiously to capture the moment, Kim and Moon duly posed. When Moon said that someday he would like to visit the North, Kim invited him to step over to the North's side of the MDL. This was not in the script of this highly orchestrated event, but a surprised Moon warmly accepted and stepped over the line, the entire gesture delighting the press, drawing admiring oohs and aahs.

Over the course of the summit, the two men sipped tea under the trees as they conversed privately. It was an odd juxtaposition on many levels. Moon was the son of poor North Korean refugees; his father worked in a prisoner-of-war camp and his mother sold eggs to make ends meet. As a student activist leader, he protested South

Korea's authoritarian government in the 1970s and was arrested. A former special forces paratrooper and a human rights lawyer with a "distinctly nerdy style," according to a colleague, he became a top aide to President Roh Moo-hyun from 2003 to 2008. Moon had worked his way to the top to become president in 2017. Sitting across from him in a forest glade was Kim, who was born into privilege with access to extreme wealth and power. He had murdered two close relatives and was the torchbearer for a decades-old repressive regime, with a demonstrated track record of torture and rape and use of slave labor, including the exploitation of children. He was also designated by the United States as a violator of human rights in 2016.

They were smiling and nodding at each other, deep in conversation. Through the course of the summit, they received flowers from two South Korean children, planted a memorial tree, and had dinner together. Kim even brought a noodle-making machine with him and a top chef from a Pyongyang restaurant—North Korea touts its *naengmyun,* a cold buckwheat noodle dish—and told Moon, "There is a lot of attention on our dinner menu for tonight, so I brought Pyongyang *naengmyun* for you from a long way." The picture of the two leaders slurping the beloved noodle dish lit up South Korean social media. Inspired South Koreans waxed poetic about the noodles, and a cold-noodle mania swept the country, with long lines forming outside restaurants that served the dish. Kim and Moon even held hands at one point and capped off the summit by watching a concert. The cognitive dissonance was overwhelming.

Kim's metamorphosis had begun.

A THAW AT THE WINTER OLYMPICS

Kim Jong Un's image rehabilitation began with his New Year's address, the same speech in which he barked about the "nuclear button" on his desk, celebrated North Korea's "powerful nuclear deterrent," and uttered not-so-veiled hints about being able to hit the United States, given the regime's professed successes in developing intercontinental ballistic missiles during the previous year. But he also expressed a desire to improve ties to South Korea, which had been frozen at least since he had taken over, and made his priorities the nuclear weapons program and consolidating power rather than forging international relations. Not that the previous South Korean presidents, conservatives Lee Myung-bak and Park Geun-hye, were willing to bow in the least to Kim's provocative actions, especially in light of North Korea's deadly attacks in 2010, scores of missile tests, and multiple nuclear tests, in addition to threats about hitting the Blue House with a missile and schoolyard name-calling.

But in Moon, a progressive who became president after a year-long series of massive popular protests that ousted Park, Kim finally had a sympathetic ear in the South Korean Blue House. Moon came into office promising to put Seoul in the "driver's scat of the Korean Peninsula," an approach consistent with South Korean progressives' efforts over decades to seek more autonomy from the United States, especially regarding North Korea policy, a position that would invite charges of anti-Americanism and appeasement toward Pyongyang. Though North Korea's belligerence and refusal to engage and Kim's confrontation with Trump left him with little choice but to endorse U.N. sanctions and U.S. efforts at maximum pressure, including more robust military drills and demonstrations, Moon consistently offered North Korea an exit ramp. Following Trump's "fire and fury" comments in August, President Moon in a televised address delivered a blunt message: "Only [South Korea] can make the decision for military action on the Korean Peninsula." He said that he would support the U.S. policy on economic and diplomatic isolation of North Korea, but "the purpose of enhanced sanctions and pressure against the North is not to heighten military tensions but to bring it back to the negotiating table."

A month later, amid the name-calling between Kim and Trump, Trump's threats to "totally destroy" North Korea, and the North Korean foreign minister's statement warning about a possible hydrogen bomb test over the Pacific Ocean in late September, Moon tried to tame tensions during his own U.N. General Assembly speech. "Finding a fundamental way to end this vicious circle of provocations and sanctions is the most important task confronting the UN," he declared. "We will not pursue any form of unification by absorption nor artificial unification. We are ready to help North Korea with the international community if it decides to stand at the right side of history." Moon faced the challenge of balancing his alliance with the United States, denuclearizing North Korea, and improving inter-Korean ties, and he avowed that throughout his presidency he would commit to parallel advancements in denuclearization and a peace treaty to put an end to the Korean War.

So when Kim expressed his desire to improve ties to the South in his New Year's address after months of ignoring Seoul's entreaties for rapprochement, the Moon administration saw an opportunity. Kim also said he was willing to send a delegation to the February Winter Olympics in Pyeongchang, South Korea, "since we are compatriots of the same blood as south Koreans, it is natural for us to share their pleasure over the auspicious event and help them." The leadership in Seoul immediately seized the moment and quickly extended an invitation to North Korea to attend the Olympics, set to open on February 9, while conveniently ignoring North Korea's threats in that same speech. Alarmed by Trump's tough talk and fearful about what other provocative actions Kim might next take, not to mention tepid Olympic ticket sales in part because of U.S.–North Korean tensions—South Korea had sold only around 30 percent of available tickets by December—Moon jumped at the chance to lower the temperature and take the reins. (He was probably also worried about what North Korea might do to thwart the success of the Olympics. In 1987, a year before the Seoul Olympics, Kim Jong Il dispatched two spies to plant a bomb on Korean Air Flight 858; 115 people were killed. A declassified CIA memo from that year assessed that "Pyongyang's public threats against the 1988 Seoul Summer Olympics and its sabotage of a South Korea airliner last November clearly point to North Korea as the greatest challenge to the security of the Games.")

The Moon administration's eagerness made some Korea watchers cringe, as they warned that Kim's offer was a trap, a well-worn regime tactic designed to drive a wedge in the U.S.–South Korean relationship and dampen sanctions enforcement, all while buying time for Pyongyang to continue developing nuclear weapons. Critics charged that Moon handed Kim a propaganda victory, as South Korean and international media showcased the North's Masikryong ski resort, a possible venue for Olympics training, and gushed over Hyon Song Wol, a singer in North Korea's all-female Moranbong Band, as she scouted for potential venues for her compatriots' Samjiyon Orchestra. Indeed, if one were to view North Korea through the euphoric lens of the "peace Olympics," the cruel, impoverished, and isolated regime seemed almost normal and, frankly, upscale and modern—exactly what Kim wanted the world to see.

While the Moon administration touted the thaw in inter-Korean relations as laying the foundation for U.S.–North Korean dialogue on denuclearization, Pyongyang did not budge an inch, continuing to refuse talks about the nuclear issue, belittling Seoul's efforts to avoid violating sanctions in its plans for North Korea's participation, and gearing up for a massive military parade on the eve of the Olympics. And as the Koreas engaged in talks and issued comments about reconciliation and cooperation, Washington, for its part, held firm on maximum pressure, rolled out sanctions, and insisted that unless North Korea showed interest in "serious and credible" denuclearization negotiations, the United States would not entertain plans to meet with its officials before or after the Olympics. Secretary of State Tillerson in mid-January 2018 declared that "the pressure campaign will continue until North Korea takes decisive steps to denuclearize." He emphasized the importance of being steadfast: "I think we all need to be very sober and clear-eyed about the current situation. . . . We have to recognize that the threat is growing."

Meanwhile, Kim dispatched his younger sister, Kim Yo Jong, a member of the Politburo and vice director of the party's Propaganda and Agitation Department—and designated as a violator of human rights by the United States—and Kim Yong Nam, the ninety-year-old president of the Presidium of the Supreme People's Assembly, to the opening ceremony of the Olympics, along with North Korean athletes and cheerleaders. Yo Jong's attendance at the event was the first time a Kim family member had visited South Korea and it signified Kim Jong Un's trust in his sibling. Vice President Mike Pence and his wife, along with Otto Warmbier's father, attended the event; in his meeting with President Moon, Pence emphasized that South Korea should continue to apply maximum pressure after the Olympics. He refused to acknowledge Yo Jong and the North Korean delegation, keeping U.S.–North Korean ties on ice. Pence was reported to be planning to meet with them, but the delegation didn't follow through, probably because they recognized that Pence was not in the mood to be conciliatory. The divergence in messaging— with Moon determined to open dialogue with North Korea and the Trump administration holding steadfast to maximum pressure and confrontation—fueled speculation of an open rift in the alliance.

And that was probably Kim Jong Un's goal. His more friendly attitude and the unprecedented—and cordial—meeting between his sister and the South Korean president let the air out of U.S. maximum pressure and undermined calls for giving North Korea a "bloody nose." The more Kim engaged, the more difficult it was to make the argument for a preventive strike, especially as Seoul was trying to couch the Olympic thaw as the beginning of a new era in inter-Korean ties.

KIM'S MAXIMUM PRESSURE AND ENGAGEMENT

During his first six years of rule, Kim relentlessly and unapologetically accelerated his nuclear and ballistic missile programs to highlight North Korea's strategic relevance and create leverage; now he seemed to be doing the same for engagement. Not only was he good at exerting maximum pressure, but he was also proving adroit at maximum engagement, exploiting the national priorities of the regional players to weaken sanctions pressure.

Kim's New Year's address and the "peace Olympics" kicked off a veritable "summit spring." Van Jackson, an Asia specialist and former Pentagon official, described the thaw in his book *On the Brink*: "The Olympics helped make the dominant narrative on Korea a hopeful one, about diplomatic progress, with South Korea leading the way." Kim's shedding of his isolation "drowned out" the warlike rhetoric coming from Washington. Kim's sister passed Moon a letter from her brother inviting Moon to visit Pyongyang. Soon after the Olympics, Moon sent National Security Adviser Chung Eui-yong and National Intelligence Service Director Suh Hoon to Pyongyang to meet with Kim. They had "openhearted talk" for more than four hours.

Buoyed by Kim's comments about improving inter-Korean ties, easing military tension on the Korean Peninsula, and being willing to denuclearize, the envoys released a triumphant statement: "The North Korean side clearly stated its willingness to denuclearize. . . . It made it clear that it would have no reason to keep nuclear weapons if the military threat to the North was eliminated and its security guaranteed." North Korea also said it wanted a "heartfelt dialogue with the United States on the issues of denuclearization and normalizing relations with the United States," and that it would refrain from nuclear and ballistic missile tests "while dialogue is continuing." Beijing welcomed the development, calling for "all relevant parties to seize the current opportunity." And so did President Trump, who tweeted, "Possible progress being made in talks with North Korea. For the first time in many years, a serious effort is being made by all parties concerned. The World is watching and waiting! May be false hope, but the U.S. is ready to go hard in either direction!" Trump then stunned his advisers, the South Korean envoys, the academic and think tank communities, and the global media when he agreed, in March, apparently on the spur of the moment, to accept Kim's offer to meet and that he wanted to do so by the end of May.

In the meantime, Kim would hold summits with Moon, in which the two sides would issue the Panmunjom Declaration, which included working toward unification of the Korean Peninsula "led by the Koreans"; fulfilling economic projects; easing military tension by practicing restraint along the DMZ and the disputed Northern Limit Line in the Yellow Sea, a site of numerous clashes; establishing a peace regime and "bringing an end to the current unnatural state of armistice"; and supporting "denuclearization of the Korean peninsula." Moon and Kim also agreed to have regular meetings and direct telephone conversations to "strengthen mutual trust."

Kim's statements about a peace regime, denuclearization, economic cooperation, and security guarantees were not new—his father had uttered similar comments as part of his effort to dampen sanctions enforcement and drive a wedge between the United States and its allies. But it was still viewed as an astonishing turn of events that Kim, who had rejected engagement for his entire tenure, would do a 180. Kim's actions and Moon's and Trump's easy acceptance of his statements at face value and their insistence on his "sincerity" muddled conventional thinking about North Korea's intentions, confused and frustrated Trump's own advisers and Korea experts who argued that the regime would never fully denuclearize, and energized those who had long believed that political and economic carrots and U.S. security guarantees were the only path toward North Korea's abandonment of nuclear weapons. Almost everyone who had been worried about a nuclear war breaking out on the Korean Peninsula was relieved at this off-ramp for Kim, Trump, and Moon to tone down the rhetoric. But as Jackson pointed out, "South Korea, the United States, and the media were responding to North Korean overtures radically differently than in decades past, but the style and substance of North Korea's overtures were entirely consistent with what it had historically done." He called the scenario "collective amnesia disguised as a hubristic refusal to be bound by history."

What was behind Kim's pivot to diplomacy? The president and others in Washington were convinced it was Trump's tough talk and maximum pressure policy that got Kim to cave. After all, the South Korean envoys who delivered Kim's invitation told him so, and Trump seemed excited about the opportunity, tweeting, "Great progress being made but sanctions will remain until an agreement is reached. Meeting being planned!" The Republican chairman of the House Foreign Affairs Committee stated, "Kim Jong Un's desire to talk shows sanctions the administration has implemented are starting to work." And Senator Lindsey Graham stated, "I am not naive. I understand that if the past is an indication of the future, North Korea will be all talk and no action. However, I do believe that North Korea now believes President Trump will use military force if he has to." The president and these officials were expressing a very human tendency to look for causal explanations—something Heuer cautioned his analysts against accepting at face value—and as a consequence, this assumption inclined them to overestimate the power of the United States to influence Kim. "When another country's actions are consistent with US desires, the most obvious explanation," Heuer wrote, "is that US policy effectively influenced the decision."

Washington was right, but only to a certain degree. Kim doubtless understood that international sanctions had never been sharper and global unity on pressuring North Korea had never been greater than they were under the U.S. maximum pressure campaign, which had its genesis in the last year of the Obama administration. But he could hardly have been surprised at this response, given the scope and pace of his strategic provocations in 2017 and accompanying belligerent language. U.N. sanctions cut off North Korea's most lucrative exports, including coal, iron ore, seafood, and textiles, worth approximately $2.7 billion, and reduced North Korea's importation of oil.

Intensive diplomacy by Washington with countries that had political, economic, and military ties to North Korea led to more than twenty of them closing Pyongyang's embassies, downgrading or expelling North Korean ambassadors, and clamping down on the ability of businesses owned by the North Korean government to make money to fund regime priorities, such as the nuclear weapons program, and to purchase luxury items for the elite. A September 2017 U.S. executive order authorizing broad secondary sanctions against individuals and companies that did business with the rogue country had the potential to squeeze North Korea's ability to generate enough revenue to fund the nuclear weapons program and Kim's other priorities. Maximum pressure also had the potential not only to suppress the ability of the elites to make money for themselves, and therefore to make loyalty payments to the regime, but also to undermine Kim's ability to reward the elites, a key element of keeping them invested in his rule. North Korea does not publish its own statistics, but the South Korean central bank estimated that in 2017 the North's economy shrank by 3.5 percent, its worst performance since 1997, during the famine. North Korea's most important exports—coal, iron ore, and textiles—declined by 40 percent.

The sanctions pressure surely played a role in Kim's decision to pivot, a standard North Korean tactic to ease international pressure, even as the regime continued to covertly develop its weapons program. Kim's reported agreement to denuclearize and focus on turning the armistice into a peace treaty is an iteration of his father's and grandfather's playbook, and an attempt to divide and conquer through bilateral exchanges with South Korea, China, the United States, and potentially Russia, while keeping Japan at arm's length. For example, Kim's agreement to work with South Korea to advance peace is reminiscent of past attempts by his predecessors to entangle Washington in long, drawn-out discussions on nonnuclear issues. Pyongyang calculates that these discussions serve to solidify the North's claimed status as a nuclear weapons power, garnering the prestige of being in negotiations with a world power. These pivots toward diplomacy also tend to hamper or at least weaken sanctions implementation, tamp down international demands for human rights, and of course buy time for North Korea to advance its strategic capabilities. And when called out for its illegal and inhumane activities, Pyongyang has a convenient excuse—the sanctions themselves—to assail Washington and critics for dragging their feet, while reneging on its own obligations.

Kim also had a receptive party in Seoul, finally having in South Korea a progressive government after ten years of hard-line conservative presidents whose focus was pressure rather than inducements. When Moon Jae-in was elected in May 2017 in a special election following the impeachment and removal of conservative president Park Geun-hye, the new progressive president emphasized trust building and "coexistence and co-prosperity"; in one of his first major speeches, he called for inter-Korean economic cooperation even as he called for North Korea's denuclearization. The former chief of staff to liberal president Roh Moo-hyun—who had continued the Sunshine Policy toward the North of his predecessor, Kim Dae-jung—Moon exhorted Pyongyang to join Seoul to make the Pyeongchang Winter Olympics an "Olympic of Peace," claiming that "sports have the power of connecting one heart to another." Moon, who was also spooked by the tension of the summer and fall of 2017, eagerly seized on Kim's willingness to participate in the Olympics as a positive sign to move forward on engaging the North.

But having declared that he had completed the country's nuclear weapons program, Kim might have already been planning a pivot toward focusing on his country's economy, regardless of maximum pressure and Trump's threats to destroy the regime. He said in his 2018 New Year's address that 2017 saw the "accomplishment of the great, historic cause of perfecting the national nuclear forces . . . [and] proving before the eyes of the world its definite success. . . . Our Republic has at last come to possess a powerful and reliable war deterrent, which no force and nothing can reverse." At a rare party meeting of the Central Committee in April 2018, Kim said North Korea had "verified the completion of nuclear weapons," announced that he would suspend nuclear and missile tests starting that month, and pledged North Korea would not proliferate or use nuclear weapons unless faced with a nuclear threat. He also declared that he would shutter the Punggye-ri test site where the regime conducted six nuclear tests: "We no longer need any nuclear test or test launches of intermediate and intercontinental range ballistic missiles." In short, Kim's aggressive push to demonstrate ICBM capabilities might have been driven by his plan to subsequently focus on the economy side of the dual-track *byungjin* policy he had announced in

2013, and that now that North Korea had fulfilled the nuclear weapons prong of it, the nation was turning to the economic development prong.

And he probably saw his pivot as an opportunity to advance his strategic goals of cementing North Korea's nuclear status and weakening the U.S. presence in East Asia, including its alliance with South Korea, perceiving that he had a receptive partner in Moon, who favored inducements over pressure, and Trump, who publicly derided the U.S.–South Korean alliance. Still, Trump took credit for the rapprochement, championing Kim's declarations and expressing admiration for the inter-Korean summit. On the day of Kim's speech to the party in April, Trump tweeted, "North Korea has agreed to suspend all Nuclear Tests and close up a major test site. This is very good news for North Korea and the World—big progress! Look forward to our Summit." He saw Kim's action as the direct result of his successful pressuring. In response to skepticism about Kim's intentions—observers noted that he did not indicate any intent to abandon his nuclear weapons and critics excoriated the president for handing Kim a key concession, a meeting with a sitting U.S. president—Trump tweeted, "Funny how all of the Pundits that couldn't come close to making a deal on North Korea are now all over the place telling me how to make a deal!"

Whatever Kim's exact motivations for shedding his isolation, he learned that the old playbook still worked, at least in the immediate aftermath of his pivot. As a result of Kim's reported intentions about working toward a new era of peace, the South Korean government agreed to stop broadcasting propaganda via loudspeakers along the border, and President Moon apparently gave Kim a USB containing a document outlining a "new economic map" and ideas for future cooperation, including potential energy assistance. And China, for its part, started to loosen sanctions implementation, and some reports indicated that North Korean laborers were being allowed to return to China, in potential violation of U.N. sanctions. For the first time, Kim in early May 2018 hosted the Chinese foreign minister, Wang Yi, who pledged Beijing's support for North Korea's focus on economic development and the resolution of Pyongyang's "legitimate security concerns," reinforcing Kim's confidence that he still had China's backing. Moreover, Kim's metamorphosis from "Rocket Man" to international statesman fueled hopes among the South Korean public and in the United States that he is "sincere." Kim almost certainly relished the favorable media attention, as his trustworthiness among South Koreans soared to an astonishing 78 percent after the inter-Korean summit in April, according to a Korea Research Center poll; it had been a dismal 10 percent earlier in 2018. His reported sense of humor, his show of deference to President Moon, and his self-deprecation as evidenced in the televised inter-Korean summit—he reportedly told Moon "I feel embarrassed about [North Korea's] poor transit infrastructure"—also engendered hope that Kim was no longer a blustery dictator but a chastened, humble young man who wanted to do the right thing.

The ensuing months showed how much Kim could abruptly change the dynamic in East Asia and constrain U.S. options by exploiting underlying fissures in the U.S.–South Korean relationship and manipulate the national priorities of regional stakeholders to his advantage. He would successfully alter his image from a stern and unyielding dictator threatening nuclear strikes to a smiling, approachable young man whom some held up as a transformational figure with the potential to make history. And he would get help in doing so, not just from President Moon but also from his wife, Ri Sol Ju.

FOURTEEN

THE QUEEN OF PYONGYANG

WHEN MOON JAE-IN SAT down with Kim Jong Un in that forest glade during their first inter-Korean summit, Kim appeared to be in listening mode, paying close attention to Moon's comments. South Korean media consulted lip-readers who noted that the two appeared to mention "Trump," "nuclear facilities," and "the United States" the most. But things got personal as well, as the two sides sought to build rapport. "Father looked at me and told me to marry that woman," Kim reportedly said, "so I trusted him." It was a moment of extraordinary candor, given Kim Il Sung's and Kim Jong Il's preference and practice of keeping their personal lives hidden and the details of their family members shrouded in mystery. Perhaps Kim's comment was calculated to build rapport and intimacy with President Moon. He also might have talked about his wife during this conversation to introduce Ri Sol Ju in anticipation of that evening's banquet in which both wives would be present.

Ri's presence at the summit in April 2018 and subsequent meetings with Moon and Chinese president Xi Jinping suggest that Kim sees her as another component of his power. As the First Lady of

Pyongyang, she has personified the charm in the proverbial North Korean charm offensive, normalizing Kim's status not just as a leader of a nuclear power but as a husband, father, and legitimate ruler on a par with the likes of Presidents Xi, Moon, and Trump. The carefully curated public appearances of Ri Sol Ju—who keeps her maiden name, per Korean custom—provide the regime with a softer side, a thin veneer of style and good humor to mask the brutality, starvation, and deprivation endured by the people, while reports about the existence of possibly multiple children hint at the couple's fecundity and the potential for the birth of another male heir to the Kim family dynasty. For the toiling masses as well as for the elite, Ri, the glamorous and devoted wife, is an aspirational figure. For outside scholars, Ri's public appearances offer something else—a glimpse of an emerging material and consumer culture, which Kim seems to be actively promoting. Thus, Kim's showcasing of his wife indicates that she serves both a domestic and an external purpose, and is consistent with his desire to portray himself as a modern leader.

THE WOMAN IN BLACK. AND GREEN. AND PINK. AND BLUE.

Just seven months after Kim Jong Un became leader of North Korea, the regime's state news agency published photos of Kim at a concert with a mysterious woman. The concert, which included North Korean pop stars and Disney characters, was a surprising choice and sparked optimism that Kim was more Westernized than his reclusive father and might be inclined toward opening North Korea. The woman's physical proximity to Kim—she sat next to him at the concert—generated intense buzz in South Korean and U.S. media about her identity and role. The regime later identified her as Kim's wife, "Comrade Ri Sol Ju," during coverage of Kim and Ri's visit to the Rungra People's Pleasure Ground, where they walked arm in arm, waving at bathing-suit-clad pleasure seekers at the new amusement park. The way Ri looked was also a striking departure from past practices. Kim's grandfather had once decried "make-up," "hair-curlers," "pretty dresses," and "fancy hats" as distracting to the revolutionary struggle, even as he made contradictory demands that "women should be feminine after all." And under the rule of Kim Jong Il, it was illegal for women to wear trousers when not at work or even to ride bicycles, reminiscent of nineteenth-century American and European beliefs that bicycling was too sexual for women, violated gender norms, and contributed to female liberation.

In 2012, when analysts were piecing together Kim's background, fragmentary information made it even more difficult to cobble together a coherent narrative about Ri, with rumor and speculation further clouding whatever meager facts might be available. According to information gathered by the South Korean government, Ri was born in 1989 and married Kim in 2009. Like his father, Kim had apparently married an entertainer. Ri was reportedly a member of the Unhasu Orchestra, an elite troupe composed of members who are handpicked by the state for looks, loyalty, and talent. She came from a "normal home" and went to South Korea in 2005 as a cheerleader to support North Korean athletes.

If Kim Jong Un's intention was to create buzz and elicit commentary about Ri to show that he was determined to change the impression of North Korea as a bleak, threatening, and authoritarian dictatorship, he succeeded. Her youth, attractiveness, and fashion sense inspired reams of media coverage. Given the paucity of information about her, it was impossible not to focus on how she looked. The comparison to other prominent women was inevitable. Was she evoking the storied elegance of Jackie Kennedy? Was she taking fashion cues from Kate Middleton, the Duchess of Cambridge? At the July 2012 concert, she wore a smart, short black skirt and matching jacket, and her cropped bob made her look decidedly modern. When touring the water park, she wore a bright green blouse with a fitted skirt and peep-toe black pumps—"She is stylish indeed!" declared *The Huffington Post*. There she is in 2014, watching a flight contest among commanding officers of the Korean People's Air Force: Her longer hair is partly pulled back, her lipstick is a muted pink shade, and she is wearing a blue dress and three-quarter-length suit jacket embellished with a sparkly brooch.

In a sea of men wearing beige military uniforms or dark suits, her colorful attire provided a dramatic—and pleasant—contrast.

LIVING THE NORTH KOREAN DREAM

Given the highly orchestrated nature of the North Korean regime, both its portrayal of Ri and her unusually visible role are almost certainly not accidental. Ri's unabashed femininity, her fashion choices, modern style, and relationship with her husband are probably reflections of existing trends in North Korean society, how Kim Jong Un sees himself and his country's place in the world, and his vision for the future. In using Ri as a representation of those ideals, as an aspirational figure, and shaping her persona so soon after Kim ascended to power, it seemed that he was literally and figuratively grooming her to be Pyongyang's First Lady.

For decades, the regime extolled Kim Il Sung's mother, Kang Pan Sok, and Kim Jong Il's mother, Kim Jong Suk, as the embodiment of the North Korean feminine ideal. As Korea scholars Bronwen Dalton, Kyungja Jung, and Jacqueline Willis have articulated in their fascinating article on fashion and the social construction of femininity in North Korea, these two women "are eulogized as both passionate revolutionary fighters and the epitome of self-sacrificing and loving mothers." Kang's importance is linked to the fact that she gave birth to the nation, figuratively and literally, by being the mother of Kim Il Sung. Kim Jong Suk's role is that of a woman who not only nurtured Kim Jong Il but also served to reinforce her son's military-first ideology. Kang is usually shown in regime hagiography wearing native Korean dress, while Kim Jong Il's mother is shown in a military uniform—appropriately feminized with a skirt and cinched waist—to symbolize the revolution.

When Kim Jong Un came to power, the regime also elevated the status of his mother, Ko Yong Hui, calling her "Our Respected Mother" to cement her position and Kim Jong Un's legitimacy by anchoring the young leader in history and biology. The regime downplayed Ko's problematic background—she was born in Japan, which would make her less "pure" and of a low status in the revered *songbun* classification system, not to mention the fact that she was Kim Jong Il's third wife. Instead the regime mythologized Ko in 2011, with a documentary on her life. The film shows Ko as a woman who waits for her son to come home from school, knits sweaters, and is good with guns. "The mother role embodies the symbolic roles women should play for the nation," the Korea researcher Darcie Draudt wrote, and Ko's importance was in her ability to "reproduce Kim Jong-il in the form of Kim Jong-un (a form that extends from Kim Il-sung) that makes her an esteemed citizen worthy of praise." According to the historian Suzy Kim, the mother becomes an "ideal, selfless public servant, a model for everyone in the North Korean nation to follow in performing their social duties."

Although the elevation of Ri is consistent with the regime's construction of femininity, she looks different from the revolutionary, militaristic motherhood portrayal of the previous Kim women figures. Placing her in the current North Korean narrative suggests that she serves Kim Jong Un's priorities and preferences, consistent with his desire not only to hew closely to the legacies of his father and his grandfather but also to create his own brand for the twenty-first century.

In their article, Dalton, Jung, and Willis argued that "the ongoing collapse of the command economy, the emergence of capitalism, increasing exposure to foreign pop culture and the growth of a new moneyed elite are influencing the construction of femininity in ways that depart from earlier state prescribed and policed ideals." As Kim Jong Un sought to craft an alternative narrative of North Korea as a modern, prosperous country and built physical structures like water parks and ski resorts to reinforce that vision, Ri provided a walking advertisement for his program. Her glamour, esteemed position (in April 2018, the regime declared her "Revered First Lady"), and complete devotion to her husband made her an aspirational figure for elite and ordinary North Koreans to adore and mimic. Ri's role as the First Wife provides Kim the gravitas and grounding as a married man in a society in which an unmarried man would still be considered a boy, as Draudt observed.

The couple, walking hand in hand, waving at adoring North Korean citizens and holding squirming babies (not their own) at a nursery, cut a compelling image of youth, vigor, and confidence. Her colorful outfits, sparkling accessories, and effervescence reinforced that image of hope. John Park, a Korea expert at Harvard University, likened Kim and Ri as protagonists in a North Korean version of Camelot—the much-admired world of the youthful John F. Kennedy and his graceful wife, Jacqueline, that encapsulated so much of post–World War II optimism. "There's this idea of a North Korean dream, and Kim Jong Un being the creator of this dream and his wife, Ri Sol Ju, being essentially the face of this dream," he explained. "This type of dynamic is sort of an analogy for the future of North Korea overall."

That future of North Korea includes the fulfillment of *byungjin,* the dual-track policy of developing both nuclear weapons and the economy. Ri appears with her husband in a wide variety of locations: military facilities, construction sites, factories, manufacturing plants, schools, and orphanages. During the peak of tensions with the United States, in October 2017, Kim still found time to tour a cosmetics factory in Pyongyang with his wife. A smiling, appreciative Kim praised the "world-class" products and their packaging, as his wife primly looked on, observing the machines and displays. The regime's showcasing of his ability to pivot from threatening war to inspecting women's makeup, with his wife at his side, suggests that it was seeking to show the complementarity—indeed, the necessity—of nuclear weapons to North Korea's prosperity and that the people can have both, as Kim has been promising since he came to power. Ri's presence underscores that message, given her place as an aspirational figure.

Ri as First Lady also provides an opportunity for the regime to channel the consumerist energies of the North Korean people, especially nonelite women who fill the formal and informal markets while their husbands are occupied with regime-directed factory work or military duties. One defector told the online periodical *Daily NK* that "Pyongyang women are influenced by Ri Sol Ju . . . so they like to wear strappy heels." But Ri is not the only trendsetter for North Koreans, as increased information penetration and the North Korean appetite for South Korean and Chinese soap operas also shape fashion choices. Suki Kim, the journalist who went undercover as a teacher at the Pyongyang University of Science and Technology, observed that "on the streets of Pyongyang, the people looked Chinese to me. . . . Women's hair was inevitably permed and pinned with sparkling barrettes the way I had seen women style their hair in China." Defectors from North Korea have reported how they covertly binge-watched foreign media and adopted fashion based on the female characters; one defector featured in a documentary made by the NGO Liberty in North Korea said that his compatriots would watch foreign movies and sitcoms and then ask a smuggler to acquire the goods they saw, which they would then sell in the markets. People copied haircuts, hairpins, clothes, and accessories. The regime sought to promote Ri as a model for the domestic alternative: Her implicit endorsement of products made in North Korea, as demonstrated in her visits to cosmetics and shoe factories, was used to encourage her compatriots to look inside their own country for coveted items.

But there is an inherent tension in all of this. As the people's interest in fashion and outward appearance grows, so do their expectations about being able to enjoy the fruits of economic development. The dangers of not being able to meet those expectations follow not far behind. A North Korean source put it this way to *Daily NK:* "Using the latest South Korean products indicates social class and living standard so people are desperate to keep up." Defector memoirs hint at social conflict and the growing gap between the haves and have-nots, with cliques forming among children and families of the *jangmadang* generation who are demonstrably better off than their neighbors, a not unusual phenomenon, of course, in other societies. Despite the Kim regime's best efforts to create a North Korean brand and an aspirational model in Ri, it struggles to compete with goods from more sophisticated companies in China and South Korea that are more adept at churning out the latest consumer trends. Kim almost certainly recognizes this deficiency, and it probably just reinforces his belief that he needs to maintain control of the flows of foreign products and cultural influences.

A WOMAN'S TOUCH

Ri Sol Ju made her diplomatic debut on March 5, 2018. Kim Jong Un was hosting his first ever South Korean delegation, consisting of National Security Adviser Chung Eui-yong and other top officials. They were in Pyongyang to set up the first Moon–Kim summit, which would occur a month later, so there was a weighty significance to the meeting, with a lot at stake. Whether emboldened by the alcohol served at the dinner, amity generated by the meeting, or a sense of mentoring a much younger man, Chung reportedly told Kim, "How about stopping smoking? It's bad for your health."

Those at the table froze, according to media reports. No one criticizes Kim, who can do no wrong in a country that considers him, his father, and his grandfather entirely above reproach. One can imagine the color draining from people's faces as the air became thick with tension. Instead, lovely Ri clapped her hands and said, "I always ask him to quit smoking, but he won't listen to me." And just like that, she defused the tension, potentially keeping the two sides on track for the leadership summit on April 27.

Ri has been present with her husband at other summit meetings, traveling with Kim to Beijing to meet with President Xi in March 2018—Kim's first trip outside the country as leader and his first meeting with Xi, whom he had ignored for the first six years of his rule. She also attended the inter-Korean summit in September 2018 in Pyongyang and joined subsequent trips to China, providing a First Lady counterpart for President Moon's wife, Kim Jung-sook, and President Xi's wife, Peng Liyuan.

Chinese and South Korean media were ablaze with commentary about her outfits, indicating North Korea's success in trying to export the Kim family brand overseas. Since Ri was seen, and not heard, it was once again inevitable that the focus would be on her appearance. The *South China Morning Post* declared Ri an "instant hit in China with her fashionable looks" during that first visit to Beijing in March. The paper reported that Chinese Internet users were full of praise for Ri's appearance, to the chagrin of the Chinese censors, who promptly removed all discussions of Ri from social media platforms that favored her over President Xi's wife. On Weibo, one of China's biggest social media platforms, one post gushed, "Ri Sol-ju is indeed beautiful and amiable. I can tell she would be good at 'first-lady diplomacy.'" Another post compared her to South Korean celebrities—Chinese viewers are avid consumers of South Korean movies, music, and sitcoms—and said that Ri was "as pretty as Song Hye-kyo," a well-known South Korean actor who is popular in China. For the most part, the three outfits she wore during the meetings won approval. A camel-colored cropped jacket and matching skirt, a green dress with a white jacket, and an ivory peplum jacket with flared three-quarter-length sleeves garnered rave reviews. Stylishly dressed, smiling graciously with Xi and Peng, and waving warmly at the Chinese leader and his wife as she and Kim got into their car to leave Beijing, Ri imparted a friendly and familiar tone to a state visit, as if she and her husband were a young couple leaving a dinner party at a much older neighbor's house.

Ri also garnered favorable attention when she and Kim Jung-sook, South Korea's First Lady, held their own meetings during the third Moon–Kim summit in Pyongyang. While their husbands dealt with state affairs, the two women visited the Pyongyang University of Music and Dance—perhaps in acknowledgment of their shared history in music (Kim studied vocal music at South Korea's Kyung Hee University). They also visited the city's Okryu Children's Hospital. Their tours of educational and medical institutions in Pyongyang showed off North Korea's modern facilities, providing an appropriate, apolitical, and noncontroversial backdrop. The venues also highlighted the normality of North Korea, allowing the nuclear and ballistic missile programs, the executions and purges, and the military threats to fade into the background.

Kim Jong Un and Ri Sol Ju's marriage is thus a metaphor for the *byungjin* policy, the organic, natural union of militarism and economic development, and a promise for the future of North Korea and its place as an equal on the world stage. She smoothed the edges of what could have been contentious leadership meetings, taking media attention away from North Korea's nuclear weapons and assassinations and directing it toward her hair and clothing, a young female presence allowing for opportunities for soft power engagement and offering—or teasing—the promise of a different North Korea, more peaceful, pliant, and charming.

FAMILY PLANNING

The regime's glorification of Ri and her growing public profile provide some clues about Kim's intentions for the future. Kim is well aware of the machinations of various groups to jockey for supremacy through alliances with potential successors, given his own experience as the son of a father who had multiple children with multiple wives and consorts. Ri's public elevation may be a deliberate attempt to fend off any potential challengers and preempt any further palace intrigue by securing Kim and Ri's union as the only legitimate one, thereby ensuring that their offspring will succeed him. It suggests that even in his midthirties Kim is planning for the long haul and plotting a strategy for the duration of not just his life but his children's lives as well. The couple have at least one confirmed child whom Dennis Rodman held on his second visit; but according to South Korean government information, they have two others. And given Kim's evident desire to hand down an independent, powerful North Korea, nuclear weapons will surely be a part of his successor's inheritance.

Of course, Ri's own status and prestige depend completely on

Kim. Without him, she would be just another performer with a pretty face. And while she has supported his desire to re-create North Korea's brand and supplemented the image he wants to project to the outside world, Kim's ultimate validation would come from another man—Donald Trump. In June 2018, Kim would get what his grandfather and his father were never able to obtain— a meeting with a sitting U.S. president.

FIFTEEN

WHEN TRUMP MET KIM

KIM'S MEETINGS WITH PRESIDENTS Xi and Moon were mere opening acts for the main event: his summit with Donald Trump. When Trump, who had once dreamed of going into show business instead of real estate, having planned to study filmmaking, according to biographer Tim O'Brien, met Kim Jong Un, the son of a cinephile dictator and a former dancer, drama and entertainment were almost guaranteed.

And the ratings were gold. The global media televised the unprecedented meeting between a sitting U.S. president and the leader of North Korea at 9:00 P.M. Eastern Standard Time, prime time for those watching in Washington and New York. Whatever the hour—it was 9:00 A.M. in Singapore for Trump, Kim, and the three thousand journalists—the world sat transfixed before their televisions and commented on social media as pundits analyzed every gesture and utterance of the two main players and their supporting casts. Trump's biographers Michael Kranish and Marc Fisher said that he harnessed his decades of appearing on talk shows and sitcoms, at WrestleMania, and on *The Apprentice* for fourteen years, his cinematic skills fully evident in his latest gambit with Kim, who was more than willing to play his part.

Even the preparations for the summit had all the elements of a good drama. There were two outsize leading actors known for their penchant for disruption and unpredictability. There was surprise, when then CIA director Mike Pompeo went to Pyongyang over the Easter holiday in late March to meet with Kim Jong Un. There was speculation: Where would they meet? What would they discuss? How would they get along? There were spies who played big roles in arranging the meeting. There was a triumphant hostage release, as North Korea freed three Americans who had been detained for various acts of "espionage and hostile acts against the government." There was even audience participation: Trump tweeted on April 30, "Numerous countries are being considered for the MEETING, but would Peace House/Freedom House, on the Border of North & South Korea, be a more Representative, Important and Lasting site than a third country? Just asking!"

There were other tweets and statements from the U.S. president touting the coming meeting with Kim rather than managing expectations. Trump had good reason to play up the regime's rather meager utterances about denuclearization of the Korean Peninsula and its conditionality on positive U.S. actions toward North Korea, utterances that over the decades had proven meaningless, given North Korea's observable actions to the contrary and its history of reneging on previous agreements. A Pew Research Center poll from late April/early May 2018 found that 71 percent of Americans supported direct talks with North Korea. A CNN poll that was taken around the same time echoed the Pew findings, when it reported that a whopping 77 percent of Americans approved of Trump's plans to meet with Kim, even though just seven months prior, at the height of tensions, only 35 percent approved of Trump's handling of the North Korea issue. South Koreans also viewed Trump positively as a result of the planned summit; his favorability rating climbed to 32 percent, up from 9 percent just a year prior.

For Trump, his decision to meet with Kim was a foreign policy success that crossed party and geographical boundaries, and he relished chatter about his winning the Nobel Peace Prize. Similarly, Kim enjoyed a boost in his favorability rating that reflected hopes that North Korea was finally willing to change its course. His enhanced global profile was thanks to the unsolicited help he was getting from the U.S. president, who was intent on selling his mastery of the situation, linking his political success to the vague assurances that Kim was making to reinforce the narrative, and getting the public involved and invested in their leaders' success. According to Trump (and Moon), Kim was now "honorable" and "sincere" in his desire to denuclearize and commit to a peaceful Korean Peninsula; their statements helped to humanize Kim and assisted in his effort to shed his image as the irrational madman and murderer from Pyongyang.

In the months that followed, Trump and Kim would meet multiple times, exchange letters, and tout their personal chemistry, even as the world would see little movement on the nuclear issue.

KNOW YOUR ADVERSARY

As the world counted down the days before the first Kim-Trump summit—on May 10, President Trump announced that the meeting would be in Singapore on June 12—warnings, optimism, premature declarations that peace was afoot, policy advice, and expert observations saturated the airwaves and print media. And given the extraordinary events that led up to Kim's remarkable pivot toward engagement, and the unsubstantiated claims by Trump and Moon that Kim was committed to abandoning his nuclear arsenal, Korea watchers were understandably examining their assumptions about Kim's motivations and whether he had, indeed, made a strategic change in his views about nuclear weapons.

While Korea experts were discussing privately and publicly their assumptions about how North Korea's history of breaking past agreements might be coloring their assessments, and whether there were signposts of real change in Pyongyang's approach, the only person who apparently wasn't questioning anything was President Trump himself. In fact, his seemingly unwavering confidence that he could solve the North Korea problem once and for all, where other presidents had failed, could well have been rooted in his mirror-imaging—the notion that he knew what would work with Kim because, ultimately, he was like Trump or like the many businessmen with whom Trump had worked in the past.

Former CIA officer Richards Heuer described mirror-imaging as a situation where an individual "fill[s] gaps in . . . assuming that the other side is likely to act in a certain way because that is how the US would act under similar circumstances." Because Heuer found that "a constant source of problems in intelligence analysis" was the "failure to understand that others perceive their national interests differently from the way we perceive those interests," within the intelligence community, our decision-making had inherent guardrails and safety nets—diverse opinions, creativity, structured analytic thinking processes, and depth of expertise, not to mention the input of policymakers who would challenge our analysis. Our jobs also required a constant shifting of perspectives, including interpreting an event and the other side's intentions from a foreign leader's point of view.

"Minds are like parachutes. They only function when they are open," Heuer wrote. President Trump was willing to try something different, jettisoning conventional guidance about not rewarding the North Korean leader with a summit, as had been done in past administrations, for dealing with Kim directly, to tease out how denuclearization could be advanced. Trump's unconventional approach in his willingness to pursue and test an alternative vision and change the paradigm of the relationship with North Korea was a reminder to seasoned analysts about the blinders of expertise. *A Tradecraft Primer: Structured Analytic Techniques for Improving Intelligence Analysis,* one of the reference documents familiar to all CIA analysts, warns that "seasoned analysts may be more susceptible to these mind-set problems as a result of their expertise and past success in using time-tested mental models." The handbook also lists "the key risks of mind-sets": "analysts perceive what they expect to perceive; once formed, [mind-sets] are resistant to change; new information is assimilated, sometimes erroneously, into existing mental models; and conflicting information is often dismissed or ignored." Engaging directly with Kim, the top decision-maker in a highly centralized authoritarian state, was logical and made sense, especially since Kim made it clear that he alone controlled the nuclear weapons program.

But Trump had been making foreign policy in an erratic fashion, often without consulting his advisers, convinced by the mythology of his personal business acumen, which was cultivated by himself and bolstered by reality television producers whose economic motivations and quest for viewership converged with Trump's own ego, that he alone knew what the best course of action was. As *The New Yorker*'s Patrick Radden Keefe observed, "By 2003 he had become a garish figure of local interest—a punch line. . . . 'The Apprentice' mythologized him anew, and on a much bigger scale, turning him into an icon of American success" despite the fact that Trump's business had been on a sharp downhill slope. Trump dismissed reports from the CIA and other intelligence organizations, criticizing and swatting away their inconvenient assessments; meanwhile, Director of National Intelligence Dan Coats testified in his annual threat assessment for 2019 that North Korea is "unlikely to completely give up its nuclear weapons and production capabilities," which Kim considers "critical to the regime's survival." The media reported that Trump was "enraged" and considered the DNI as being "not loyal," apparently for undercutting his more rosy outlook for engaging with Kim Jong Un.

Trump had consistently assessed his approach to Kim through the lens of a New York City businessman. In November 2017, when he addressed the South Korean National Assembly, Trump extolled the nation's transformation from a devastated, war-torn country to an economic powerhouse—and the U.S. role in helping its advancements—and compared it to the North Korean "hell that no person deserves." He promised that the United States was ready to show North Korea "a brighter path . . . if its leaders cease their threats and dismantle their nuclear program," and, as it had with South Korea, Washington would partner with Pyongyang to achieve the same levels of economic success. In May 2018, he was more blunt, reassuring Kim that he was not seeking the Libya model in which Muammar al-Qaddafi gave up his nascent nuclear weapons program but was subsequently captured and killed by pro-U.S. rebels. Speaking from the Oval Office, Trump said, "The Libyan model is not a model that we have at all when we are thinking of North Korea. . . . With Kim Jong Un . . . he would be there, he'd be in his country, he'd be running his country, his country would be very rich." (Secretary of State Pompeo, also a businessman before he entered politics and was elected to Congress, echoed similar points. After his first meeting with Kim in April 2018, he told *Face the Nation* that the United States would make it financially worthwhile for Kim if he abandoned his nuclear weapons: "What Chairman Kim will get from America is our finest. Our entrepreneurs. . . . They will get private capital that comes in." He also promised "American know-how, knowledge entrepreneurs, and risk takers working alongside the North Korean people to create a robust economy.")

In stamping his own preferences onto Kim, Trump appeared to have reinforced his own confidence that he could make a deal, in contrast to all the failed nuclear negotiations of the past. "Vision is my best asset," he told *Playboy* in 1990. "I know what sells and I know what people want." Before the meeting with Kim, *Time* magazine, citing a senior official, reported in mid-May that President Trump did not think that he needed to prepare. A Republican adviser admitted to *HuffPost* that "he thinks that all he needs to do is get into a room with Kim for two hours, and he thinks he can get it all worked out." The adviser also said that Trump knows almost nothing about disarmament issues or the background of why Kim would want a summit with a sitting U.S. president to advance his own ambitions. And less than a week before the actual meeting in Singapore, Trump even boasted about his lack of preparation— "I think I'm very well prepared. . . . I don't think I have to prepare very much. It's about the attitude. It's about willingness to get things done"—suggesting that he believed that the sheer force of his charm and deal-making prowess could finally convince Kim to see the light and give up his nuclear weapons. Apparently, the White House had not convened a cabinet-level meeting to discuss the summit with North Korea, as President Trump continued to eschew the traditional decision-making processes, which had been designed to ensure a whole-of-government approach to national security problems. These were worrisome developments, because when Trump was in the room with Kim, there would be no one to check his assumptions about what Kim wanted and what Trump could deliver.

If Kim were a businessman, like one of the many contractors, land developers, and investors Trump had dealt with over the years, this type of man-to man approach to negotiations might have worked. One can imagine that the real estate mogul in Trump saw Kim as wanting the same wealth, glory, and acclaim that he had once promised his business partners. "I truly believe North Korea has brilliant potential and will be a great economic and financial Nation one day," the president tweeted in the run-up to the summit. His administration held fast to this theme after Singapore, even though there was little to suggest that Kim saw this as a compelling reason to give up his nuclear weapons. Before the second summit, which was held in Hanoi on February 27–28, 2019, the White House announced, "The President has made clear that should North Korea follow through on its commitment to complete denuclearization, we will work to ensure there are economic development options." Four months later, the president continued to see resolution of this complicated national security issue as revolving around his personal rapport with Kim. Just hours before their third meeting, this time at the DMZ, Trump touted his "chemistry" with Kim and underscored its importance: "And sometimes that can lead to very good things."

But Kim is not a businessman, and wealth—in Trump's sense of the word—is not what he was looking for as he continued his maximum engagement strategy. Trump's mirror-imaging had the potential to lead to policymaking that did not comport with the realities of this thorny problem. Kim is highly unlikely to give up his nuclear weapons in order to get a McDonald's franchise in Pyongyang. And we are well aware by now that his pivot toward engagement was most likely aimed at trying to reduce sanctions implementation and his country's economic and political dependence on China, even as he tries to maintain China's support. Kim Jong Un has declared that he has completed the nuclear project that his grandfather started and his father nurtured. North Korea's identity is wrapped up in the idea of being a nuclear state—it is in the constitution, its monuments, its rhetoric, and its culture. To trade that away for money from Americans would have been the ultimate form of dishonor and betrayal to one of his country's founding principles.

So when the Trump administration framed the first summit with Kim as American capitalism helping to develop North Korea, Kim probably saw it as American "imperialists" seeking to exploit his country's people and resources. A senior North Korean official said in response to such U.S. declarations: "We have never had any expectation of US support in carrying out our economic construction and will not at all make such a deal in [the] future." At the same time, Kim might see it as worthwhile to make use of U.S. comments about sending investment and American know-how to North Korea, and the president's optimism about their personal chemistry, hoping to coax other countries to follow suit so that he can pocket the benefits of engagement without making real concessions on his nuclear program.

One's own assumptions are hard to identify and even harder to check without a willingness to learn and incorporate new or different information. While President Trump was openly stating that he wasn't preparing very much for the meeting, Kim was busy doing his homework.

KNOWING TRUMP

Trump believed "improvising was his strength," according to Bob Woodward, and that foreign policy was about personal relationships. Meanwhile, Kim was preparing, not having anticipated that he would spend the first half of 2018 planning for a meeting with the U.S. president. After Trump's surprise announcement in March that he would be willing to meet with Kim, North Korea did not publicly acknowledge the possibility of a Kim-Trump meeting until a month later. Kim told a Politburo meeting on April 9 that he had "made a profound analysis and appraisal of the orientation of the development of the north-south relations at present and the prospect of the DPRK-U.S. dialogue." The delay suggests that Kim, surprised by Trump's first move, was calculating his response. And he used his meetings with President Moon to gather information about President Trump. Lip-readers who watched Moon and Kim hold their private dialogue at the March 2018 summit reported that Kim asked Moon about U.S. intentions and expressed his desire for "positive results" from a meeting with Trump. During his trip to Beijing in late March, Kim almost certainly spoke with President Xi about the United States and the president's agenda before he finally confirmed publicly that he would be willing to sit down with Trump.

This series of summits and meetings in advance of the Singapore event gave Kim a decided advantage. Before he met with Trump on June 12, Kim met twice with Moon and Xi. And as speculation about a meeting with Putin swirled, Abe's insistence on maintaining maximum pressure and resolving the controversy over the abduction of Japanese citizens by North Korea made him an outsider in the era of reconciliation and historical forgetfulness. In essence, Kim squeezed a couple of years' worth of summits into the first six months of 2018, without having had to make any concessions on North Korea's nuclear weapons program, appalling human rights violations, or ongoing cyberattack operations. On top of that, Kim's every move dominated regional and global headlines. Images of him blanketed the media: walking side by side with Xi on a red carpet, smiling ear to ear with Trump in Singapore, hanging out with South Korean K-pop musicians, warmly gripping the hand of a visiting senior Chinese official, and enjoying the banter at a wine-soaked banquet with President Moon's envoys.

In meeting with South Korean and Chinese leaders, Kim was no doubt seeking, in part, to shape and bound the agenda of his meeting with Trump and validate his own assumptions about the U.S. president and the intentions of regional leaders. His goals were probably to shore up support from Seoul and Beijing on removal of international sanctions and to elicit their assistance to put pressure on the United States to provide incentives for North Korean denuclearization and maintain the mood of diplomacy. His engagement included the familiar bromides that Korea watchers and policymakers were used to hearing from his father and grandfather—pledging "denuclearization of the Korean Peninsula" and a willingness to resolve issues through dialogue while expressing admiration for China's developments in science and technological fields in order to trigger as yet unrequited Chinese hopes for North Korean economic reform.

Kim's success in winning over Beijing was evident in Xi's reported comment that "China sticks to the goal of denuclearization of the peninsula [using North Korea's preferred term]" and "calls on all parties to support the improvement of inter-Korean ties, and take concrete efforts to facilitate peace talks." The four subsequent meetings with the Chinese leader, in May and June 2018 and then in January and June 2019, undoubtedly cemented Kim's confidence. Xi's "all parties" construction had been used by Chinese leaders in the past, reflecting their belief that Washington is as responsible as Pyongyang for inflaming tensions. These words were almost certainly directed at Trump to condemn and discourage his return to his "fire and fury" of late 2017. Kim must have been reassured by Xi's reported comment prior to the Singapore summit that "no matter how the international and regional situation changes, we will both firmly grasp the global development trend and the overall situation of the China-DPRK relationship, strengthen our high-level exchanges, deepen our strategic communication, and expand our exchanges and cooperation, and benefit the people of both countries and the people of all countries." Even after North Korea's shunning and defying Beijing for more than six years, Xi had not abandoned the nation after all.

With the wind at his back—and the expressed support of Xi and Moon—Kim had another reason to believe that he could claim a position of strength before he went to Singapore. Although the world was able to gather some insight about Kim as he engaged in diplomacy, his intentions and preferences remained opaque. But for Kim, there were tens of thousands of Donald Trump's tweets at his disposal, along with multiple biographies and memoirs of former administration officials, and decades of statements and interviews about foreign relations and his approach to negotiations—most of which have been consistent over that time—to glean clues about his adversary. In late 2017, Kim dispatched his diplomats to query U.S. think tank experts and former officials in their work "figuring out the unconventional president's strategy," as *The Washington Post* reported. By mid-2018, Kim probably had a solid understanding of the president's personality and mindset, based on his conversations with Xi and Moon and the handful of meetings that he and his senior officials had with Secretary of State Mike Pompeo. In an interview with *Face the Nation* after having met with Kim, Pompeo said, "He is very knowledgeable in the sense of he knows the files. He's very capable of engaging in [a] complex set of discussions. When I ask him a question about something . . . there's no notecards. It is Chairman Kim in this case interacting with me directly having a robust discussion about what the outlines of a successful negotiation between our two countries might ultimately be."

Pompeo's observations about Kim's mastery of the issues and how to manage the Trump administration were probably also colored by the North Korean leader's perception that it paid to focus attention on Trump himself, taking advantage of the president's ownership of the issue, his desire to show progress in the negotiations, and the fact that he was personally driving the policy. Kim almost certainly saw the ousting of Rex Tillerson as secretary of state in mid-March—a Trump loyalist, Mike Pompeo, who had been the director of the CIA, was named as his successor—and the replacement of National Security Adviser H. R. McMaster with John Bolton in April as signs of tumult and policy dysfunction in the Trump administration. At the same time, he might have interpreted Trump's actions as those of a tough, confident leader, unafraid and unconstrained and willing to buck convention—qualities that Kim himself surely believed he possessed.

Those qualities in the two men came to a head briefly in late May, when North Korea, reacting viscerally to repeated comments about the "Libya model" by Vice President Pence and National Security Adviser Bolton—Pyongyang called Pence a "political dummy"—hinted at a possibility of calling off the summit. Its negotiators also stood up their U.S. counterparts for a planning meeting in Singapore, fueling concerns that Kim might pull out at the last minute. Instead, President Trump canceled the summit in a publicized letter to Kim: "Based on the tremendous anger and open hostility displayed in your most recent statement, I feel it is inappropriate, at this time, to have this long-planned meeting." Trump's tone, however, strongly suggested that he wanted the summit to happen. "I was very much looking forward to being there with you," he wrote, ending the letter with "If you change your mind . . . please do not hesitate to call me or write."

Kim then sent Kim Yong Chol, North Korea's former chief intelligence officer, who was taking on a new role as his top U.S. negotiator, to meet with Trump in the White House for almost two hours. Many Korea experts were dismayed by the appointment of Kim Yong Chol, whom they considered responsible for both masterminding a deadly attack on a South Korean corvette in 2010 that killed forty-six sailors and orchestrating the Sony attack in 2014; they asserted that neither he, nor the regime he represented, could be trusted. It was the first time that a North Korean official had been hosted at the White House in two decades. In what appeared to be a friendly meeting—with Kim handing Trump a jumbo-size letter from Kim Jong Un, which seemed to have pleased Trump—the two sides cemented the commitment to go forward with the Singapore summit.

But then in what probably came as a surprise to Kim—and to Korea watchers and even to Trump's own advisers—the president followed this last-ditch negotiation by painting a rosy picture of the relationship to the press, stating that North Korea and the United States were "getting along" and that "the relationship we have right now with North Korea is as good as it's been in a long time." He said that he did not "even want to use the term 'maximum pressure' anymore," and urged the North Koreans to "take your time"—presumably on denuclearization—batting away previous statements from his senior officials about the urgency of the issue. Trump also admitted that he did not raise human rights (which he had once held up as a central part of his North Korea policy) in his meeting with Kim Yong Chol, an issue that always elicits harsh comments from Pyongyang. Rather, he had reiterated his long-held doubts about the utility of a U.S. presence in East Asia ("And, look, we're very far away. . . . It's their neighborhood") and said he was open to signing a document to end the war ("Can you believe that we're talking about the ending of the Korean War? You're talking about 70 years").

If Kim took away one impression from his negotiator's White House meeting, it was that he and the U.S. president at least had a potential convergence of interests that made the summit attractive. Given the history of Trump's long-held suspicions about U.S. alliances, his apparent infatuation with bringing "peace" to Korea, and his jettisoning of the human rights issue, Kim had reason to be optimistic about the Singapore summit.

FANTASY ISLAND

Sentosa Island in Singapore (a city-state with a population of six million in around 280 square miles) is a lush resort area of only two square miles, "a good-time island . . . dedicated to unabashed fun," according to the travel website Lonely Planet, with theme parks, aquariums, golf and beach clubs, restaurants, and bars. It was hot and muggy on June 12, 2018, when Donald Trump and Kim Jong

Un met. The journalists reporting from the location were seen wiping their sweaty brows and fanning themselves. At the luxurious Capella Hotel, where the summit took place, peacocks roamed the grounds—a sign of new beginnings, suggested the management in a promotional tweet.

Kim Jong Un took center stage even before the summit started. The night before, after having borrowed an Air China Boeing 747 because his own aging jet could not have flown the nearly three thousand miles between Pyongyang and Singapore, Kim went on a surprise evening stroll, while the media (including North Korea's regime mouthpiece) and curious onlookers took photos and applauded. He even took a selfie with the Singaporean foreign minister and education minister, the three men smiling broadly. Kim waved to the crowds, the camera flashes lighting up his face. He admired Singapore's development—"Singapore is clean and beautiful and every building is stylish"—and said that he was going to "learn a lot from the good knowledge and experience of Singapore in various fields in the future." Kim seemed to revel in the attention, elevating himself as a celebrity and a statesman on a par with the U.S. president and setting the tone of the meeting that was to occur twelve hours later.

Set against the rather jarring juxtaposition of the North Korean and U.S. flags lining a bright red carpet, Kim Jong Un and Donald Trump, both dressed in their signature clothing—Kim in his Mao suit and Trump in a dark blue suit with a red tie—approached each other and shook hands, Trump using his left hand to grasp Kim's right arm. They exchanged pleasantries and then turned to the cameras for a photograph; three thousand journalists were there, broadcasting the historic meeting to all corners of the globe. Later, in a more intimate scene with their backs to the cameras, Kim through his translator said to Trump, "Many people in the world will think of this as a scene from a fantasy . . . science fiction movie." His comment presumably reflected the historical significance of the two sitting leaders from North Korea and the United States meeting for the first time and the extreme change from the confrontation of just a few months before the summit. Perhaps it betrayed his own incredulity about what it took to get him to that point in space and time, all of the historical forces that had to converge to propel him into this position, standing shoulder to shoulder with the president of the United States, a feat that neither his grandfather nor his father was able to accomplish in his lifetime. Kim had done it in less than seven years, at the age of thirty-four. In a rare move, the regime, keen to share Kim's victory with North Korea's twenty-five million people, transmitted the summit on live television through the Korean Central News Agency instead of the usual delayed broadcast.

During the nearly hour-long private conversation, facilitated by two interpreters, President Trump showed Kim a video, a fictional movie trailer that seemed to underscore the fantastical nature of the meeting. Kitschy, sensational, and dramatic, the four-minute video showed the two men as leading actors who would define the future, its soaring language intended to endow their encounter with immense historical significance and casting them as exceptional heroes among seven billion people in this narrative: "Featuring President Donald Trump and Chairman Kim Jong Un. In a meeting to remake history. To shine in the sun. One moment. One choice." While Trump and Kim were the protagonists, the film made it clear that Kim was the one who had to make a stark choice. It showed promise and peril. "History is always evolving," the solemn narrator intoned. "The past doesn't have to be the future. Out of darkness can come the light." A montage of fully stocked supermarkets, a bustling city with skyscrapers, scientists making breakthroughs at state-of-the-art laboratories, and men and women busily at work in factories and manufacturing plants accompanied the narration. On the other hand, if Kim chose his nuclear weapons over economic prosperity and "friendship," he would face war and deepening poverty.

Although Trump said, "I think he loved it," Kim might have seen the video as condescending and a reinforcement of his view about why he needed nuclear weapons to prevent the United States from taking the actions that it was threatening not only in the fall of 2017 but in the video itself. The film reflected the mirror-imaging apparent in Trump's prior statements and those of his senior officials that they could buy their way out of the nuclear impasse with North Korea. Trump later described what he told Kim. "As an example, they have great beaches. You see that whenever they're exploding their cannons into the ocean, right? I said, 'Boy, look at the view. Wouldn't that make a great condo behind?' And I explained, I said, 'You know, instead of doing that, you could have the best hotels in the world right there.' Think of it from a real estate perspective. You have South Korea, you have China, and they own the land in the middle." Of course, from Kim's perspective, it was building nuclear weapons, not condos, that got him to this summit.

Moreover, the Singapore joint communiqué, Trump's apparently unilateral concessions announced at his press conference, and his victory lap in the weeks following the summit negated whatever effect his administration was hoping would be achieved by the film. The communiqué, widely panned by Asia experts for its vague aspirational content, stated that the United States and North Korea would "commit to establish new U.S.-DPRK relations" and "build a lasting and stable peace regime on the Korean Peninsula." It also stated that the two sides would work toward recovering and repatriating remains of American service members killed during the Korean War. Most significantly, and most disappointingly, as it turned out, North Korea pledged to "work toward complete denuclearization of the Korean Peninsula," a sparse statement that pointed to the weakness of the U.S. position and showcased Trump's lack of understanding and the administration's inability to obtain a more detailed set of steps that North Korea should take to demonstrate Pyongyang's sincerity about denuclearization. The communiqué fell far short of previous ones, such as the 2005 Joint Statement of the Fourth Round of the Six-Party Talks that included Pyongyang's commitment to "abandoning all nuclear weapons and existing nuclear programs and returning, at an early date, to the Treaty on the Nonproliferation of Nuclear Weapons and to IAEA safe-guards."

Beneath the frothy statements, smiles, and handshakes, the summit produced little of substance, with no accountability for Kim Jong Un to cease and dismantle his nuclear weapons program. Trump crafted a narrative of success, saying in Singapore, "We had a really fantastic meeting, a lot of progress. . . . Better than anybody could have expected." He brushed away questions about the abductions issue that was a priority for Japan, as well as North Korea's human rights violations, which he had emphasized just a few months earlier. Trump also cast doubt on U.S. commitments to its alliances with South Korea and Japan, criticized U.S.–South Korean military exercises, and questioned the future of a U.S. troop presence in South Korea and Japan, breaking with U.S. policy and blindsiding the Pentagon and South Korean officials who then had to scramble to do damage control.

Instead, he made gratuitous comments complimenting Kim— "He is very talented. Anybody that takes over a situation like he did, at 26 years of age, and is able to run it, and run it tough. . . . Very few people, at that age—you can take one out of ten thousand, probably couldn't do it"—and raised the possibility of additional giveaways to Kim, such as a visit to the White House. Trump dismissed questions about more concrete measures, such as inspections and how he would measure Kim's sincerity and progress, by implying that the strength of their personal relationship and the president's deal-making prowess would lead to denuclearization. And the president seemed to take Kim's word for it, saying that Kim "said we have never gone this far. I don't think they've ever had the confidence, frankly, in a President than they have right now for getting things done and having the ability to get things done. And he was very firm in the fact that he wants to do this." On the way back from Singapore, Trump would tweet, "Just landed—a long trip, but everybody can now feel much safer than the day I took office. There is no longer a Nuclear Threat from North Korea," astonishing for its dishonesty or naïveté or both, in accrediting Kim's recycled talking points, trotted out by the regime over the past two decades to delay and deflect denuclearization, as a national security success.

Although certainly in line with his personal style, Trump's display of confidence was also a product of what Heuer called "vividness" bias: that "information that people perceive directly, that they hear with their own ears or see with their own eyes, is likely to have greater impact than information received secondhand that may have greater evidential value." Trump's personal interaction with Kim, physically and through the letters that Kim would send the president, weighed more in his mind than the cool, objective analyses of his intelligence agencies and the warnings from seasoned national security experts. Trump emphasized his confidence in his success in the ensuing days and months, stating that North Korea was "doing so much. And now we're well on our way to denuclearization." He took the opportunity to jab again at our ally South Korea: "I hated [the joint military exercises] from the day I came in. I said, why aren't we being reimbursed?" Moreover, Trump referred to the joint exercises as "war games," a favorite term of the North Korean regime because it implies the drills are belligerent and a preparation for invasion.

Kim Jong Un, for his part, said very little in public. Given the fact that he was able to secure statements from Trump that advanced his goal of chipping away at U.S. alliances in the region and obtain recognition as a nuclear weapons power, perhaps Kim perceived that he did not have to offer very much. After having declared the completion of his nuclear weapons program and demonstrated his capabilities, he had little to lose by publicizing the high-profile shuttering of the nuclear test site at Punggye-ri and agreeing to dismantle a missile test site at Sohae. These reversible and symbolic moves, eagerly embraced by President Trump and President Moon and others as signs of Kim's sincerity in making good on his promise to denuclearize, also probably only reinforced his belief that the theater of denuclearization was more important than doing anything actual or verifiable. At the summit, Kim ignored a question about whether he agreed to give up his nuclear weapons and spoke in generalities: "The world is going to see a major change. . . . It was not easy to get here. The past worked as fetters on our limbs, and the old prejudices and practices worked as obstacles on our way forward. But we overcame all of them today, and we are here today."

Kim might have been talking simply about the fact of the unprecedented meeting itself. But he might have been looking back with pride and self-satisfaction about how he had brought North Korea center stage despite the early criticisms and doubts about his leadership. As President Trump stood beside him, telling reporters that Kim was "a very worthy, very smart negotiator," perhaps Kim did believe that he was the hero in this fantasy that appeared to be gelling into reality.

But optics, spin, and performance aside, reality keeps puncturing the narrative of progress that the Trump and Moon administrations are trying to champion. Washington and Seoul continue to downplay reports that show Kim has been enriching uranium, expanding long-range missile bases, building new ballistic missiles, and upgrading nuclear weapons–related facilities, with Trump choosing to narrowly define progress on denuclearization as the absence of nuclear and ballistic missile testing. And even if it were true that Kim came to the negotiating table as a result of maximum pressure, his elevation as a star on television and in social media since 2018 has eroded the sanctions infrastructure that took herculean efforts to build. As maximum pressure morphed into maximum flexibility for North Korea, Kim is probably learning that both his in-your-face provocative actions and his passive-aggressive diplomatic intransigence are enough to ensure his survival and his country's relevance and independence. The North Korean threat still exists, and Trump's disingenuous claims otherwise mask the multiple dimensions of risk that it poses to regional and global security.

As the Trump administration started gearing up for a second Trump-Kim summit, National Security Adviser John Bolton admitted in early December that North Korea had not taken steps to move closer to denuclearization since Singapore. Vice President

Pence similarly acknowledged the lack of progress, when he told *Fox News Sunday* that at the next summit President Trump would urge Kim to take "concrete steps" toward denuclearization and that he would "lay out our expectations for North Korea."

In the months following the Singapore summit, nuclear negotiations between the United States and North Korea remained deadlocked. Kim made it clear that he does not intend to give up his nuclear weapons. As if in frustration over the insistence by Trump administration officials that North Korea's "fully and final verified denuclearization" must precede sanctions removal, the regime issued a commentary in late December that reiterated its existing position about refusing "unilateral disarmament" and showed how far apart Washington and Pyongyang were on an agreement of what "denuclearization" meant: "The proper definition of Korean Peninsula denuclearization is 'completely removing the United States nuclear threat against North Korea' before it is getting rid of our nuclear deterrent."

To underscore what he wants, Kim reiterated the regime's longstanding demands in his 2019 New Year's address—an end to the U.S.–South Korean military exercises, a peace mechanism to replace the 1953 armistice that ended the military conflict of the Korean War without formally ending the war, and the removal of sanctions—while declaring that he is ready "to meet the US president again anytime." Kim stressed Korean unity in an us-versus-them framework, most likely in an effort to appeal to ethnonationalism in both the North and the South. "We will never tolerate the interference and intervention of outside forces who stand in the way of national reconciliation," Kim said, and stressed that Koreans are "the master[s] of peace on the peninsula." President Moon touted the speech as having a "positive effect on resolving the Korean Peninsula issue smoothly in the new year," while President Trump tweeted, "I also look forward to meeting with Chairman Kim who realizes so well that North Korea possesses great economic potential!"

Trump and Kim met again in Hanoi for a second summit on February 27–28, 2019. Despite the weather—the temperature was

73 degrees but with a steaming, uncomfortable humidity over 90 percent—Kim was much more at ease in this meeting, as was Trump. Their body language was in sync: Both men rested their elbows casually on the table placed between them. They touched each other's elbows when they spoke and laughed easily, as if they were old friends. When they walked from one venue to another, Kim's gait was more confident, his arms swaying, his hand gestures easy and relaxed. In fact, he seemed to have gained weight since Singapore, his plumpness stretching his skin smooth, his growing size a metaphor for his enlarged stature since the start of his experiment with summitry. He smiled contentedly and appreciatively at President Trump's repeated statements about his desire to see North Korea become an "economic powerhouse." And Kim almost certainly took note of how Trump downplayed denuclearization when he reiterated that "speed is not that important to me. . . . What is important is that we do the right deal," and hinted at future summits ("I'm sure over the years we'll be together a lot"). Indeed, they would meet again just a few months later.

But the summit ended early. And there was no joint statement, as had been widely anticipated. Thousands of bewildered journalists who had camped out to capture the spectacle packed up and left, and Kim's motorcade departed quickly, as members of his entourage scrambled to jump into moving cars. Given the gaping hole between U.S. and North Korean expectations, the summit was little more than a vanity project, a product of both leaders' hubris and overconfidence that the sheer force of their charisma and their budding friendship could get them a good deal, even though they almost certainly were briefed by their working-level negotiators about the limited parameters of what the other side was asking for and willing to give. Like Trump, Kim miscalculated by gambling that he had a more malleable partner. Both his assessment that he could stymie working-level talks on the more sensitive issues of denuclearization and his coolness toward a peace declaration, including the U.S. proposal for establishing liaison offices in Washington and Pyongyang—an important step toward normalizing diplomatic ties—also laid bare that Kim was not serious about "peace" and that sanctions removal was more important than improving North Korea's relationship with the United States. Instead, he walked away after having failed to trade the closure of some unidentified portion of his aging Yongbyon nuclear research site in exchange for the lifting of the bulk of the more effective sanctions on North Korea's export industries, which would have amounted to billions of dollars in revenue that the regime could then have funneled back into the programs proscribed by the United States.

Yet Trump's mindset about the effectiveness of his positive relationship with Kim and his affinity and talent for big symbolic moves, improvisation, and drama were hard to shake. Four months after Hanoi, the president, in keeping with his personal brand of diplomacy, tweeted an offer to meet the North Korean leader at the DMZ just to "say hello." Trump was going to be on the Korean Peninsula that weekend anyway for a summit with Moon, but by crossing the MDL to meet with Kim, he became the first sitting U.S. president to set foot in the North. As they had in Singapore and Hanoi, the two men smiled broadly for the cameras, greeted each other warmly, and pledged to continue negotiations. Having learned the effectiveness of appealing to Trump's penchant for the theatrical, Kim played along, as he also surely recognized the value of creating the illusion of progress, even though the dictator's promises of economic prosperity for his people were growing increasingly hollow. Trump's preference for the top-down approach and strong hints about a future summit—he invited Kim to the White House again—without any nuclear concessions from Kim, only incentivized the regime to continue advancing its military capabilities and hew closely to its Trump-centric diplomacy.

So after impressive motorcades in Singapore and Hanoi, historic "firsts," flag-waving onlookers, media buildup, and expressions of mutual respect and admiration between President Donald Trump and Kim Jong Un, the U.S.–North Korean meetings produced . . . the status quo.

CONCLUSION

—▪—

THE METASTASIS

N NOVEMBER 2018, EBS, a South Korean public broadcasting channel, sparked a controversy when it released a 3-D puzzle in which children could create a figure of Kim Jong Un. The puzzle described Kim as "the youngest head-of-state in the world" and "a leader who took one more step to achieve world peace by denuclearizing the Korean Peninsula." Moon's political opponents, who had been criticizing Seoul's rapprochement with Kim, excoriated EBS for promoting "a dictator, whom children should never look up to." In response, EBS quickly backed down, saying the product would be discontinued and the puzzles that had been sold would be recalled.

The fact that EBS even thought to issue a children's puzzle softening Kim's image and celebrating his leadership showed a dramatic change in perceptions. It reflected the efforts of the Moon administration to transform Kim's role from adversary to partner in the quest for peninsula peace and unity and demonstrated the effectiveness of Kim's own efforts to shed his reputation as a murderous dictator through diplomacy and vague declarations about denuclearization. President Trump had also played a part, of course, in advancing Kim's image makeover since the Singapore summit and the flurry of diplomatic activity.

And the reduction of Kim Jong Un to a caricature does seem hard to resist. In fact, if you look at this children's puzzle, it might even be easy to forget that in 2019 Director of National Intelligence Dan Coats testified before Congress that North Korea "has for years underscored its commitment to nuclear arms," poses a "significant cyber threat," has shown a willingness to kill using chemical weapons, and has "conventional capabilities [that] continue to pose a threat" to the region and U.S. forces there. The problem arises when we derive policies from these softened caricatures and lose sight of who the man really is and the true nature of his strategic goals, while either overreacting or underreacting to his tactics and giving him space to continue to drive events on the Korean Peninsula.

KIM'S GOALS

Amid all the uncertainty and subterfuge surrounding one of the most intractable U.S. national security concerns, this much is clear: Kim Jong Un sees the possession of nuclear weapons as vital to achieving the development of North Korea's economy and cementing his country's strategic relevance and autonomy. These are key ingredients to solidifying his own power and ensuring the perpetuation of the Kim family dynasty. Judging from regime actions and propaganda since 2011, Kim has taken ownership of the program not only to highlight his power, independence, and unity of national purpose but to draw a contrast between North Korea and South Korea, which despite its wealth and international standing relies on an alliance with the United States for its national security. Kim Jong Un sees his country's military programs as a national symbol of prestige and modern progress, and has pegged his personal legacy and the Kim family dynasty to them. Moreover, he has elevated and embedded nuclear weapons into both the popular consciousness and the ideological, physical, and cultural landscape, enshrining them in the constitution and linking them to North Korea's prosperity.

Externally, Pyongyang wields its nuclear weapons program to deter a U.S. attack and invasion and to conduct coercive diplomacy—including the use of limited violence—to weaken Washington's alliances with Seoul and Tokyo, retain independence of action from Beijing, and maintain North Korea's strategic relevance amid wealthier and more powerful neighbors. Kim Jong Un has manufactured and exploited crisis situations by conducting provocative actions and cleverly uses the perception of the regime's unpredictability and volatility to extract economic and political concessions. Kim's technological advances and demonstrated capability to potentially hit the United States with a nuclear-tipped intercontinental ballistic missile locks in Washington's attention, which in turn affords him leverage to shape and drive the relationship with his neighbors. He can engage on his terms by exploiting Beijing's desire for stability and concern about being sidelined in nuclear or peace negotiations; Seoul's domestic priorities, such as the reunions of families separated by the Korean War and its current ambition to interweave the economies of the two Koreas; and Japan's fears of looking in from the outside and its priority of resolving the abductee issue. Kim—like his father—has preferred bilateral relationships, which give him the opportunity to play off regional rivalries, strategic competition, and historical animosities. And he has had some success in undermining sanctions through evasion techniques and with diplomacy.

Kim inherited much of his mindset and approach from his father, Kim Jong Il, but Jong Un has managed to accelerate and exploit North Korea's capabilities, despite deepening isolation and a growing list of sanctions. His brazenness and high risk tolerance emanate from the fact that he came to power with an advanced nuclear weapons program already in place. Kim Il Sung and Kim Jong Il sought to develop nuclear weapons; Kim Jong Un claims he completed the program. Kim Il Sung and Kim Jong Il aspired to international standing; Kim Jong Un scored three meetings with a sitting U.S. president as of this writing. Kim Jong Il downplayed the prospects for economic development and exhorted people to tighten their belts; Kim Jong Un created a socialist fairyland and told his people that they can have both nuclear weapons and prosperity. Kim Jong Il worked his way through the North Korean bureaucracy; Kim Jong Un landed at the top. Kim Jong Il shied away from the spotlight and was relatively more cautious, but like his grandfather, Kim Jong Un embraced publicity and actively marketed his image as a charismatic man of the people. And luckily for Kim Jong Un, his father was able to "maintain . . . control of the regime as the economy recovered from the famine, demonstrated a functioning nuclear device for national security, and bequeathed an intact polity for his son," as U.S. State Department analyst Patrick McEachern noted.

All of this indicates that Kim is highly unlikely to abandon his nuclear weapons program: precisely the intelligence community's long-held assessment. In fact, its conclusion is probably more valid now than ever before. Kim Jong Il was more willing to negotiate over his nuclear weapons in exchange for economic aid, probably to buy time as he covertly advanced his capabilities, but this approach might also have been an acknowledgment of the relative weakness of the regime's leverage due to its moribund economy and the fledgling nature of the strategic programs. However, to date, it is unclear if Kim Jong Un would even consider putting any part of the program on the negotiating table, given the regime's consistent refusal to "bargain" away its weapons, Kim's personal identification with them, their linkage to economic prosperity and national security, and the fact that they afford him a place on the international stage.

At the same time, Kim is not an irrational young dictator who is determined to start a war with the United States. Senator Lindsey Graham declared, "We're not going to let this crazy man in North Korea have the capability to hit the homeland." Nikki Haley, the U.S. ambassador to the United Nations, said at a meeting of the U.N. Security Council that Kim Jong Un was "begging for war" and called for the "strongest possible measures." Secretary of Defense James Mattis said that "any threat to the United States or its territories, including Guam, or our allies will be met with a massive military response." Such language was probably an effort to warn Pyongyang about the consequences of its actions and to assure allies and reflect the tensions of that moment, but it also expresses a strain of thinking that Kim is irrational and reckless, a notion that has stubbornly clung to discussions about him since he took the reins in 2011. However, this belief conflates capabilities with intentions, and assumes a strategic intent—that Kim seeks a nuclear war with the United States—that almost certainly does not exist.

Over the years the intelligence community has reiterated that Kim is rational and that his primary purpose for nuclear weapons is deterrence and international status toward securing regime survival. Kim is most likely to use his nuclear weapons against the United States or a U.S. ally only if he assesses that an attack on the North is imminent. Kim's personal stamp on the program, the regime's public celebration of various technical milestones through parades, the promotion of scientists and technicians, and the photographs and media statements all suggest that nuclear weapons are a source of great domestic pride and a vital part of Kim's brand. Moreover, the regime has consistently asserted, as it did in 2013 legislation "consolidating possession of nuclear weapons," that its nuclear arsenal is for deterrence and that the reason for the North's position is the United States. Kim stated at the time:

> When one is firmly equipped with the capability to make precision strikes with nuclear weapons against aggressors and strongholds of aggression, no matter where they are on the face of the earth, no aggressor can dare to attack recklessly, and the greater and more powerful the nuclear strike capability, the greater the power of deterring aggression will be. Especially in the case of our country, whose opponent is the United States . . . it is necessary to firmly bolster the nuclear armed forces both quantitatively and qualitatively.

Subsequent statements by the regime have continued to hew to a similar line. In his 2018 New Year's address, Kim said that North

Korea "as a peace-loving nuclear power . . . will not use a nuclear weapon as long as the aggressive hostile forces do not infringe upon our country's sovereignty and interests, and will not threaten any country or region with nuclear [weapons]. However, we will resolutely respond to any act of destroying peace and security on the Korean Peninsula." Kim has been punctuating this message while carefully constructing his image as a statesman, an identity that has certainly been enhanced by his repeated summits with regional leaders and the U.S. president. His 2019 New Year's address seemed designed to advance his standing as a responsible head of state. He addressed his country on television wearing a suit and tie, as he had since 2017, instead of a dark Mao jacket as in previous years, but now comfortably seated in an overstuffed leather chair. His appearance reinforced the speech's softer tone and message: Kim is a modern leader, relatable, powerful, and a responsible steward of a nuclear state. Evans Revere, a former top Asia expert in the State Department, presciently wrote in 2017, "The new goal, as Pyongyang sees it, is to discuss the terms under which the United States will accept and live with a nuclear-armed North Korea and agree to end 'hostility.' "

Given Kim's purported completion of his nuclear program, he is more unlikely than his father to give up something he owns that bolsters his own legitimacy and legacy. And in a way, Kim Jong Un's position in the world today vindicates Kim Jong Il, who labored through the hardest years so that he could bequeath to his son the gift of security and stature.

EXAMINING ASSUMPTIONS

Having been inured to expect belligerence from Kim Jong Un, analysts' mindsets were challenged by his abrupt turn toward diplomacy in early 2018. "Once an observer has formed an image . . . a mind-set or expectation," cautioned Richards Heuer, "this conditions future perceptions." In 2017, U.S. experts were calling Kim "crazy" and "irrational"; the next year the pendulum swung in the other direction, as many Korea watchers advocated measures that would assuage Kim's security concerns and integrate him into the international community. Visions of a North Korean "madman" wielding nuclear weapons against the United States alternated with glimpses of a North Korean statesman whose comments about a "new era" of peace and foreign relations aroused optimism about the potential for genuine improvements in U.S.–North Korean relations. The debates within and among the security communities in the region and in the United States still reflect these widely differing opinions about North Korea's intentions.

Some Korea experts, intrigued by the possibilities of diplomacy, have placed a higher priority on inducements rather than pressure. North Korean outreach can look like a gambit for peace, especially when amplified by the U.S. president's friendly tweets, social media postings of a smiling Kim Jong Un and his lovely, stylish wife, and televised summits that show him acting like a global leader who is an old hand at conducting foreign negotiations.

The thought of peace on the Korean Peninsula and an economically integrated North Korea is tantalizing. In the minds of well-meaning peace activists and academics encouraged by Kim's turn to diplomacy, North Korea has always wanted a security guarantee from the United States, and its development of nuclear weapons is a logical reaction to the perceived threat that Washington poses to Pyongyang, which fears a second war if it does not have the armaments to deter a military strike. For some of these peace advocates, the United States bears responsibility for the division of the Korean Peninsula because the nature of its alliance with South Korea, especially the mutual defense treaty and overwhelming U.S. military might, created and perpetuated the emergence of a paranoid and repressive state in North Korea. They and others have argued the logic of North Korea's resistance to denuclearization without a peace treaty and sanctions removal, given that the two sides are technically in a state of war. Using the pain of sanctions as leverage, the Moon and Trump administrations hoped to turn Kim's focus toward economic development, in an attempt to lure North Korea into denuclearizing if it received enough economic incentives. Some academics insist that Kim wants to be a great *economic* reformer; according to one Asia scholar, Kim wants "North Korea to become a normal East Asian economy, catch up with and integrate into the region."

They might be right, but only if we accept the assumption that North Korea perceives the United States as its only threat and the nuclear weapons program was set up strictly for defensive and deterrence purposes. But that's not the case. In fact, the Kim family sees a multitude of threats to its survival: the United States, to be sure; South Korea; China; and ultimately, its own people. And since he came to power in December 2011, Kim Jong Un has systematically tackled these challenges through the regime's nuclear weapons program, coercive diplomacy, and repression.

Let me explain why I believe that Kim is not looking for a peace treaty with the United States. First, the case for getting the United States to agree to a peace declaration and to grant security guarantees depends on the key assumption that Kim's idea of peace is linked to relinquishing his nuclear weapons. Indeed, a peace declaration and the exchange of a liaison office in Washington and Pyongyang were both under consideration at the Hanoi summit, until the meeting ended abruptly, in part because Kim placed a higher priority on the removal of sanctions rather than on steps that would move the two countries toward a more normal relationship. The history of North Korea's nuclear ambitions, the ideological infrastructure that the Kim dynasty has built over the decades, and the regime's own public statements strongly suggest that peace— from Pyongyang's perspective—is achievable *because* it has nuclear weapons.

The regime requires a "hostile" outside world to justify the diversion of scarce resources into military programs, to be able to cast blame on others for the problems in its economy, and to maintain the mythology of the Kim family as the protectors of North Korea's existence. Sheila Miyoshi Jager, a professor of East Asian Studies, has argued that "the *disruption* [emphasis in original] of peace has been North Korea's main strategic goal since 1950, when it invaded South Korea." The goal of its propaganda, education, and monuments to the Korean War and the guerrilla struggles is to continually revisit and revive fear of the United States. For Kim Jong Un in particular, who overcame the succession odds and doubts about his age and faced down "fire and fury" from the United States, the purported completion of the nuclear weapons program was "a great victory," and a "powerful treasured sword for defending peace" that would "reliably guarantee" North Korea's security and prosperity. Following the sixth nuclear test in September 2017 and the tests of intercontinental ballistic missiles that year, NK News reported that North Korean state media held rallies to celebrate the "completion of the state nuclear force" and showed officials giving thanks to Kim for providing for the "eternal rosy future of the country."

Kim must see good reason to seek to preserve his garrison state. Self-reliance and his political will and leadership got him to the place where his regime could boast about multiple meetings with the U.S. president after having obtained strategic equivalence. He trusts only himself to safeguard North Korea's security and his own survival. Kim was explicit that the nuclear button is on *his* desk. If he has learned anything from his country's history, it is that *no one* can be trusted, even allies like China and Russia that chose to normalize relations with South Korea and signed on to United Nations sanctions. Japan, the former imperial power and colonizer, cannot be trusted, of course; neither can South Korea, whose various presidents have chosen to punish the regime for terroristic activities and its nuclear weapons program. Add to the mix the tumultuous politics of democratic governments in the United States, South Korea, and Japan—the United States holds presidential elections every four years, with corresponding policy changes; South Korea elects a president who is limited to a single five-year term—which contribute to a low likelihood of long-term sustainability for policies that might be favorable to North Korea. That risk is probably too much for North Korea to entertain.

Kim doesn't trust his own people either, and like his father and grandfather, he fears the penetration of information that would accompany economic integration with North Korea's regional powers. He doesn't have to look too far for examples of what happens when the people are empowered and connected. The yearlong candlelight protests in South Korea, inspired by legitimate grievances against the Park Geun-hye government for its corruption, and fueled by social media wielded by a vibrant civil society, toppled the former dictator's daughter—the nation's first female president—in 2017. Kim's tightening of borders; his draconian punishment for those who attempt to defect, engage in unsanctioned market activities, or consume South Korean soap operas, films, books, and music; and his extensive surveillance networks point to his understanding of the potentially destabilizing effects that reforms and relaxation of his regime's repressive measures might inflict on his country. In addition to these defensive measures, Kim's creation of his own intranet, his support for a consumer culture and the domestic production of luxury goods and services, and his efforts to modernize regime propaganda to make it more palatable to a population increasingly attracted to South Korean and Chinese tastes reflect his offensive efforts to shape and control his citizens' minds.

Moreover, as much as the young leader wants prosperity for North Korea, economic reforms and integration would require foreign investment, innovation, entrepreneurship, and attendant incentives to foster development. It would mean greater information flows into the country and among the populace, which would be likely to lead to an unraveling of the mythology that has enshrouded and buttressed the Kim family rule. A prosperous South Korea— a country with an economy that ranks among the global leaders, that shares a border, history, and language, whose people are supposed to be living under the suffocating yoke of American imperialism— poses an existential threat to the Kim regime. Jager concisely sums up this argument: "South Korea's miraculous story of economic growth and democratic progress threatens the regime's hold on power precisely because the more North Koreans know about the South, the less likely they are to put up with the conditions of pov-

erty and repression at home." Moreover, in a post-unification scenario, the elite party and military officials who control the trading
companies and the smaller-scale market players would also lose out
to more sophisticated, organized, and educated South Korean capitalists.

Kim's interests thus lie in conflict not peace, in autarky rather
than integration, and in the possession of nuclear weapons, which
make his survival and long-term Kim family control of the country
possible, not denuclearization.

HUBRIS

In fact, we should be concerned that Kim might move toward a
more expansive vision of how he could use his nuclear and missile
programs to advance offensive objectives—such as creating conditions conducive to the unification of the Korean Peninsula, his
grandfather's dream. He has grown significantly bolder since 2011,
having expanded the boundaries of international tolerance for his
bad behavior and stopping just short of actions that might lead to
U.S. or allied military responses that would threaten his regime.
Rather than striving for nuclear war or peace and normalization
with the United States, North Korea's actions, statements, history,
and ideology are more consistent with the country's long-held aspi-
ration for reunification on its own terms. Kim Jong Un's efforts to
diversify nuclear weapons, develop a second-strike nuclear capability, upgrade conventional armaments and training, and improve
surveillance and reconnaissance competence certainly appear to be
above and beyond North Korea's stated desire for mere deterrence.
A panel of former security officials, academic experts, and CIA analysts concluded in 1998—but it still holds true today—that "the regime derives its ideological legitimacy from its mission to unify
Korea."

Richard Bush, a Brookings scholar and former national intelligence officer for East Asia, wrote in 2017 that "the real danger [of
North Korea's pace and success in its nuclear developments] stems

from the possibility of weakened alliances and unchecked escalation in the Korean Peninsula that could spiral out of control." Bush raised alarms about the "decoupling" issue—the possibility that if North Korea has the capability to hit the United States, Washington would be unwilling to risk San Francisco in order to save Seoul, thus undermining U.S. credibility and influence in the region. Moreover, Kim's confidence about his ability to deter the United States could lead him to believe that he can conduct conventional attacks against South Korea to probe Seoul's resolve, expand the space for his maneuvers, sow division within South Korea, and drive a wedge between the United States and its ally. North Korea could do all of these things without using any nuclear weapons—or for that matter, firing artillery. Kim has already succeeded in wielding the peace and diplomacy card to chip away at the U.S. alliance with South Korea and rehabilitated his global image by normalizing North Korea's nuclear status and repugnant human rights violations, and we know he will continue to do so.

His confidence may be bolstered by the fact that he has yet to face a real "crisis" of the kind that his grandfather and his father had to confront. Kim's belief that he can, in the future, repeat his tactic of renewing provocative actions to get his way and then turn on the charm to deflate or mitigate international punishment has undoubtedly been reinforced by his success in securing summits without making concessions on his nuclear weapons program. His perceptions about his freedom of action depend on his likely assumptions that Washington would be deterred from taking military actions; Beijing and Moscow would not abandon his regime; the United States and China would seek to rein in aggressive South Korean or Japanese military actions against North Korea; and Washington would restrain Seoul and Tokyo from developing their own nuclear inventories.

So far, since Kim has come to power, these assumptions have been confirmed, even during the period of Kim's most blustery rhetoric and provocations. Over the years, Beijing's leaders have stuck to their line about "all sides"—meaning not just North Korea but also the United States and South Korea—needing to "remain calm and exercise restraint" and resolve issues through dialogue to "maintain regional peace and stability." Xi Jinping's first visit to Pyongyang in June 2019—despite the lack of progress on North Korean denuclearization—and his pledge that Beijing will strengthen its ties with the North, surely assuaged any concerns in the Kim regime about its neighbor's commitment to it. Russia, too, has been a relatively reliable partner of the regime; for example, at the U.N. Security Council in September 2018 and again in December 2019, Russia joined with China to call for the easing of sanctions and to encourage concessions for North Korea, despite reports of its ongoing nuclear weapons activities. Moscow's 2014 cancellation of 90 percent of North Korea's $11 billion debt and Kim's first meeting with Putin in April 2019 probably showed Kim that his attempts to build support from his two powerful neighbors are bearing fruit as both signal that they would not abandon his country.

Kim has also witnessed how Washington has no desire for a military conflict and that South Korea and the United States would restrain each other from taking actions that could potentially spark a war. President Moon has been vocal in his opposition to a U.S. military strike against the North. All previous U.S. administrations had considered nuclear or conventional military strikes against the North, but backed down because the cost in lives would have been devastating, and Kim certainly knows this. Washington has also been resistant to potentially escalatory actions by South Korea. During Kim Jong Un's grooming process in 2010, North Korea fired artillery against a South Korean island, Yeonpyeong-do, while Seoul was conducting military drills. After North Korea's sinking of the South Korean warship *Cheonan* earlier that year, South Korea was in no mood to back down from Pyongyang's threats that it would respond if Seoul went ahead with these prescheduled drills. As recounted in Van Jackson's *On the Brink,* the Obama administration was worried about what the conservative Lee Myung-bak government might do and successfully pleaded with the South Koreans not to take retaliatory action against the North.

Once these assumptions are cemented in his mind as fact, Kim will probably continue to conduct limited acts of aggression, using cyber and other coercive tools to keep North Korea's rivals off balance. We should be worried about how he could be emboldened to take provocative actions to test the hypothesis that he won't suffer any consequences. Even if Washington once again seriously contemplates the military strike option, the United States faces an increased risk of a miscalculation that spirals into an unintended clash if Kim misreads a potential next confrontation as a paper tiger, like the "fire and fury" of 2017 turned out to be. Moreover, if U.S.–North Korean relations deteriorate to that degree, and the United States stands alone, unsupported by its allies, Kim's self-assurance and perception of his relative strength will only be bolstered.

But Kim is not invulnerable. "North Korea's fundamental liabilities are systemic and enduring," longtime North Korea expert Jonathan Pollack has argued, and "the vision of a self-reliant country bears little relation to North Korea's actual needs," particularly given Kim's lofty promises of economic development *and* nuclear weapons. The consequences of the regime's actions and the country's isolation are taking a toll: The pool of trading partners has shrunk to essentially one—China, which accounts for more than 90 percent of North Korea's trade.

And the maximum pressure sanctions are adding to North Korea's troubles. In 2017, North Korea's number two trading partner, India, accounted for only slightly more than $7 million of imports and exports (a decrease of 10 percent from the prior year), and Russia was a distant number three at around $2 million (a 70 percent decrease). Inter-Korean trade plummeted to about $1 million that year, down from $333 million in 2016, deepening the gap between the Koreas and undoubtedly exacerbating North Korea's fears about absorption in a unification scenario. (According to market research firm IHS Markit, North Korea's total trade was around $6.4 billion in 2016, less than that of Malta, which has a fraction of the population—less than half a million compared with North Korea's twenty-five million. Total trade in South Korea was $835 billion,

130 times more than in the North.) North Korea's trade deficit with China ballooned to almost $2 billion in 2017, with exports to China down almost 90 percent to $210 million—the lowest since 2001—and imports down 33 percent to $2.2 billion. In 2018, as a result of Beijing's sanctions implementation, North Korea's trade with China dropped almost 50 percent from the prior year, resulting in a similar decline in the country's overall foreign trade volume, given its overwhelming dependence on its powerful neighbor. North Korea's economy overall shrank by about 5 percent in 2018, reducing it to a level comparable to the regime's economic situation in 1997, when the country was in the midst of a devastating famine. And for the first time since he came to power, Kim saw his country's foreign trade fall below $3 billion. Kim is almost certainly aware of the toll that his weapons program has taken on his push for economic prosperity.

North Korea does not publicize its own economic statistics, of course, but anecdotal information and reports trickling out of the country in early 2019 suggest that the regime is shuttering or suspending activity and production at government-backed factories and mines amid a drying up of trade and restrictions on flows of oil into the country, and that it is trying to squeeze more from North Korean overseas laborers to fund various projects in the country. North Korea's dispatching of its diplomats to cultivate relationships with its neighbors, as well as with Europe and Southeast Asia, is surely intended to drum up investment and trade ties. These internal developments and trends, such as greater information penetration, marketization, and the growth of a newly wealthy class driven more by money than ideology, are probably stressing Pyongyang and adding to concerns that these conditions could potentially overwhelm the regime as it buckles under the weight of internal contradictions and rising expectations.

Kim Jong Un no doubt understands at least the broad contours of the challenges he faces. And he is likely to use diplomacy to mitigate the negative effects of his actions, including ensuring that China will not turn its back on his country, exploiting any cleavage among the regional players, encouraging foreign investment and aid from South Korea and other countries to lessen Pyongyang's dependence on China, and reducing the world's appetite for sanctions implementation. There is little doubt that Kim wants to stimulate North Korea's economic development, not just muddle through like his father, especially since he is probably planning to be in power for the next few decades and pass down a stable, thriving, nuclear-armed North Korea to one of his children. Amid rising expectations— especially among young people and the *jangmadang* generation, who are more individualistic than their elders—the crippling effects of sanctions, and North Korea's intentional isolation, it will be difficult for Kim to sufficiently match reality with his aspirations and rhetoric.

But his ability to quickly pivot to diplomacy and secure a slew of summits with the United States, China, South Korea, and Russia in just a matter of months has probably boosted his confidence that he can accomplish these goals at little or no cost to his weapons program. Kim's calibration of provocations and diplomacy, as well as his adroit use of ambiguity and flattery, also underscore how we must be clear-eyed about his goals, while also maintaining analytic agility in our assessment of his intentions and identifying risks and opportunities in a given scenario.

THE EVOLVING PUZZLE

If figuring out Kim's intentions is like completing a jigsaw puzzle, crafting a solution to the North Korea problem should be likened to solving the Rubik's Cube. This 3-D puzzle befuddles players with seemingly endless permutations, only to frustrate them further when they see that even though they've solved one side, the other five are a jumble of colors. Denuclearization is a primary goal of any solution; another high priority is choking off North Korea's ability to generate revenue for the regime and its nuclear weapons program, which has grown by leaps and bounds since he came to power—it is more diverse, more mobile, and more dangerous—and poses unacceptable threats to global security.

But we also have to keep an eye on the multiple dimensions of the North Korean threat that have metastasized since Kim came to power, as well as how his perception of the hazards that loom inside and outside his country is developing and changing. Kim's personalization of the nuclear weapons program and promises of a socialist fairyland—and ownership of the man-to-man diplomacy with Trump, Xi, Moon, and Putin—could put an unwelcome and dangerous spotlight on his failure to deliver on his promise to improve North Korea's economy. Shaking Kim's key assumptions about his freedom of action, maintaining a long-term strategy that breaks the cycle of provocation and reward, and raising the costs for his bad behavior will require Washington's credibility to follow through, close cooperation among the United States, the Northeast Asian countries, and the international community to defend and deter against North Korean adventurism, and, perhaps most frustratingly, time.

To intensify North Korea's internal contradictions, sharpen the choices that Kim has to make, and alter his risk calculus, the United States, its regional allies, and the global community must undertake coordinated and consistent actions—a calibration of pressure and negotiations in public and private—toward convincing Kim that nuclear weapons make his survival *less* rather than more secure. Sanctions and economic carrots—and threats of military action—are unlikely to get him to budge on abandoning his arsenal, unless we also acknowledge and exploit the totality of Kim's fears, concerns, and desires. Our policies should aim at both external pressure and methods to increase the domestic costs for Kim. The central question, then, is not how do we make Kim feel more "secure" by giving him what he demands, as some activists and academics argue, but rather, how do we alter Kim's calculus in a way that compels him to believe that nuclear weapons are a greater threat to his rule and dynastic preservation than an asset?

To do so, we must first focus on alliances. Any real or perceived fissures among allies and partners, as well as questions about U.S. credibility and commitment to the region, only play to Kim's advantage, affording him the space to disrupt regional stability and conduct acts of violence that fall just below the threshold for regional or international military retaliation that could threaten the survival of his regime. North Korea has threatened to test a hydrogen bomb in the Pacific. It continues to bolster its ability to attack Japan and South Korea and has in the past engaged in deadly attacks against South Korea. It continues cyberactivities to generate revenue for the regime. And it is a proliferator of conventional and unconventional weapons, having transferred missiles and related technologies to Iran and Syria. North Korea has used these tactics even during periods in which it was engaging in diplomacy.

Unequivocal declarations and demonstrations of U.S. commitment to its alliances and its allies' security and increased regional defense cooperation, especially between South Korea and Japan, would temper North Korea's proclivity to undertake actions that undermine regional stability. As Ryan Hass, the former China director at the National Security Council, and I have argued in a Brookings Foreign Policy Brief, the first thing that Washington and its allies Seoul and Tokyo should do is develop a menu of options that the three countries are jointly prepared to execute to minimize the North Korean threat, and also use that menu to present Beijing with the choice of either cooperating or stepping aside as the three parties move forward. The list could include covert and overt actions against North Korea, as well as steps that Seoul and Tokyo would take to strengthen their own security if certain threatening conditions are reached. Such an agreement would reduce the potential for Japan and South Korea to take unilateral actions that could undercut global efforts against North Korea, while encouraging Beijing to put pressure on Pyongyang rather than shield it.

Second, we need to maintain and build on maximum pressure sanctions designed to create leverage in negotiations, prevent the proliferation of North Korea's nuclear and ballistic missile technologies, and retard their efforts to make additional nuclear advancements. But sanctions don't implement themselves and they need time to work. They require U.S. leadership and initiative, allies and partners, including China, to maintain vigilance against North Korean violations, and a unity of purpose and understanding that sanctions implementation is necessary if there is to be any chance of North Korea abandoning its nuclear weapons.

The importance of coordinated international action was highlighted by the March 2019 release of the annual report of the U.N. Panel of Experts, the group in charge of monitoring the implementation of U.N. Security Council sanctions on North Korea. The report documents the breadth of sanctions violations and evasion tactics used by North Korea and its third-party facilitators. Singaporean companies reportedly have knowingly shipped banned luxury items to North Korea. South Korean government officials transferred petroleum products to the North, despite a U.S. warning that Pyongyang had already exceeded the cap on such imports, and Seoul also failed to report these transfers, flouting U.N. regulations and requirements. North Korean representatives of the regime's financial institutions continue to travel freely and do business in a number of different countries, including China, Syria, the United Arab Emirates, and Russia. The international community must also work harder to deter North Korean cyberattacks, which the U.N. report indicates are used to evade financial sanctions. The cooperation of Beijing in particular is required to shut down malicious cyber actors using Chinese networks or operating in China, a favored location due to its permissive environment. Together, these violations keep the Kim regime afloat and feed its defiance of international rules and norms.

Third, Washington should intensify efforts at sustained and institutionalized dialogue with regional stakeholders through five-party talks with South Korea, Japan, China, and Russia as a signal of international unity of purpose. The group can use this forum to discuss the range of economic and other benefits that the community is willing to grant if Pyongyang makes the strategic decision to abandon its nuclear weapons program, and assuage Pyongyang's concerns about the sustainability of any deal beyond electoral events and leadership changes in the region and in the United States. The stakeholders should also develop scenarios and responses in anticipation of potential future North Korean actions designed to surprise, confuse, and diminish international cooperation.

Fourth, we must direct our efforts to erode the infrastructure of repression that the Kim family has built and Kim Jong Un has buttressed with modern tools and techniques. The United States and the global community should seek to increase stress on the North Korean regime, and the U.S. president should appoint a special envoy on human rights, a position that the Trump administration jettisoned. A lifting of sanctions without a discernible loosening of Kim's cruel grip on his people would make it impossible to verify any potential denuclearization steps in the absence of an open information environment in North Korea, in which scientists, technicians, and military officials are free to provide accurate data without fear of reprisal from the government.

Finally, the United States should invest in programs that encourage information penetration into North Korea, as well as craft and disseminate a credible, alternative vision for a post-nuclear era that would help to increase regime fragility or Kim's perception of regime fragility to encourage him and his leadership to be more responsive to internal pressures. The goal would be to tap into a mostly neglected group of stakeholders—the North Korean people. After ten years of study and countless hours interviewing hundreds of North Korean defectors, Jieun Baek, author of *North Korea's Hidden Revolution,* has stressed the necessity of increasing the flow of information into North Korea in order to create positive change: "Information dissemination is significant because North Koreans are demanding it. . . . Access to more information gives North Korean people the agency, self-determination, and knowledge to write their own future and destiny as a nation." The former director of national intelligence James Clapper, for whom I served as the deputy national intelligence officer for Korea at the National Intelligence Council, would have concurred with this assessment. In his memoir he lamented that we had "limited means to satisfy the [North Korean] citizens' hunger for information" and concluded, "I believe, and have advocated, that to counter North Korea, the United States needs to consider capitalizing on our greatest strengths: openness and information." Empowering the North Korean people toward creating an internal environment to shape Kim's choices in a positive direction is a necessary component of the external pressures of sanctions and diplomacy.

There are no silver bullets, and any policy must be sustained over time before it shows any demonstrable effect. A policy along the lines I've just enumerated also requires U.S. leadership, disciplined implementation, and an international coalition with a common understanding of the accompanying risks and opportunities. These steps should also be paired with U.S. willingness to keep the window open for talks with the North.

Kim's return to provocative actions is a matter of when, not if. Since the Hanoi summit, Kim's "plan B" seems to be taking shape, and it looks a lot like the coercive diplomacy of his father's days: trying to cast North Korea as the aggrieved party, calibrating provocative actions and statements to attempt to put the pressure on Washington to budge, and engaging bilaterally with regional leaders. While touting his good personal relationship with Trump and the importance of dialogue and negotiations, Kim emphasized in an April 12, 2019, speech to the Supreme People's Assembly that "the United States will not be able to move us one iota nor get what it wants at all, even if it sits with us a hundred times, a thousand times." He warned of a "bleak and very dangerous" situation if the United States does not change its "hostile" policies toward North Korea and claimed that "we will be patient and wait till the end of this year to see whether the United States makes a courageous decision or not."

Kim had already been following through on his tough talk, providing hints about how he seeks to fortify his leverage. In April 2018, he observed the test of a new tactical guided weapon, which the regime media claimed could carry a powerful warhead. The following month, North Korea announced that Kim Jong Un had supervised a drill along the East Sea that demonstrated "large-caliber, long-range multiple rocket launchers and tactical guided weapons," the first ballistic missile tests since November 2017, violating existing U.N. sanctions and the Panmunjom Declaration in which the two Koreas pledged to "alleviate the acute military tension." In July 2019, North Korea's state media reported that Kim inspected a newly built submarine that might be intended for launching ballistic missiles, and instructed his officials to "steadily and reliably increase the national defense." Three months later, in October 2019, the North tested a ballistic missile from a sea-based platform, suggesting that Kim is continuing to improve the regime's military capabilities despite his diplomatic engagement. And he presided over a series of missile tests that same month. In all, as of December 2019, North Korea has conducted two dozen ballistic missile tests. We should expect more aggressiveness from Kim. As he rang in the New Year, Kim defiantly declared that "the world will witness a new strategic weapon" and hinted at a return to nuclear and ICBM tests. Kim seems to be intent on improving his military options, underscoring for us the limits of diplomacy and more clearly defining the outlines of his ambitions.

In the shadow of "fire and fury," the potential for a catastrophic miscalculation is higher, as Kim has learned by now that U.S. threats of military action are not credible. In any future confrontation with the United States, Kim might be more inclined to keep escalating tensions, not realizing that the threat calculus of Washington, Beijing, Seoul, and Tokyo has changed and that these countries' threshold for responding militarily may have lowered. War is simply not an option, as much as the current, past, and future U.S. administrations might have considered or will consider it, but neither is accommodation with a young, aggressive, and risk-tolerant dictator on whose whims and personal preferences our security cannot depend. As his skyscrapers and missiles triumphantly pierce the sky, Kim risks, like Icarus flying too close to the sun, making promises that he can't fulfill and overestimating how high he can soar.

EVEN THOUGH WE HAVE gleaned more insights about North Korea's dictator, there are still lots of unknowns and gaps in our knowledge that will keep Korea experts busy scrutinizing the latest regime statements; Kim's personal health and habits; who's in and who's out in the never-ending cycles of purges, demotions, and promotions; the capabilities of the latest weapons; the attitudes of the market generation toward the government; the impact of sanctions on elite support for the regime—the list goes on. New leaders will come and go in the capitals of the United States, South Korea, and Japan, and even in Russia and China, but a nuclear-armed Kim dynasty is likely to endure for the foreseeable future.

My copy of Heuer's book is dog-eared, with several passages underlined and multiple pages flagged with colorful Post-it notes. As Kim Jong Un nears his second decade as North Korea's leader in 2021, the relevance of Heuer's now twenty-year-old book will endure because the players, events, and circumstances will change, altering regional dynamics and policies, and requiring new research and fresh analysis, as well as a revisiting of assumptions. His warnings about recognizing our biases will never cease to resonate for analysts because, as he noted, "mind-sets are neither good nor bad; they are unavoidable." Heuer, who passed away at the age of ninety-one in August 2018, wrote that our perception of reality is inescapably influenced by "past experience, education, cultural values, role requirements, and organizational norms." This reminder applies equally to the dictator in Pyongyang. Kim Jong Un's mindset has been shaped by his understanding of the history of his family and country and his role in it, his neighbors' actions, his experiences in manipulating his internal and external environments, and his awareness about his relative strengths and weaknesses vis-à-vis the political, military, and economic challenges he faces.

Yet Kim is still in the process of becoming—learning, adapting, and adjusting. We have to shape and constrain his ambitions and illusions, as his visions about his legacy and North Korea's future reach new, and more dangerous, heights.

ACKNOWLEDGMENTS

Writing this volume has been thrilling and humbling. In the process, I have come to realize how lucky I am to have the support, guidance, and friendship of so many individuals, whose generosity, scholarship, and sense of humor nourish me and give me strength.

I am grateful for Strobe Talbott, then president of Brookings, who encouraged me to write the Brookings Essay, "The Education of Kim Jong Un," from which this book grew, and dedicated the organization's resources and the enormous talent of the editorial, creative, and communications teams to make it a success. Bruce Jones has invested in me from the moment I stepped through the doors and ensured that I had everything I needed to thrive at Brookings. Mike O'Hanlon has been my champion, mentor, and friend, who read the manuscript in full and facilitated the external review process with three anonymous reviewers whose thoughtful suggestions made this a better book. The wisdom of Richard Bush and Mireya Solis is a daily source of strength and inspiration, and I am also thankful for their comments on the initial draft. My dear friends and colleagues Ryan Hass and Jonathan Pollack read parts of the manuscript and offered their insights. Nat Kretchun generously read a chapter and contributed important comments, and Mark Lippert gave helpful suggestions and encouragement. I am also thankful for SK Group, the Korea Foundation, and other donors for their generous financial support of the Korea Chair.

I am indebted to Paul Park, a gifted researcher, writer, and administrator, who helped me in my transition to the think tank world, as well as in juggling my multiple Korea projects. Jasmine Zhao, Eun Dubois, Sam Crosby, and Ethan Jewell also provided valuable assistance for the book, and Brookings librarians Laura Mooney and Sarah Chilton patiently fielded my requests for obscure articles and books. All errors are mine.

Outside of Brookings, I have been thrilled to find a collegial community of Korea watchers and Asia and nonproliferation experts, many of whom were former colleagues in the U.S. government.

Although I left the intelligence community (IC), it has not left me. I still have that sense of mission: to provide objective, rigorous, policy-relevant analysis. It was a privilege to serve in the Central Intelligence Agency and at the National Intelligence Council. To my mentors, sponsors, managers, and colleagues still in the IC— thank you. And sincere thanks to the officers at the CIA's Publications Review Board, who reviewed this manuscript in the requested time.

My agent, Bridget Matzie, shepherded me through the entire process and cheered me on the whole way. My editor, the brilliant Susanna Porter, and her team at Ballantine made masterful contributions to the manuscript and made the volume so much better than I could have imagined.

Finally, I thank my husband, Jay, and my children, who bring me so much joy and fill my days with hugs and laughter, and Dick and Carol Habermann, who have warmly welcomed me into their lives and treat me like I am one of their own children. Nothing would have been possible without my parents, Ok Sook and Kwan S. Pak, who sacrificed everything to immigrate to the United States and taught me courage and perseverance.

NOTES

ABBREVIATIONS

AP   Associated Press
LAT   *Los Angeles Times*
NYT   *The New York Times*
SCMP *South China Morning Post*
WP   *The Washington Post*
WSJ   *The Wall Street Journal*

PROLOGUE

xii   *Everyone knew that Kim:* Steven Erlanger, "Doctor Confirms Kim Jong-il Stroke," *NYT,* December 11, 2008.

xii   *South Korea convened:* "North Korean Leader Kim Jong Il Dead after Heart Attack, State Media Reports," CNN, December 19, 2011.

xii   *Japan set up a crisis:* "Reactions to Kim Jong Il's Death," *The Huffington Post,* December 19, 2011; "North Koreans Mourn Kim Jong-il after 'Heart Attack,'" BBC News, December 19, 2011.

xii   *"At the head of our revolution today":* "North Korea Agency Officially Informs Citizens about Dear Leader's Death," *BBC Monitoring Asia Pacific,* December 19, 2011, accessed via LexisNexis.

xiii   *The U.K. ambassador:* Choe Sang-Hun, "North Korea's 'Dear Young General' Has Made His Mark," *NYT,* September 30, 2011.

xiii   *Octogenarian elites bowed:* Ibid.

xiii   *"North Korea as we know it":* Victor Cha, "China's Newest Province?," *NYT,* December 19, 2011.

xiv   *Most experts saw:* Andrew Salmon, "Power Behind Kim Jong-Un's Throne: The 'Gang of Seven' Emerges from the Shadows," *The Telegraph,* December 31, 2011.

xiv   *In the journal* Asian Perspectives: Patrick McEachern, "Centralizing North Korean Policymaking under Kim Jong Un," *Asian Perspectives* 43, no. 1 (2019): 60–61, doi:10.1353/apr.2019.0001.

xiv   *Within the first two years:* Chico Harlan, "In North Korea, Kim Jong Un Rises and Advisers Are Shoved Aside," *WP,* December 13, 2013.

ONE: FROM TEN-FOOT-TALL BABY TO INTERNATIONAL STATESMAN

4   *"must quickly sift":* Central Intelligence Agency, "Analytic Positions," Careers & Internships, last updated April 12, 2019, https://www.cia.gov/careers/opportunities/analytical.

5   *One of his key points:* Richards J. Heuer, Jr., *Psychology of Intelligence Analysis* (Washington, D.C.: Center for the Study of Intelligence, Central Intelligence Agency, 1999), 10.

6   *An article in* The Washington Post: Marc Fisher, "Too Much Power for Young Hands?," *WP,* December 23, 2011.

6   *Citing an East German:* Don Oberdorfer, *The Two Koreas: A Contemporary History* (New York: Basic Books, 2001), 349.

7   *North Korean media released:* Martin Fackler, "On North Korean TV, a Dash of (Unapproved) Disney Magic," *NYT,* July 9, 2012.

7   *He threatened to turn:* "North Korea Threatens 'Sea of Fire' for South Korea Presidential Office," *The Telegraph,* November 22, 2013.

8   *He called the U.S. president:* Anna Fifield, "Kim Jong Un Calls Trump a 'Mentally Deranged U.S. Dotard,'" *WP,* September 21, 2017.

9   *Are those who tout:* Zachary Cohen and Kevin Liptak, "Trump Praises Kim Jong Un as Honorable, Refuses to Explain Why," CNN, April 25, 2018.

TWO: GUERRILLAS AND GODS

11   *"To North Koreans":* Bradley K. Martin, *Under the Loving Care of the Fatherly Leader: North Korea and the Kim Dynasty* (New York: Thomas Dunne Books, 2006), 1.

11   *"like many religious believers":* Helen-Louise Hunter, *Kim Il-song's North Korea* (Westport, Conn.: Praeger, 1999), 27.

12   *He was the* suryong: Martin, *Under the Loving Care of the Fatherly Leader,* 5.

13   *An American missionary:* Jung H. Pak, "Disoriented in the Orient: A

U.S. Historian Goes Transnational," in *Why We Write: The Politics and Practice of Writing for Social Change,* ed. Jim Downs (New York: Routledge, 2006), 56.

13   *her description of conditions was uncharitable:* Isabella Bird Bishop, *Korea and Her Neighbours: A Narrative of Travel, with an Account of the Recent Vicissitudes and Present Position of the Country* (1898; repr., Seoul: Yonsei University Press, 1970), 40.

14   *Boasting of the advance:* Horace G. Underwood, "Korea's Crisis Hour," *Korea Mission Field,* September 15, 1908.

14   *The Japanese legation's:* Bishop, *Korea and Her Neighbours,* 43–44.

14   *The United States helped:* Carter J. Eckert, Ki-baik Lee, Young Ick Lew, Michael Robinson, and Edward W. Wagner, *Korea Old and New: A History* (Cambridge, Mass.: Harvard University Press, 1990), 238.

15   *His father, Kim Hyong Jik:* Martin, *Under the Loving Care of the Fatherly Leader,* 14.

15   *His son would witness: Kim Il Sung: Condensed Biography* (Pyongyang: Foreign Languages Publishing House, 2001), 5.

15   *Profoundly affected by the sight:* Kim Il Sung, *With the Century* (Pyongyang: Korea Friendship Association, 2003), chap. 1, http://www.korea-dpr.info/lib/202.pdf.

16   *To honor the patriarch: Kim Il Sung: Condensed Biography,* 7.

16   *But whatever legitimate connection:* Dae-sook Suh, *Kim Il Sung: The North Korean Leader* (New York: Columbia University Press, 1988), 5.

16   *Kim and his brigade:* Ibid., 37–38.

16   *The historian Bruce Cumings:* Bruce Cumings, *Korea's Place in the Sun: A Modern History* (New York: W. W. Norton, 1997), 196.

16   *In his memoir:* Kim Il Sung, *With the Century,* chap. 1.

17   *Having experienced repression:* Ibid.

17   *Although Kim apparently:* Eckert et al., *Korea Old and New,* 341.

18   *The division was arbitrary:* James F. Schnabel, *Policy and Direction: The First Year* (Washington, D.C.: Center of Military History, United States Army, 1992), 11, https://history.army.mil/html/books/020 /20-1/CMH_Pub_20-1.pdf.

18   *He had been away from Korea:* Victor Cha, *The Impossible State: North Korea, Past and Future* (New York: HarperCollins, 2013), 70.

18   *Kim declared the founding:* Cumings, *Korea's Place in the Sun,* 231–35.

19   *George Kennan, the architect:* Quoted in Paul J. Heer, *Mr. X and the Pacific: George F. Kennan and American Policy in East Asia* (Ithaca, N.Y.: Cornell University Press, 2018), 141.

19   *North Korea attacked:* Schnabel, *Policy and Direction,* 39.

19   *By the end of that summer:* Eckert et al., *Korea Old and New,* 344.

19   *Just a week before the invasion:* Central Intelligence Agency, "The Korean War Controversy: An Intelligence Success or Failure?," last updated June 25, 2015, https://www.cia.gov/news-information/featured -story-archive/2015-featured-story-archive/korean-war-intelligence -success-or-failure.html.

19   *That was enough to trigger:* Minnie Chan, "China's Korean War Veterans Still Waiting for Answers, 60 Years On," *SCMP,* July 28, 2013.

20   *As the Pulitzer Prize–winning journalist:* David Halberstam, *The Coldest Winter: America and the Korean War* (New York: Hyperion, 2007), 631.

20   *Despite MacArthur's removal:* Cumings, *Korea's Place in the Sun,* 290–93. See also Schnabel, *Policy and Direction,* 288.

20   *The war's casualty figures:* Charles K. Armstrong, "The Destruction and Reconstruction of North Korea, 1950–1960," *Asia-Pacific Journal* 7 (March 16, 2009), https://apjjf.org/-Charles-K.-Armstrong/3460 /article.html.

20   *Around 900,000 Chinese:* Oberdorfer, *Two Koreas,* 9–10.

20   *Nearly 34,000 U.S. troops:* Walter G. Hermes, *Truce Tent and Fighting Front: United States Army in the Korean War* (Washington, D.C.: Center of Military History, United States Army, 1992), 501, https:// history.army.mil/html/books/020/20-3/CMH_Pub_20-3.pdf.

20   *The historian Charles Armstrong:* Armstrong, "Destruction and Reconstruction of North Korea."

21   *"I have never seen":* Military Situation in the Far East: Hearings before the Committee on Armed Services and the Committee on Foreign Relations, to Conduct an Inquiry into the Military Situation in the Far East and the Facts Surrounding the Relief of General of the Army Douglas MacArthur from His Assignments in That Area, 82nd Congress, 1st sess. (Washington, D.C.: U.S. Government Printing Office, 1951), 82, https://babel.hathitrust.org/cgi/pt?id=ucl.$b643205&view= 1up&seq=11.

21   *A veteran of the Korean War:* "G.I.s Tell of a U.S. Massacre in Korean War," *NYT,* September 30, 1999.

21   *As Armstrong argued:* Armstrong, "Destruction and Reconstruction of North Korea."

21   *While people lived:* Martin, *Under the Loving Care of the Fatherly Leader,* 91.

22   *Sung-Yoon Lee, a professor:* Sung-Yoon Lee, "Welcome to the Showdown over South Korea's Seoul," *National Interest,* November 5, 2018.

23   *As documented by the Russian scholar:* Andrei Lankov, "Kim Takes

Control: The 'Great Purge' in North Korea, 1956–1960," *Korean Studies* 26, no. 1 (2002): 87–119, doi:10.1353/ks.2002.0010.

23   *Driven by self-importance:* James Person, ed., "New Evidence on North Korea in 1956," *Cold War International History, Project Bulletin,* issue 16, https://www.wilsoncenter.org/sites/default/files/CWIHP Bulletin16_p51.pdf.

23   *In a 1955 speech:* Andrei Lankov, *The Real North Korea: Life and Politics in the Failed Stalinist Utopia* (New York: Oxford University Press, 2015), 69.

25   *This project required:* Robert Collins, *Marked for Life: Songbun, North Korea's Social Classification System* (Washington D.C.: Committee for Human Rights in North Korea, 2012).

25   *The CIA analyst:* Helen-Louise Hunter, "The Society and Its Environment," in *North Korea: A Country Study,* 5th ed., ed. Robert L. Worden (Washington, D.C.: Library of Congress, Federal Research Division, 2008), 122.

26   *"We learn[ed] by rote answers":* Kang Chol-hwan and Pierre Rigoulot, *The Aquariums of Pyongyang: Ten Years in the North Korean Gulag* (New York: Basic Books, 2001), 4–5.

26   *Hunter wrote that:* Hunter, *Kim Il-song's North Korea,* 26.

26   *"Thinking of North Korea":* Central Intelligence Agency, *North Korea: A Sociological Perspective,* January 1983, https://www.cia.gov /library/readingroom/document/cia-rdp84s00553r000100010001-7.

26   *Such efforts paid dividends:* Hunter, *Kim Il-song's North Korea,* 26–27.

26   *"Right away we felt":* Kang and Rigoulot, *Aquariums of Pyongyang,* 5.

27   *"We killed Americans":* Cha, *Impossible State,* 7.

27   *"to take turns beating":* Yeonmi Park, *In Order to Live: A North Korean Girl's Journey to Freedom* (New York: Penguin Press, 2015), 49.

27   *"We could never just say":* Ibid.

27   *"uniquely vulnerable child race":* B. R. Myers, *The Cleanest Race: How North Koreans See Themselves—and Why It Matters* (Brooklyn, N.Y.: Melville House, 2010), 47.

28   *embalming by Russian specialists:* Christine Kim, "North Korea's Kim, the Second of His Line to Be Embalmed," Reuters, December 20, 2011.

THREE: THE INHERITANCE

29   *"It was impossible":* Anna Fifield, "The Secret Life of Kim Jong Un's Aunt, Who Has Lived in the U.S. Since 1998," *WP,* May 27, 2016.

30   *North Korea's dire food:* Cha, *Impossible State,* 188.

31   *"the father of the Korean nation":* *Kim Jong Il: Brief History* (Pyongyang: Foreign Languages Publishing House, 1998), 1.

31 *"leader of the anti-Japanese":* Ibid.

31 *"revolutionary fighters":* Ibid., 1–2.

31 *Kim was walking:* Paul Fischer, *A Kim Jong-Il Production: The Extraordinary True Story of a Kidnapped Filmmaker, His Star Actress, and a Young Dictator's Rise to Power* (New York: Flatiron Books, 2015), 34.

31 *Official biographies:* Choe In Su, *Kim Jong Il: The People's Leader,* vol. 1 (Pyongyang: Foreign Languages Publishing House, 1983), 46, 75.

32 *In her haunting memoir:* Park, *In Order to Live,* 47.

32 *"Even when he was a child":* Ibid.

32 *In the early 1980s:* Jae-Cheon Lim, *Kim Jong Il's Leadership of North Korea* (London and New York: Routledge, 2009), 11–12; see also Kwang Joo Sohn, "Kim Jong Il's Birth and Growth," *Daily NK,* February 11, 2005.

32 *She was a teenager when she joined:* Suh, *Kim Il Sung,* 51.

32 *"She snatched me":* Kim, *With the Century,* chap. 23.

32 *In a 1999 interview:* Martin, *Under the Loving Care of the Fatherly Leader,* 204.

33 *Less flattering accounts:* Ibid., 187.

33 *Kim Jong Il's early childhood:* John Cha and K. J. Sohn, *Exit Emperor Kim Jong-il: Notes from His Former Mentor* (Bloomington, Ind.: Abbott Press, 2012), 17.

33 *A year or so later:* Martin, *Under the Loving Care of the Fatherly Leader,* 208.

33 *Jong Il reportedly complained:* Lim, *Kim Jong Il's Leadership,* 23–28.

33 *He initially refused:* Ibid., 23.

33 *The situation was frustrating:* Ra Jong-yil, *Inside North Korea's Theocracy: The Rise and Sudden Fall of Jang Song-Thaek,* trans. Jinna Park (Albany: State University of New York Press, 2019), 2.

34 *The most prominent member:* Martin, *Under the Loving Care of the Fatherly Leader,* 196

34 *"Any place deemed":* Ibid.

34 *Secured by small armies:* Hunter, *Kim Il-song's North Korea,* 136–37.

34 *Hwang recalled that:* Martin, *Under the Loving Care of the Fatherly Leader,* 216–17.

34 *As an adolescent:* Fischer, *A Kim Jong-Il Production,* 42–43.

34 *His schoolmates said:* Lim, *Kim Jong Il's Leadership,* 27.

34 *In fact, a senior South Korean:* Lim Dong-won, *Peacemaker: Twenty Years of Inter-Korean Relations and the North Korean Nuclear Issue* (Stanford, Calif.: Walter H. Shorenstein Asia-Pacific Research Center, 2012), 64.

34   *"One can imagine":* Hunter, *Kim Il-song's North Korea,* 133–34.

35   *Despite Jong Il's complaints:* Lim, *Kim Jong Il's Leadership,* 23–28.

35   *For those surrounding:* Martin, *Under the Loving Care of the Fatherly Leader,* 195.

35   *Hwang recalled:* Ra, *Inside North Korea's Theocracy,* 2.

35   *declassified 1978 CIA document:* Central Intelligence Agency, *The North Korean Succession: An Intelligence Assessment,* October 1978, https://www.cia.gov/library/readingroom/document/cia-rdp81b004 01r002100110012-7.

35   *"By guiding the movement":* Ibid.

36   *And as the "keeper of the faith":* Ibid.

36   *"In order to show his father":* Peter Maass, "The Last Emperor," *NYT Magazine,* October 19, 2003.

36   *Still, in a 1982 paper:* Central Intelligence Agency, *North Korea: The Dynasty Takes Shape,* March 3, 1982, https://www.cia.gov/library /readingroom/document/cia-rdp08s02113r000100210001-5.

36   *For his father's seventieth birthday:* Andrei Lankov, *North of the DMZ: Essays on Daily Life in North Korea* (Jefferson, N.C.: McFarland, 2007), 82–83.

37   *That same year:* Ibid.

37   *Soon after graduating:* Cha and Sohn, *Exit Emperor Kim Jong-il,* 28–30.

37   *The regime released a statement:* Mark Savage, "Kim Jong-il: The Cinephile Despot," BBC News, December 19, 2011.

38   *Six months later:* "Choi Eun-Hee: South Korean Actress Who Was Kidnapped by North Dies," BBC News, April 17, 2018.

38   *The couple secretly taped:* Barbara Demick, "Secret Tape Recordings of Kim Jong Il Provide Rare Insight into the Psyche of His North Korean Regime," *LAT,* October 27, 2016.

38   *"like any ordinary young man":* Fischer, *A Kim Jong-Il Production,* 273.

38   *"social realist docudramas":* Ibid.

39   *fourth-largest standing army:* Cha, *Impossible State,* 53.

39   *In the 1970s:* Central Intelligence Agency, *North Korean Military Capabilities and Intentions: A Special National Intelligence Estimate,* May 23, 1979, https://www.cia.gov/library/readingroom/docs/DOC _0001171647.pdf.

39   *Additional investment:* Ibid.

40   *CIA intelligence analysts:* Ibid.

40   *"is a form of warfare":* Quoted in Max Boot, *Invisible Armies: An Epic History of Guerrilla Warfare from Ancient Times to the Present* (New York: Liveright, 2013), xxiii.

40   *the "weak [to] compensate":* Samuel Huntington, *The Clash of Civili-*

zations and the Remaking of World Order (New York: Simon & Schuster, 1996), 187–88.

41 *A December 1991:* National Intelligence Council memorandum, *North Korea: Likely Response to Economic Sanctions,* December 10, 1991, https://www.cia.gov/library/readingroom/docs/DOC_000538 0437.pdf.

42 *As Jonathan Pollack:* Jonathan Pollack, *No Exit: North Korea, Nuclear Weapons and International Security* (New York: Routledge, 2011), 53–56.

42 *In February 1993, the director:* Joel Wit, Daniel Poneman, and Robert Gallucci, *Going Critical: The First North Korean Nuclear Crisis* (Washington, D.C.: Brookings Institution Press, 2004), 38; National Intelligence Council, *Foreign Missile Developments and the Ballistic Missile Threat to the United States through 2015,* September 1999, https://www.dni.gov/files/documents/Foreign%20Missile%20 Developments_1999.pdf.

42 *The defector Hwang Jang Yop:* Kevin Sullivan, "N. Korea Has A-Weapons, Defector Quoted as Saying," *WP,* April 23, 1997.

42 *Compounding the concern:* National Intelligence Council, *Foreign Missile Developments and the Ballistic Missile Threat.*

43 *In 1998, after denying U.S. charges:* Kevin Sullivan, "N. Korea Admits Selling Missiles," *WP,* June 17, 1998.

FOUR: THE SON RISING

45 *Many defectors described:* Jang Jin-sung, *Dear Leader: My Escape from North Korea,* trans. Shirley Lee (New York: Atria Books, 2014), 111–12.

46 *Song's sister, who used to:* Lim, *Kim Jong Il's Leadership,* 100.

46 *"meticulous and humorous comedian":* Ra, *Inside North Korea's Theocracy,* 16.

46 *"From what I heard":* Martin, *Under the Loving Care of the Fatherly Leader,* 686.

46 *The young boy:* Ibid., 686–88.

46 *He had a ten-thousand-square-foot playroom:* Cha and Sohn, *Exit Emperor Kim Jong-il,* 34.

46 *The situation understandably:* Jenny Lee, "Death of North Korea's Onetime Heir Sheds Light on Secretive Kim Dynasty," VOA News, February 17, 2017.

46 *Li said that:* Kim Hakjoon, *Dynasty: The Hereditary Succession Politics of North Korea* (Stanford, Calif.: Walter H. Shorenstein Asia-Pacific Research Center, 2015), 109.

46 *Despite his official second marriage:* Ralph Hassig and Kongdan Oh,

The Hidden People of North Korea: Everyday Life in the Hermit Kingdom (Lanham, Md.: Rowman & Littlefield, 2009), 50–51.

47 *He co-slept with him:* Martin, *Under the Loving Care of the Fatherly Leader,* 688.

47 *In fact, even though Kim's agents:* Ibid.

47 *One of Jong Nam's cousins wrote:* Cha and Sohn, *Exit Emperor Kim Jong-il,* 36.

47 *She would later say:* Martin, *Under the Loving Care of the Fatherly Leader,* 689.

47 *Having once been:* Kim, *Dynasty,* 109.

47 *between 1978 and 1988:* Ibid., 109–11; Lee, "Death of North Korea's Onetime Heir."

47 *He had taken up a new lover:* Kim Yo Jong's birth year can be found in U.S. Treasury Department, "North Korea Designations," Office of Foreign Assets Control, Special Designated Nationals List Update, January 11, 2017, https://www.treasury.gov/resource-center/sanctions/OFAC-Enforcement/Pages/20170111.aspx.

47 *At the end of World War II:* Cumings, *Korea's Place in the Sun,* 177; see also Tai-hwan Kwon, "International Migration of Koreans and the Korean Community in China," *Korea Journal of Population and Development* 26, no. 1 (July 1997): 6, http://s-space.snu.ac.kr/bitstream/10371/85280/1/1.INTERNATIONAL_MIGRATION_OF_KOREANS_AND_THE_KOREAN_COMMUNITY_IN_CHINA%5DTAI-HWAN%20KWON.pdf.

48 *Jong Nam began working:* Lee, "Death of North Korea's Onetime Heir."

48 *While in Geneva:* Kim, *Dynasty,* 110.

48 *In the early 1990s in Pyongyang:* Ibid., 110–11.

49 *In a 2012 interview:* "Kim Jong-Nam Says N. Korean Regime Won't Last Long," *Chosun Ilbo,* January 7, 2012.

49 *Fujimoto recalled:* Kim, *Dynasty,* 144.

49 *The cumulative tuition:* Ibid., 145.

49 *Jong Chol, the older:* Ra, *Inside North Korea's Theocracy,* 139.

50 *One of Jong Chol's friends:* Kim, *Dynasty,* 146.

50 *According to Thae Yong Ho:* Choe Sang-Hun, "Book Explores Kim Jong Un's Feelings about His Mother, and Other Family Tales," *NYT,* May 24, 2018.

50 *Thae was in charge:* James Pearson, "Wonderful Tonight: Taking Kim Jong Un's Brother to a Clapton Concert," Reuters, February 3, 2017.

50 *Unlike the temperate:* Fifield, "The Secret Life of Kim Jong Un's Aunt."

50   *But apparently because:* Kim, *Dynasty,* 145–47.

50   *Jong Un's friend and classmate:* Allan Hall, " 'He Couldn't Speak English, Didn't Pass Any Exams and Was Obsessed with Basketball and Computer Games': Kim Jong Un's Swiss School Days Revealed," *Daily Mail,* December 22, 2011.

51   *Perhaps he just wasn't interested:* Andrew Higgins, "Who Will Succeed Kim Jong Il?," *WP,* July 16, 2009; Anna Fifield, *The Great Successor: The Divinely Perfect Destiny of Brilliant Comrade Kim Jong Un* (New York: PublicAffairs, 2019), 58–59.

51   *"He was very explosive":* Higgins, "Who Will Succeed Kim Jong Il?"

51   *Ra Jong-yil, a former:* Ra, *Inside North Korea's Theocracy,* 139.

51   *A former teacher said:* Keir Simmons, Amy Perrette, Serena Tinari, and Stella Kim, "Trump Can Win over Kim Jong Un by Appealing to Sense of Humor, Teacher Says," NBC News, June 11, 2018.

51   *"We lived in a normal house":* Fifield, "The Secret Life of Kim Jong Un's Aunt."

52   *Micaelo recalled:* Kim, *Dynasty,* 147.

52   *During school vacations:* Fifield, "The Secret Life of Kim Jong Un's Aunt."

52   *Although exact numbers:* Cha, *Impossible State,* 188.

53   *As the anthropologist Sandra Fahy and others:* Sandra Fahy, *Marching through Suffering: Loss and Survival in North Korea* (New York: Columbia University Press, 2015), 106.

53   *Fahy claims that avoiding:* Ibid., 11.

53   *High government officials:* Stephan Haggard and Marcus Noland, *Hunger and Human Rights: The Politics of Famine in North Korea* (Washington, D.C.: U.S. Committee for Human Rights in North Korea, 2005), 14, https://www.researchgate.net/publication/40904797_Hunger_and_Human_Rights_The_Politics_of_Famine_in_North_Korea.

53   *For example, trade with the Soviet Union:* Cha, *Impossible State,* 355.

53   *Both the confrontation with:* Fahy, *Marching through Suffering,* 10.

53   *Korea experts:* Haggard and Noland, *Hunger and Human Rights,* 14.

54   *Although the international community:* Ibid., 8.

54   *Instead, 10 to 30 percent:* Ibid., 28.

54   *One defector told Fahy:* Fahy, *Marching through Suffering,* 40.

54   *When asked why:* Ibid., 120.

55   *People of all ages:* Amnesty International, "Starving North Koreans Forced to Survive on Diet of Grass and Tree Bark," July 15, 2010.

55   *One defector recalled that the hungry:* Fahy, *Marching through Suffering,* 83.

55   *Another said:* Ibid., 71.

55 *A woman who defected:* Barbara Demick, *Nothing to Envy: Ordinary Lives in North Korea* (New York: Spiegel & Grau, 2009), 169.

55 *The timing of Kim Il Sung's death:* Fahy, *Marching through Suffering,* 53.

55 *In 1996, CIA director John Deutch:* Terry Atlas, "CIA Director Fears N. Korea's Collapse, New War," *Chicago Tribune,* December 12, 1996.

56 *"We are now in a period":* Mary Jordan, "Speculation Grows on Demise of N. Korea," *WP,* April 6, 1996.

56 *In 1998, a group of CIA analysts:* Central Intelligence Agency, *Exploring the Implications of Alternative North Korean Endgames: Results from a Discussion Panel on Continuing Coexistence between North and South Korea,* Intelligence Report, January 21, 1998, https://www.cia.gov/library/readingroom/docs/DOC_0001085294.pdf.

57 *According to Fujimoto:* Kim, *Dynasty,* 147.

58 *He cited as evidence:* Ibid., 155.

FIVE: THE EDUCATION OF KIM JONG UN

60 *The streets were lined:* "Kim Jong-Un Attends North Korean Military Parade," *The Guardian,* October 10, 2010.

60 *The military vice marshal:* Chico Harlan, "North Korean Ruler and Heir Attend Parade," *WP,* October 11, 2010.

60 *Following the parade:* "N. Korean Official: Nation Will Serve Kim Jong Un," NPR, October 8, 2010.

61 *As the journalist:* Mark Bowden, "Understanding Kim Jong Un, the World's Most Enigmatic and Unpredictable Dictator," *Vanity Fair,* March 2015.

63 *"an axis of evil":* The White House, The President's State of the Union Address, January 29, 2002, https://georgewbush-whitehouse.archives.gov/news/releases/2002/01/20020129-11.html.

63 *For two decades prior:* Mary-Beth Nikitin, "North Korea's Nuclear Weapons: Technical Issues," Congressional Research Service Report for Congress, RL34256, April 3, 2013, https://fas.org/sgp/crs/nuke/RL34256.pdf.

64 *"facing up to them":* R. Jeffrey Smith, "Perry Sharply Warns North Korea," *WP,* March 31, 1994.

64 *In fact, the Pentagon:* Oberdorfer, *Two Koreas,* 306; see also Jamie McIntyre, "Washington Was on Brink of War with North Korea 5 Years Ago," CNN, October 4, 1999.

64 *Combined with the fact:* Oberdorfer, *Two Koreas,* 313.

64 *Kim agreed to a temporary freeze:* Ibid., 328–29.

64 *As part of the Agreed Framework:* Cha, *Impossible State,* 254–55.

64 *The North Korea analyst:* Myers, *Cleanest Race,* 51.

65 *That was when North Korea:* "N. Korea Withdraws from Nuclear Pact," BBC News, January 10, 2003.

65 *A few weeks later:* Eric Schmitt, "North Korea MIG's Intercept U.S. Jet on Spying Mission," *NYT,* March 4, 2003.

65 *When North Korea announced:* Nikitin, "North Korea's Nuclear Weapons," 4.

66 *Most important, Pyongyang:* Full text of the September 19, 2005, Joint Statement of the Six Party Talks, https://www.ncnk.org/resources /publications/September_19_2005_Joint_Statement.doc.

66 *The optimism engendered:* U.S. Department of the Treasury, "Treasury Designates Banco Delta Asia as Primary Money Laundering Concern under USA Patriot Act," September 15, 2005, https://www .treasury.gov/press-center/press-releases/Pages/js2720.aspx.

66 *The missile failed:* "North Korea Missile Tests—a Timeline," CBS News, September 6, 2017.

66 *These actions elicited quick condemnation:* Sue Mi Terry, "North Korea's Strategic Goals and Policy towards the United States and South Korea," *International Journal of Korean Studies* 17, no. 2 (Fall 2013), http://www.icks.org/data/ijks/1482461379_add_file_3.pdf.

67 *But as a student:* Kim, *Dynasty,* 148.

67 *His father would later:* Ibid., 168.

67 *The Foreign Ministry declared:* Quoted in Emma Chanlett-Avery and Sharon Squassoni, "North Korea's Nuclear Test: Motivations, Implications, and U.S. Options," Congressional Research Service Report for Congress, RL33709, October 24, 2006, https://fas.org/sgp /crs/nuke/RL33709.pdf.

67 *After the test:* "North Korea Claims Nuclear Test," BBC News, October 9, 2006.

67 *The Congressional Research Service:* Chanlett-Avery and Squassoni, "North Korea's Nuclear Test."

68 *It eased sanctions:* Terry, "North Korea's Strategic Goals," 71.

68 *In a statement released:* "North Korea Says Its Nuclear Weapons State Status Will Remain Unchanged," *BBC Monitoring Asia Pacific,* January 17, 2009.

69 *Using the ensuing sanctions:* Choe Sang-Hun, "North Korea Says It Tested Nuclear Device," *NYT,* May 25, 2009.

69 *The regime did not waste:* Glenn Kessler, "During Visit by Bill Clinton, North Korea Releases American Journalists," *WP,* August 5, 2009.

70 *When the conservative politician:* Cha, *Impossible State,* 388.

70 *One resident described:* Jack Kim and Lee Jae-won, "North Korea

Shells South in Fiercest Attack in Decades," Reuters, November 23, 2010.

70 *Yet at nearly the same time:* David Sanger, "North Koreans Unveil New Plant for Nuclear Use," *NYT,* November 20, 2010.

70 *This meant a refusal:* Mark Manyin, "Kim Jong-il's Death: Implications for North Korea's Stability and U.S. Policy," Congressional Research Service Report for Congress, R42126, January 11, 2012, https://fas.org/sgp/crs/row/R42126.pdf; Ian E. Rinehart, Steven A. Hildreth, and Susan V. Lawrence, "Ballistic Missile Defense in the Asia-Pacific Region: Cooperation and Opposition," Congressional Research Service Report for Congress, R43116, April 3, 2015, https://fas.org/sgp/crs/nuke/R43116.pdf.

SIX: BIGGER, BADDER, BOLDER

72 *The documentary quotes:* "North Korean TV Shows Young Kim Threatening War in 2009," *The Journal,* January 8, 2012, http://www.thejournal.ie/north-korean-tv-shows-young-kim-threatening-war-in-2009-323104-Jan2012/#slide-slideshow3.

73 *Just a week earlier:* Jack Kim and Sung-won Shim, "North Korea Calls for 'Human Shields' to Protect New Leader," Reuters, December 31, 2011.

73 *Elder brother and erstwhile successor:* "Report: Kim Jong Un Won't 'Last Long,' Half-Brother Says," NBC News, January 17, 2012.

74 *"an inferiority complex":* Ernesto Londoño, "North Korean Leader Kim Jong Un Offers Many Faces, Many Threats," *WP,* April 13, 2013.

75 *Within hours of the launch:* Barbara Demick and Jung-yoon Choi, "North Korea Satellite Launch Fails Quickly after Liftoff," *LAT,* April 13, 2012.

75 *As six road-mobile:* Jonathan Marcus, "New ICBM Missiles at North Korea Parade 'Fake,'" BBC News, April 27, 2012; Jeffrey Lewis and John Schilling, "Real Fake Missiles: North Korea's ICBM Mockups Are Getting Scary Good," 38 North, November 4, 2013.

75 *"the days are gone forever":* Choe Sang-Hun, "North Korean Leader Stresses Need for Strong Military," *NYT,* April 15, 2012.

75 *As longtime North Korea expert:* Chico Harlan, "New North Korean Leader Kim Jong Eun Speaks Publicly for First Time," *WP,* April 15, 2012.

76 *Eight months later:* Choe Sang-Hun and David Sanger, "North Koreans Launch Rocket in Defiant Act," *NYT,* December 11, 2012.

76 *"demonstrate North Korea's commitment":* James R. Clapper, Director of National Intelligence, "Statement for the Record. Worldwide

Threat Assessment of the US Intelligence Community," Senate Committee on Armed Services, April 18, 2013, https://www.dni .gov/files/documents/Intelligence%20Reports/UNCLASS_2013 %20ATA%20SFR%20FINAL%20for%20SASC%2018%20Apr %202013.pdf.

77 *Posted on its Web portal:* Leon Watson, "We ARE a Nuclear Power: North Korea's Chilling Claim in New Constitution," *Daily Mail,* May 31, 2012.

77 *There is Kim smiling:* Will Ripley and Mariano Castillo, "Report: North Korea Tests Ballistic Missile," CNN, May 9, 2015.

77 *There is Kim with scientists:* "Kim Jong Un's Media Moments," CBS News, multiple dates, https://www.cbsnews.com/pictures/kim-jong -un-media-moments/2/.

77 *There is Kim observing:* Ibid.

78 *The North has thousands:* U.S. Office of the Secretary of Defense, "Report to Congress: Military and Security Developments Involving the Democratic People's Republic of Korea," 2017, https://fas.org /irp/world/dprk/dod-2017.pdf.

78 *Around the time of Kim's ascension:* Barbara Demick, "North Korea Has Long Put Weapons Ahead of Food for Its People," *LAT,* April 13, 2012.

79 *Kim watched a night-combat:* "N.K. Leader Watches Rocket Firing Contest, Combat Flight Drill," Yonhap News Agency, December 21, 2016.

79 *The regime has also demonstrated:* U.S. Office of the Secretary of Defense, "Military and Security Developments Involving the Democratic People's Republic of Korea."

79 *In 2013, the regime also used:* Ibid.

79 *Kim could also rely:* Ibid.

79 *In 2016, the regime publicized:* Ibid.

79 *Within Kim's first year and a half:* Choe Sang-Hun, "North Korea Threatens South with Military Action," *NYT,* April 23, 2012.

79 *The most important aspect:* Bonnie Berkowitz, Laris Karklis, and Tim Meko, "What Is North Korea Trying to Hit?," *WP,* July 25, 2017.

80 *To protest annual U.S.–South Korean military drills:* "North Korea Suspends Works at Kaesong Industrial Zone," BBC News, April 8, 2013.

80 *The tension also had an impact:* Choe Sang-Hun, "U.S. and South Korea Put Forces on Alert for Missile Test by North," *NYT,* April 11, 2013.

80 *The United States and regional allies:* Ibid.

81   *With a range of between:* Center for Strategic and International Studies, "Musudan at a Glance," last modified June 15, 2018, https://missilethreat.csis.org/missile/musudan/.

81   *China, claiming prescheduled:* Bill Gertz, "On the Border: China Confirms Military Exercises near N. Korean Border," *The Washington Free Beacon,* April 8, 2013.

82   *Whether the result:* Center for Strategic and International Studies, "Musudan at a Glance."

82   *In 2014, North Korea:* Jack Kim, "South Korea Extending Ballistic Missile Range to Counter North's Threat," Reuters, April 3, 2014.

82   *"His father and his grandfather":* Londoño, "Kim Jong Un Offers Many Faces, Many Threats."

83   *"weaknesses and biases":* Heuer, *Psychology of Intelligence Analysis,* 1.

84   *Director of National Intelligence Dan Coats:* Jon Schwarz, "Trump Intel Chief: North Korea Learned from Libya War to 'Never' Give Up Nukes," *The Intercept,* July 29, 2017.

84   *"A dazed and confused Gaddafi":* Peter Beaumont and Chris Stephen, "Gaddafi's Last Words as He Begged for Mercy: 'What Did I Do to You?,'" *The Guardian,* October 22, 2011.

85   *The North's Foreign Ministry:* Schwarz, "Trump Intel Chief."

SEVEN: A TWENTY-FIRST-CENTURY DICTATORSHIP

87   *"with . . . new urgency":* Adam Cathcart, "Kim Jong-un Syndrome: North Korean Commemorative Culture and the Succession Process," in *Change and Continuity in North Korean Politics,* ed. Adam Cathcart, Robert Winstanley-Chesters, and Christopher Green (London: Routledge, 2017), 13.

87   *Suzy Kim, a professor of Korean history:* Suzy Kim, "Specters of War in Pyongyang: The Victorious Fatherland Liberation War Museum in North Korea," *Cross-Currents: East Asian History and Culture Review,* E-journal no. 14 (March 2015), 145, https://cross-currents.berkeley.edu/sites/default/files/e-journal/articles/s._kim.pdf.

88   *"a simple building":* Jean H. Lee, "For North Koreans, the War Never Ended," *Wilson Quarterly,* Spring 2017, https://wilsonquarterly.com/quarterly/trump-and-a-watching-world/for-north-koreans-the-war-never-ended/.

88   *"In North Korea, the Korean War":* Kim, "Specters of War in Pyongyang," 145.

88   *"This is a man comfortable":* Cathcart, "Kim Jong-un Syndrome," 15.

90   *The sushi chef Fujimoto claimed:* Choe Sang-Hun and Martin Fackler, "North Korea's Heir Apparent Remains a Mystery," *NYT,* June 14, 2009.

90 *Though his father had begun:* "North Korea Propaganda Slogans Urge 'Socialist Fairyland,'" *BBC News,* February 12, 2015.

90 *Kim waves as he walks:* Megan Willett, "North Korea Releases Photos of Colorful New Water Park in Pyongyang," *Business Insider,* October 17, 2013.

90 *At the Mirim Riding Club:* "Mirim Riding Club," Tongil Tours, accessed September 26, 2018, https://tongiltours.com/travel-guide /pyongyang/attractions/mirim-riding-club.

90 *Another tour company:* "New DPRK Site Spotted: Mirim Equestrian Riding Club," Uri Tours, accessed September 26, 2018, https://www .uritours.com/blog/new-dprk-site-spotted-mirim-equestrian-riding -club/.

90 *If horse riding:* Oliver Wainwright, "The Pyonghattan Project: How North Korea's Capital Is Transforming into a 'Socialist Fairyland,'" *The Guardian,* September 11, 2015.

90 *The Masikryong ski resort:* Kim Wall, "A Tourist in North Korea," *The Atlantic,* October 30, 2014.

91 *Kim is buckled in:* Mike Firn, "British Diplomat Takes Roller Coaster Ride with North Korea's Leader Kim Jong-un," *The Telegraph,* August 2, 2012.

91 *The Changjon Street Apartments:* Wainwright, "Pyonghattan Project."

91 *Since Kim came to power:* Rüdiger Frank, "North Korea's Economic Policy in 2018 and Beyond: Reforms Inevitable, Delays Possible," 38 North, August 8, 2018, https://www.38north.org/2018/08 /rfrank080818/; see also Elizabeth Shim, "North Korea Legalizing Marketplaces to 'Manage' Population," UPI, March 29, 2017.

91 *"mundane life":* Wall, "A Tourist in North Korea."

92 *"Kids zoom around":* Wainwright, "Pyonghattan Project."

92 *The Korea Maritime Institute:* Ju-min Park and James Pearson, "In Kim Jong Un's Summer Retreat, Fun Meets Guns," Reuters, October 10, 2017.

92 *According to a North Korean brochure:* Ibid.

93 *As a result, Kim has engaged:* Christopher Green, "Wrapped in a Fog: On the DPRK Constitution and the Ten Principles," in *Change and Continuity in North Korean Politics,* ed. Adam Cathcart, Robert Winstanley-Chesters, and Christopher Green (London: Routledge, 2017), 25.

93 *The international advocacy organization: World Report 2019,* Human Rights Watch, accessed September 12, 2019, https://www.hrw.org /sites/default/files/world_report_download/hrw_world_report _2019.pdf.

94 *A North Korean high school:* Christopher Richardson, "Hagiography

of the Kims and the Childhood of Saints," in *Change and Continuity in North Korean Politics,* ed. Adam Cathcart, Robert Winstanley-Chesters, and Christopher Green (London: Routledge, 2017), 123.

94   *In 2014, the regime released:* "N. Korean TV Shows Childhood Photos of Kim Jong-un," *Chosun Ilbo,* April 23, 2014.

94   *Christopher Richardson, a researcher:* Richardson, "Hagiography of the Kims," 123.

94   *"there is a peculiarly consistent style":* Wainwright, "Pyonghattan Project."

95   *Rüdiger Frank, a German expert:* Frank, "North Korea's Economic Policy in 2018 and Beyond."

95   *One defector who left in 2014:* Anna Fifield, "Life under Kim Jong Un," *WP,* November 18, 2017, https://www.washingtonpost.com /graphics/2017/world/north-korea-defectors/?utm_term=.2be15641 e8f4.

95   *A twenty-five-year-old:* Ibid.

95   *Another young adult:* Ibid.

96   *Kim Jong Un was populating:* Demick, *Nothing to Envy,* 61–62.

96   *In 2007, Kim Jong Il directly addressed:* John Everard, *Only Beautiful, Please: A British Diplomat in North Korea* (Stanford, Calif.: Walter H. Shorenstein Asia-Pacific Research Center, 2012), 94.

97   *"Capitalism was . . . alive and well":* Park, *In Order to Live,* 50.

97   *Teenager Kim Hyuck:* Demick, *Nothing to Envy,* 172.

97   *Ha-Young, a defector:* Jieun Baek, *North Korea's Hidden Revolution: How the Information Underground Is Transforming a Closed Society* (New Haven, Conn.: Yale University Press, 2016), 69–71.

98   *"Since her family":* Ibid., 71.

98   *"The Kim regime has survived":* William A. Brown, "North Korea's Economic Strategy, 2018," in *A Whirlwind of Change in East Asia: Assessing Shifts in Strategy, Trade, and the Role of North Korea,* vol. 29, *Joint U.S.-Korea Academic Studies,* ed. Gilbert Rozman (Washington, D.C.: Korea Economic Institute, 2018), 326–41, http://www.keia .org/sites/default/files/publications/kei_jointus-korea_2018_180801 _final_digital.pdf.

98   *The government started legalizing:* Shim, "North Korea Legalizing Marketplaces."

98   *For example, in Sinuiju:* U.S. National Geospatial-Intelligence Agency, "Developments in North Korea's Sinuiju City under Kim Jong-un," last updated April 21, 2018, https://pathfinder.geointservices .io/public_page/u-developments-in-north-koreas-sinuiju-city-under -kim-jong-un/.

99   *For example, John Everard:* Everard, *Only Beautiful, Please,* 100.

99   *North Korea's economy:* Robert E. Kelly, "A New Economy for North Korea," Centre for International Governance Innovation, August 3, 2018, https://www.cigionline.org/articles/new-economy -north-korea.

99   *"There are great":* Testimony of Minister Thae, Yong-ho, U.S. House Committee on Foreign Affairs, November 1, 2017, https://docs.house .gov/meetings/FA/FA00/20171101/106577/HHRG-115-FA00 -Wstate-Yong-hoT-20171101.pdf.

99   *Some estimates indicate:* Shim, "North Korea Legalizing Market-places"; Baek, *North Korea's Hidden Revolution,* 38.

100 *Yeonmi Park recalled:* Park, *In Order to Live,* 58.

100 *"In a sense":* Daniel Tudor and James Pearson, *North Korea Confidential: Private Markets, Fashion Trends, Prison Camps, Dissenters and Defectors* (Tokyo: Tuttle Publishing, 2015), 37.

100 *In her fascinating study:* Jean H. Lee, "Soap Operas and Socialism: Dissecting Kim Jong-un's Evolving Policy Priorities through TV Dramas in North Korea," Korea Economic Institute Academic Paper Series, November 30, 2017, http://www.keia.org/sites/default /files/publications/lee_soap_operas_and_socialism.pdf.

101 *"The first, most shocking thing":* Baek, *North Korea's Hidden Revolution,* 54–55.

102 *"seduce people":* Ibid., 59.

102 *A thirty-seven-year-old contemporary:* Fifield, "Life under Kim Jong Un."

102 *"We would hear about":* Ibid.

102 *"I hung out with the popular girls":* Baek, *North Korea's Hidden Revolution,* 70.

102 *The United Nations in 2019 reported:* United Nations, "2019 DPR Korea: Needs and Priorities," March 6, 2019, https://www.undp.org /content/dam/unct/dprk/docs/DPRK_NP_2019_Final.pdf.

EIGHT: PRUNING THE FAMILY TREE

104 *"blood-sealed ties":* The full text of the January 1, 2014, speech is at https://www.ncnk.org/resources/publications/kju-ny2014.pdf/file _view.

105 *Tall, masculine, and popular:* Ra, *Inside North Korea's Theocracy,* 29.

106 *A few days later:* The full text is in Chad O'Carroll, "North Korea Executes 'Traitor' Jang Song Thaek," NK News, December 12, 2013, https://www.nknews.org/2013/12/north-korea-executes-jang -song-thaek-for-factionalism/.

106 *Whatever remained of their bodies:* Ra, *Inside North Korea's Theocracy,* 165.

106 *After his sentencing:* Choe Sang-Hun, "In Hail of Bullets and Fire, North Korea Killed Official Who Wanted Reform," *NYT,* March 12, 2016.

107 *"The spectacle of public humiliation":* Nicholas Eberstadt, "North Korea Could Be In Store for a Purge—and Destabilization," *WP,* December 13, 2013.

107 *As Andrei Lankov and others:* Lankov, *Real North Korea,* 154.

107 *Jang's nephew:* "Pyongyang Recalls Senior Official," *Daily NK,* December 31, 2013.

107 *The regime also replaced:* Shin Hyon-hee, "N.K. Seen Spurring Leadership Shakeup," *The Korea Herald,* January 6, 2014.

108 *Since the Jang incident:* "N. Korea Purges 340 during 5-Year Rule of Kim Jong-un: Think Tank," Yonhap News Agency, December 29, 2016.

108 *Both the surprising dismissal:* Chico Harlan, "North Korea Names Kim Jong Eun 'Marshal' of the Military," *WP,* July 18, 2012.

110 *the "open warfare":* Choe Sang-Hun and David Sanger, "Korea Execution Is Tied to Clash over Businesses," *NYT,* December 23, 2013.

110 *Ra Jong-yil, a former senior:* Ra, *Inside North Korea's Theocracy,* 163.

110 *Over the past several decades:* Dick K. Nanto, "North Korean Counterfeiting of U.S. Currency," Congressional Research Service Report for Congress, RL33324, June 12, 2009, https://fas.org/sgp/crs/row /RL33324.pdf.

110 *According to Justin Hastings:* Justin V. Hastings, *A Most Enterprising Country: North Korea in the Global Economy* (Ithaca, N.Y.: Cornell University Press, 2016), 10–12.

111 *a "symbiosis" has developed:* Sheena Chestnut Greitens, *Illicit: North Korea's Evolving Operations to Earn Hard Currency* (Washington, D.C.: Committee for Human Rights in North Korea, 2014), https:// www.hrnk.org/uploads/pdfs/SCG-FINAL-FINAL.pdf.

111 *Coal is the single largest export:* Carol Morello, "U.N. Caps N. Korean Coal Sales in Bid to Deprive It of Hard Currency after Nuclear Tests," *WP,* November 30, 2016.

111 *It has about two hundred kinds:* "N.K. Mineral Resources May Be Worth $9.7 Trillion," *The Korea Herald,* August 26, 2012; see also Leonid Petrov, "Rare Earths Bankroll North Korea's Future," *Asia Times,* August 8, 2012.

111 *Seafood, one of the reasons:* U.S. Mission to the United Nations, "Fact Sheet: Resolution 2371 (2017) Strengthening Sanctions on North Korea," August 5, 2017, https://usun.usmission.gov/fact-sheet -resolution-2371-2017-strengthening-sanctions-on-north-korea/?_ga =2.127536526.220785168.1569552870-707405175.1564779131.

111 *The government also dispatches:* U.S. Mission to the United Nations, "Fact Sheet: Resolution 2397 on North Korea," December 22, 2017, https://usun.usmission.gov/fact-sheet-un-security-council-resolution -2397-on-north-korea/?_ga=2.15513014.1072312274.1569553067 -221063855.1568833043.

112 *During a rare excursion:* Suki Kim, *Without You, There Is No Us: My Secret Life Teaching the Sons of North Korea's Elite* (London: Rider Books, 2015), 101.

112 *Despite U.N. Security Council Resolution 1718:* United Nations, *Report of the Detailed Findings of the Commission of Inquiry on Human Rights in the Democratic People's Republic of Korea,* February 7, 2014, 203, https://www.ohchr.org/EN/HRBodies/HRC/CoIDPRK/Pages /ReportoftheCommissionofInquiryDPRK.aspx.

112 *In 2013, North Korea imported:* Robert Collins, *Pyongyang Republic: North Korea's Capital of Human Rights Denial* (Washington, D.C.: Committee for Human Rights in North Korea, 2016), 71, 73, https:// www.hrnk.org/uploads/pdfs/Collins_PyongyangRepublic_FINAL _WEB.pdf.

112 *That number soared to $800 million:* Hyonhee Shin, "North Korea Bought at Least $640 Million in Luxury Goods from China in 2017, South Korea Lawmaker Says," Reuters, October 22, 2018.

112 *The 2014 U.N. report also showed:* United Nations, *Report of the Detailed Findings of the Commission of Inquiry,* 203.

112 *Subsequent investigations revealed:* United Nations, *Report of the Panel of Experts Established Pursuant to Resolution 1874 (2009),* February 27, 2017, https://www.undocs.org/S/2017/150; United Nations, *Report of the Panel of Experts Established Pursuant to Resolution 1874 (2009),* August 30, 2019, https://undocs.org/S/2019/691.

112 *And in 2019:* Colin Zwirko and Oliver Hotham, "High-End Appliances, Watches on Sale at Recently-Renovated N. Korean Dept. Store," NK News, April 16, 2019.

113 *The current leadership:* Ken E. Gause, *North Korean House of Cards: Leadership Dynamics under Kim Jong-un* (Washington, D.C.: Committee for Human Rights in North Korea, 2015), 68–69; Chico Harlan, "N. Korea Says It Executed Leader's Uncle," *WP,* December 12, 2013.

113 *His sushi chef:* Cited in Ra, *Inside North Korea's Theocracy,* 157.

113 *"when analyzing Kim's lip movements":* Lee Young-jong and Kang Jin-kyu, "Pyongyang Purges More Jang Song Thaek Loyalists," *Korea JoongAng Daily,* December 1, 2014.

113 *Just months after the Jang execution:* Kim Jong Un, "Let Us Hasten the Final Victory through a Revolutionary Ideological Offensive,"

Eighth Conference of the Ideological Workers of the Korean Workers' Party, February 27, 2014, https://www.ncnk.org/resources/publications/let-us-hasten-final-victory-through-revolutionary-ideological-offensive.pdf.

114 *"The commanding officers":* "Kim Jong Un Supervises KPAN Swim Test and Inspects Hwa Islet," North Korea Leadership Watch, July 2, 2014, http://www.nkleadershipwatch.org/2014/07/02/kim-jong-un-supervises-kpan-swim-test-and-inspects-hwa-islet/.

114 *Earlier that year:* "Kim Jong-un Sends Navy Officers for a Swim," *Chosun Ilbo,* July 3, 2014.

114 *Describing the incident:* "North Korean Leader Flays Officials during Amusement Park Visit," *BBC Monitoring Asia Pacific,* May 10, 2012, accessed via LexisNexis.

115 *Kim grieved intensely:* "North Korean Minister Offers Apology over Building Collapse to Bereaved Families," *BBC Monitoring Asia Pacific,* May 18, 2014, accessed via LexisNexis.

115 *During a 2015 tour:* "North Korean Leader Flays Officials' Incompetence during Terrapin Farm Visit," *BBC Monitoring Asia Pacific,* May 19, 2015, accessed via LexisNexis.

115 *Shortly after his visit:* Kang Mi Jin, "Terrapin Farm Manager Executed Post Onsite Visit," *Daily NK,* July 7, 2015.

116 *"a monkey in a tropical forest":* Simon Denyer, "North Korea Slams U.S. over Internet Shutdown, Calls Obama a 'Monkey,'" *WP,* December 27, 2014.

116 *Park Geun-hye, South Korea's first:* Tania Branigan, "North Korea Labels South's President as 'Crafty Prostitute' after Obama Visit," *The Guardian,* April 27, 2014.

117 *Indeed, in November 2012:* Jane Perlez, "North Korean Leader, Young and Defiant, Strains Ties with Chinese," *NYT,* April 13, 2013.

117 *Kim then abruptly:* Julian Ryall, "Kim Jong-un 'Ordered Girl Group Home over Chinese Snub,'" *The Telegraph,* December 14, 2015.

118 *But he met with Dennis Rodman:* Mark Memmott, "'I Love Him,' Dennis Rodman Says of North Korean Leader Kim Jong Un," NPR, February 28, 2013; Fifield, *The Great Successor*, chap. 11.

118 *"You have a friend":* Ibid.

118 *He spent time with Kim:* Peter Walker, "Dennis Rodman Gives Away Name of Kim Jong-un's Daughter," *The Guardian,* September 9, 2013.

118 *The men partied:* Curtis Melvin, "Identifying the Ibiza of N. Korea: Where Kim Jong Un Met Rodman," NK News, October 21, 2013.

118 *This series of events:* Heuer, *Psychology of Intelligence Analysis,* 33.

119 *But instead of a hit squad:* Anna Fifield, "What Do We Know about

Kim Jong Un? Very Little. That Makes This Guy an Expert," *WP,* January 8, 2016.

120 *As many as 120,000 North Koreans:* David Hawk and Amanda Mortwedt Oh, *The Parallel Gulag: North Korea's 'An-jeon-bu' Prison Camps* (Washington, D.C.: Committee for Human Rights in North Korea, 2017), v, 57, https://www.hrnk.org/uploads/pdfs/Hawk_The _Parallel_Gulag_Web.pdf.

120 *After conducting scores of interviews:* United Nations, *Report of the Detailed Findings of the Commission of Inquiry,* 365.

121 *The U.N. report indicated:* Ibid., 232.

121 *The father of:* Hyeonseo Lee, *The Girl with Seven Names* (London: William Collins, 2015), 67.

121 *Lee also recalled:* Ibid., 66.

122 *They released him:* United Nations, *Report of the Detailed Findings of the Commission of Inquiry,* 215.

122 *The U.N. Commission of Inquiry described:* Ibid., 220.

122 *"their seed must be eliminated":* Ibid., 228–29.

122 *Former camp guards:* Ibid., 228.

122 *For the nearly three decades:* Ibid., 229.

123 *"cringed at getting too close":* Kang and Rigoulot, *Aquariums of Pyongyang,* 73.

123 *Rape and sexual torture:* "Report: Inquiry on Crimes against Humanity in North Korean Prison Camps," War Crimes Committee of the International Bar Association, December 12, 2017, https://www .ibanet.org/Article/NewDetail.aspx?ArticleUid=8ae0f29d-4283 -4151-a573-a66b2c1ab480.

124 *Adam Szubin:* U.S. Department of the Treasury, "Treasury Sanctions North Korean Senior Officials and Entities Associated with Human Rights Abuses," press release, July 6, 2016, https://www.treasury.gov /press-center/press-releases/Pages/jl0506.aspx.

124 *Six months later:* U.S. Treasury Department, "Treasury Sanctions Additional North Korean Officials and Entities in Response to the North Korean Regime's Serious Human Rights Abuses and Censorship Activities," press release, January 11, 2017, https://www.treasury .gov/press-center/press-releases/Pages/jl0699.aspx.

124 *"The more zeal they demonstrate":* Collins, *Pyongyang Republic,* 28.

124 *The hundreds of thousands:* Gause, *North Korean House of Cards.* See sect. 2, chap. 7.

125 *The goal of coup-proofing:* Sheena Chestnut Greitens, *Dictators and Their Secret Police: Coercive Institutions and State Violence* (Cambridge: Cambridge University Press, 2016), 25.

125 *"the state made accusers":* Lee, *Girl with Seven Names,* 38.

NINE: KIM'S HACKERS

129   *Paul Fischer, the author:* Paul Fischer, "North Korea's Fear of Hollywood," *NYT,* July 4, 2014.

129   *Perhaps they even read:* Martina Stewart, "Activist to Drop 100,000 Copies of 'The Interview' on North Korea by Balloon," *WP,* December 31, 2014.

129   *Jang Jin-sung, one of the North's:* Katie Engelhart, "Former North Korean Poet Laureate Says 'The Interview' Is as Explosive as a Real Bomb Being Dropped on Kim Jong-un," Vice News, January 2, 2015.

130   *During their visit to Beijing:* Martyn Williams, "Kim Jong Un Tries Out Virtual Reality," North Korea Tech, April 2, 2018.

130   *Kim is a "digital native":* Marc Prensky, "Digital Natives, Digital Immigrants," October 2001, https://www.marcprensky.com/writing /Prensky%20-%20Digital%20Natives,%20Digital%20Immigrants %20-%20Part1.pdf.

131   *"It felt like getting hacked":* Amanda Hess, "Inside the Sony Hack," *Slate,* November 22, 2015.

131   *North Korea as the culprit:* Ju-min Park, "North Korea Slams U.S. Movie on Leader Assassination Plot," Reuters, June 25, 2014.

131   *"Making and releasing a movie":* Choe Sang-Hun, "North Korea Warns U.S. over Film Mocking Its Leader," *NYT,* June 25, 2014.

131   *"People don't usually":* "North Korea Threatens War on US over Kim Jong-un Movie," BBC News, June 26, 2014.

131   *Among other reasons:* Kim Zetter, "Sony Got Hacked Hard: What We Know and Don't Know So Far," *Wired,* December 3, 2014.

131   *"North Korea is a long-running":* Alexandra Alter, "North Korea's Love-Hate of Movies," *NYT,* December 31, 2014, https://www .nytimes.com/2015/01/01/business/media/a-kim-jong-il-production - looks-at-north-koreas-film-past.html.

132   *"North Korea embodies":* Ibid.

132   *"At that point":* David Sanger, *The Perfect Weapon: War, Sabotage, and Fear in the Cyber Age* (New York: Crown, 2018), 127.

132   *"It was like a bomb":* Hess, "Inside the Sony Hack."

132   *"Everything was so completely destroyed":* Ibid.

132   *The cyberattack exposed:* Brooks Barnes and Nicole Perlroth, "Sony Films Are Pirated, and Hackers Leak Studio Salaries," *NYT,* December 2, 2014.

133   *When the FBI investigated:* Kahyun Yang and Jim Finkle, "North Korea Says Its Supporters May Be Behind Sony Attack," Reuters, December 7, 2014.

133 *The NDC statement:* As reported in Sean Gallagher, "Sony Pictures Attackers Demand: 'Stop the Terrorist Film!,'" Ars Technica, December 8, 2014.

133 *A little over a week:* Choe Sang-Hun, "North Korea Denies Role in Sony Pictures Hacking," *NYT,* December 7, 2014, https://www.nytimes.com/2014/12/08/business/north-korea-denies-hacking-sony-but-calls-attack-a-righteous-deed.html.

133 *The film debuted:* Seth Rosenblatt and Ian Sherr, "Sony to Release *The Interview* After All?" CNET, December 19, 2014.

133 *"Why are we all":* Michael Cieply and Brooks Barnes, "Quandary for Sony in Threats over 'The Interview,'" *NYT,* December 17, 2014.

134 *"without a shadow of a doubt":* James R. Clapper with Trey Brown, *Facts and Fears: Hard Truths from a Life in Intelligence* (New York: Viking, 2018), 283.

134 *The FBI press release stated:* U.S. Federal Bureau of Investigation, "Update on Sony Investigation," press release, December 19, 2014, https://www.fbi.gov/news/pressrel/press-releases/update-on-sony-investigation.

134 *President Obama criticized:* Elizabeth Weise, Kevin Johnson, and Andrea Mandell, "Obama: Sony 'Did the Wrong Thing' When It Pulled Movie," *USA Today,* December 19, 2014.

134 *"The problem now":* Jose Pagliery, "Why North Korea's Attack Should Leave Every Company Scared Stiff," CNN, December 19, 2014.

135 *"The movie offers":* Engelhart, "Former North Korean Poet Laureate."

135 *"Cyberweapons were tailor-made":* Sanger, *Perfect Weapon,* 136.

135 *Just a few months before:* U.S. Congress, House Committee on Armed Services, "Statement of General Curtis M. Scaparrotti, Commander, United Nations Command; Commander, United States–Republic of Korea Combined Forces Command, United States Forces Korea," 113th Congress, 2nd sess., April 2, 2014, https://docs.house.gov/meetings/AS/AS00/20140402/101985/HHRG-113-AS00-Wstate-ScaparrottiUSAC-20140402.pdf.

136 *His warnings about:* Aaron Boyd, "DNI Clapper: Cyber Bigger Threat Than Terrorism," *Federal Times,* February 4, 2016.

136 *Citing Kim Heung-kwang:* David Sanger, David Kirkpatrick, and Nicole Perlroth, "The World Once Laughed at North Korean Cyberpower. No More," *NYT,* October 15, 2017.

136 *"Cyberwarfare, along with nuclear weapons":* Ibid.

136 *Kim has deployed:* Matthew Ha and David Maxwell, "Kim Jong-un's 'All-Purpose Sword': North Korean Cyber-Enabled Economic

Warfare," Foundation for Defense of Democracies, October 2018, https://www.fdd.org/analysis/2018/10/03/kim-jong-uns-all-purpose -sword/.

136 *Kim has also focused:* Ibid.

137 *South Korean officials:* Emma Chanlett-Avery, Liana Rosen, John Rollins, and Catherine Theohary, "North Korean Cyber Capabilities: In Brief," Congressional Research Service Report for Congress, R44912, August 3, 2017, https://fas.org/sgp/crs/row/R44912.pdf.

137 *In 2011, North Korea:* Ha and Maxwell, "Kim Jong-un's 'All-Purpose Sword.' "

137 *It deleted credit card:* Ibid.

137 *In 2016, Kim's attacks:* "$81 Million Bangladesh Bank Heist Sparks Push for Stepped-Up Cybersecurity," NPR, May 24, 2016.

137 *The U.S. National Security Agency:* Chanlett-Avery et al., "North Korean Cyber Capabilities."

137 *In addition to the Bangladesh heist:* "North Korean Hackers Blamed for a Wave of Cyberattacks on Banks," *SCMP,* October 3, 2018.

138 *It stated that North Korea:* Ha and Maxwell, "Kim Jong-un's 'All-Purpose Sword.' "

138 *Furthermore, in December 2017:* Ibid.

138 *The White House homeland security adviser:* Ellen Nakashima and Philip Rucker, "U.S. Declares North Korea Carried Out Massive WannaCry Cyberattack," *WP,* December 19, 2017.

138 *As detailed in an August 2019 U.N. report:* United Nations, *Report of the Panel of Experts Established Pursuant to Resolution 1874 (2009),* August 30, 2019.

139 *One of the perks:* Laya Maheshwari, "Pizzas, Pony Rides and Dolphin Shows: Balms for North Korea's Elite," *NYT,* October 25, 2016; Alexander Walter, " 'Pyongyang Speed': North Korea Miraculously Cranks Out Massive Residential Development for Scientists in Only One Year," Archinect News, December 18, 2015.

139 *Nat Kretchun, an expert:* Author exchange with Nat Kretchun, February 18, 2019.

139 *In January 2016:* James Griffiths, "Inside North Korea: High-Tech Science Center Lauds Nuclear Advances," CNN, January 8, 2016.

140 *Enticed by inducements:* Sung-hui Moon, "More North Koreans Become Scientists to Reap Privileges from the Regime," Radio Free Asia, May 18, 2017.

140 *Regime propaganda regularly features:* Luke Dormehl, "Kim Jong-Un Sure Looks Happy with His MacBook Pro," Cult of Mac, February 15, 2016.

140 *As InterMedia, a Washington-based:* Nat Kretchun, Catherine Lee,

and Seamus Tuohy, "Compromising Connectivity: Information Dynamics between the State and Society in a Digitizing North Korea," February 2017, https://www.intermedia.org/wp-content/uploads/2017/02/Compromising-Connectivity-Final-Report_Soft-Copy.pdf.

141 *InterMedia found in 2012:* Nat Kretchun and Jane Kim, "A Quiet Opening: North Koreans in a Changing Media Environment," May 2012, https://www.intermedia.org/wp-content/uploads/2013/05/A_Quiet_Opening_FINAL_InterMedia.pdf.

141 *According to a UNICEF study:* UNICEF, "Multiple Indicator Cluster Survey 2017 Democratic People's Republic of Korea," June 2018, 7, https://www.unicef.org/eap/sites/unicef.org.eap/files/2018-06/2017%20DPRK%20MICS%20Survey%20Findings%20Report_July%202018.pdf.

141 *Based on his research of the borderland:* Lankov, *Real North Korea,* 105.

141 *The cell phones and tablets:* Recorded Future, "North Korea Cyber Activity," July 25, 2017, https://go.recordedfuture.com/hubfs/reports/north-korea-activity.pdf.

141 *A New York Times reporter:* Maheshwari, "Pizza, Pony Rides and Dolphin Shows."

141 *The journalists Daniel Tudor and James Pearson:* Tudor and Pearson, *North Korea Confidential,* 148–49.

142 *UNICEF found that:* UNICEF, "Multiple Indicator Cluster Survey 2017 Democratic People's Republic of Korea," 7.

142 *Suki Kim, who taught:* Kim, *Without You, There Is No Us,* 170.

142 *Martyn Williams, a technology specialist:* Martyn Williams, "How the Internet Works in North Korea," *Slate,* November 28, 2016.

142 *In 2016, North Korea had:* Rebecca Hersher, "North Korea Accidentally Reveals It Only Has 28 Websites," NPR, September 21, 2016; Eric Talmadge, "Only If It Serves the State: North Korea's Online Experience," AP, November 9, 2017.

142 *"It's no Netflix":* Williams, "How the Internet Works in North Korea."

142 *The regime in recent years:* Eric Talmadge, "Online Shopping Has Arrived in North Korea," AP, May 6, 2015.

142 *Kretchun observes:* Author exchange with Nat Kretchun, February 18, 2019.

142 *An even smaller number of North Koreans:* Recorded Future, "North Korea Cyber Activity."

143 *The Korea Computer Center:* U.S. Department of State, "Democratic People's Republic of Korea 2018 Human Rights Report," https://

www.state.gov/wp-content/uploads/2019/03/DEMOCRATIC
-PEOPLE%E2%80%99S-REPUBLIC-OF-KOREA.pdf.

143 *While the West has touted:* Peter W. Singer and Emerson T. Brooking, *LikeWar: The Weaponization of Social Media* (Boston: Houghton Mifflin Harcourt, 2018), 103.

TEN: MURDER IN MALAYSIA

145 *It is the morning:* "CCTV Footage Appears to Show Attack on Kim Jong-nam," *The Guardian,* February 19, 2017, https://www.the guardian.com/global/video/2017/feb/20/kim-jong-nam-killing-cctv -footage-appears-to-show-attack-on-north-korean. Includes video acquired by Fuji News Network.

145 *He is wearing:* James Pomfret, "Kim Jong Un's Murdered Half Brother Lived Quiet, Open Life in Macau," Reuters, February 16, 2017.

146 *As the VX seeps into his body:* U.S. Centers for Disease Control and Prevention, "Facts about VX," last modified April 4, 2018, https:// emergency.cdc.gov/agent/vx/basics/facts.asp.

146 *One of the Malaysian doctors:* "Doctor: Kim Jong Nam's Underwear Soiled, Pupils Contracted," AP, November 27, 2017.

146 *But they could see:* Pomfret, "Kim Jong Un's Murdered Half Brother."

147 *In March 2019:* Eileen Ng, "Indonesian Woman Freed 2 Years after Killing of Kim Jong Nam," AP, March 11, 2019.

147 *Two months later:* Nicola Smith and Nga Nguyen, "Doan Thi Huong: Vietnamese Suspect in Kim Jong Nam Murder Is Released," *The Telegraph,* May 3, 2019.

147 *In response to South Korean:* Ben Westcott, "Kim Jong Un 'Ordered' Half Brother's Killing, South Korean Intelligence Says," CNN, February 28, 2017.

147 *To the horde of journalists:* Julian Ryall, "North Korea 'Tightens Security at Border to Stop News of Kim Jong-nam's Death from Spreading,'" *The Telegraph,* February 23, 2017.

147 *North Korea also maintained:* "North Korea Agency Names 'Citizen' Killed in Malaysia," *BBC Monitoring Asia Pacific,* March 1, 2017, accessed via LexisNexis.

147 *The United States and South Korea:* "State Department Says North Korea Used Chemical Warfare Agent in Assassination," CBS News, March 6, 2018; Westcott, "Kim Jong Un 'Ordered' Half Brother's Killing."

148 *"He wasn't paranoid":* Anna Fifield, "For Kim Jong Nam, a Sad Ending to a Lonely Life," *WP,* February 24, 2017.

148 *The head of South Korea's:* Arthur Lim, Barney Henderson, and Ju-

lian Ryall, "Kim Jong-nam Murder: Woman Held over Assassination of North Korean Dictator's Brother amid Claims He 'Begged Kim Jong-un to Spare His Life,'" *The Telegraph,* February 15, 2017.

148 *But he tried to lead:* Ibid.

148 *He traveled regularly:* Nadja Sayej, "Kim Jong Nam's Facebook Page Offered a Glimpse into His Life outside North Korea," *Motherboard Vice,* February 28, 2017.

151 *Two decades after:* Cristina Varriale, "North Korea's Other Weapons of Mass Destruction," *Arms Control Today,* September 2018.

151 *The Office of the Director of National Intelligence:* U.S. Office of the Director of National Intelligence, "Unclassified Report to Congress on the Acquisition of Technology Relating to Weapons of Mass Destruction and Advanced Conventional Munitions, 1 January to 31 December 2006," 6, https://www.odni.gov/files/documents/Newsroom/Reports%20and%20Pubs/Acquisition_Technology_Report_030308.pdf.

151 *North Korea has an estimated reserve:* Nuclear Threat Initiative, "North Korea Chemical," last updated April 2018, https://www.nti.org/learn/countries/north-korea/chemical/.

151 *The North reportedly also has four:* Ibid.

151 *Information collected from defectors:* Joseph S. Bermudez, Jr., "North Korea's Chemical Warfare Capabilities," 38 North, October 10, 2013.

152 *Melissa Hanham, an expert on weapons:* Melissa Hanham, "Kim Jong Un Tours Pesticide Facility Capable of Producing Biological Weapons: A 38 North Special Report," 38 North, July 9, 2015.

152 *The United Nations in 2018:* United Nations, *Report of the Panel of Experts Established Pursuant to Resolution 1874 (2009),* March 5, 2018, https://www.un.org/ga/search/view_doc.asp?symbol=S/2018/171.

152 *For at least two decades:* Bermudez, "North Korea's Chemical Warfare Capabilities."

152 *In 2009, for example:* Ibid.

153 *Pyongyang had been a member:* Adam Taylor, "North Korea's On-Again-Off-Again Status as a State Sponsor of Terrorism," *WP,* November 20, 2017.

153 *"The practical effects":* Jeff Mason and David Brunnstrom, "Trump Declares North Korea State Sponsor of Terrorism, Triggers Sanctions," Reuters, November 20, 2017.

ELEVEN: TESTING TRUMP

155 *In September 2015:* Saba Hamedy and Joyce Tseng, "All the Times President Trump Has Insulted North Korea," CNN, March 9, 2018.

155 *In a February 2016 television interview:* Ibid.

155 *"I mean this guy's a bad dude":* Ibid.

155 *Despite the harsh talk:* Ibid.

155 *In his New Year's speech:* "Kim Jong Un's 2017 New Year's Address"; full text is at https://www.ncnk.org/sites/default/files/KJU_2017_New _Years_Address.pdf.

155 *Kim touted North Korea's:* "North Korea Claims Success in Fifth Nuclear Test," BBC News, September 9, 2016.

155 *Ominously, Kim also declared:* "Kim Jong Un's 2017 New Year's Address."

156 *A day later, President-elect Trump:* @realDonaldTrump, January 2, 2017, https://twitter.com/realDonaldTrump/status/81605792022384 6400.

156 *Less than a month after:* Phil Helsel, Stella Kim, and Courtney Kube, "North Korea Launches Missile into Sea, First Since Trump Took Office," NBC News, February 11, 2017.

157 *He "punched" his music teacher:* Michael Kranish and Marc Fisher, *Trump Revealed: The Definitive Biography of the 45th President* (New York: Scribner, 2016), 34–35.

157 Trump Revealed *quoted a classmate:* Ibid., 48.

157 *His favorite sport:* Ibid., 35.

158 *Fred Trump, the patriarch:* Timothy L. O'Brien, *TrumpNation: The Art of Being the Donald* (New York: Grand Central Publishing, 2016), 42.

158 *He placed his name:* Ibid., 58.

158 *In dotting the landscape:* Ibid., 170.

158 *Barbara Corcoran:* Ibid., 74.

158 *Tony Schwartz, the ghostwriter:* Jane Mayer, "Donald Trump's Ghostwriter Tells All," *The New Yorker,* July 25, 2016.

158 *Like Trump, who joined:* Kranish and Fisher, *Trump Revealed,* 52.

159 *In April 2017:* Stephen Adler, Steve Holland, and Jeff Mason, "Exclusive: Trump Says 'Major, Major' Conflict with North Korea Possible, but Seeks Diplomacy," Reuters, April 27, 2017.

159 *Trump "fancied himself":* Kranish and Fisher, *Trump Revealed,* 4.

159 *His supporters:* Ibid., 352.

160 *The Chinese are untrustworthy:* Jieun Kim, "North Korea Stokes Anti-China Sentiment in Response to Tougher Sanctions," Radio Free Asia, January 4, 2018.

160 *After reviewing Trump's statements:* Thomas Wright, "Trump's 19th Century Foreign Policy," Politico, January 20, 2016.

160 *Trump bragged:* The White House, "Remarks by President Trump on the Administration's National Security Strategy," December 18,

2017, https://www.whitehouse.gov/briefings-statements/remarks
-president-trump-administrations-national-security-strategy/.

161 *"We have 25,000 soldiers":* Louis Jacobson, "Donald Trump Mostly
Wrong That 'We Get Practically Nothing' from South Korea for
U.S. Troop Presence," PolitiFact, January 10, 2016.

161 *"How long will we go on defending":* John Power, "Donald Trump's
Problem with the US-Korea Alliance," *The Diplomat,* July 23, 2015.

161 *And as president in 2017:* Bob Woodward, *Fear: Trump in the White
House* (New York: Simon & Schuster, 2018), 264.

161 *"Fear," candidate Trump:* Ibid., front matter.

161 *Trump the businessman:* Niraj Chokshi, "The 100-Plus Times Donald Trump Assured Us That America Is a Laughingstock," *WP,*
January 27, 2016.

TWELVE: TESTING KIM

163 *After a two-month policy review:* Matthew Pennington, "Trump
Strategy on NKorea: 'Maximum Pressure and Engagement,'" AP,
April 14, 2017.

163 *Although Trump declared:* @realDonaldTrump, June 30, 2018, https://
twitter.com/realDonaldTrump/status/880892632142143490.

164 *Obama's new measures:* U.S. Mission to the United Nations, "Fact
Sheet: Resolution 2371 (2017) Strengthening Sanctions on North
Korea," August 5, 2017, https://usun.usmission.gov/fact-sheet
-resolution-2371-2017-strengthening-sanctions-on-north-korea
/?_ga=2.75938005.1950839997.1564779402-587643110.1564779402.

164 *The regime tested:* Joby Warrick, "Experts: North Korea's Missile
Was a Real ICBM—and a Grave Milestone," *WP,* July 4, 2017.

164 *According to state media:* Dagyum Ji, "North Korea Says ICBM Can
Carry 'Large-Size Heavy' Nuclear Warhead," NK News, July 5,
2017.

164 *Alarmed and surprised:* "Russia, China to N. Korea: Stop All Missile
Tests," *The Straits Times,* July 5, 2017.

165 *Secretary of State Rex Tillerson:* Elise Hu, "Tillerson Confirms North
Korea Missile an ICBM, Calls for Global Action," NPR, July 3, 2017.

165 *He tweeted, "North Korea has":* @realDonaldTrump, July 3, 2017,
https://twitter.com/realDonaldTrump/status/882061157900718081.

165 *In response to these condemnations:* Foster Klug and Hyung-jin Kim,
"Kim Vows North Korea's Nukes Are Not on Negotiation Table,"
AP, July 5, 2017.

166 *In* The Art of the Deal: Peter Economy, "11 Winning Negotiation
Tactics from Donald Trump's 'The Art of the Deal,'" *Inc.,* May 7,
2016.

166 *A few years later:* Glenn Plaskin, "Donald Trump," *Playboy,* March 1, 1990.

166 *During his June 2017 trip:* Anna Fifield, "Dennis Rodman Just Gave Kim Jong Un 'The Art of the Deal.' And It May Be a Genius Move," *WP,* June 15, 2017.

167 *In August 2017:* "N. Korea Threatens 'Physical' Actions over New U.N. Sanctions," Yonhap News Agency, August 8, 2017.

167 *While at his golf club:* Karen DeYoung and John Wagner, "Trump Threatens 'Fire and Fury' in Response to North Korean Threats," *WP,* August 8, 2017.

167 *A few days later:* @realDonaldTrump, August 11, 2017, https://twitter.com/realDonaldTrump/status/895970429734711298; Dan Merica, Kevin Liptak, and Angela Dewan, "Trump Warns North Korea: US Military 'Locked and Loaded,'" CNN, August 11, 2017.

167 *Russia boosted its air defense:* Mythili Sampathkumar, "South Korea in Plea to Avoid North Korea War after Trump's 'Locked and Loaded' Comment," *The Independent,* August 14, 2017.

167 *In China, an editorial:* "Chinese Paper Says China Should Stay Neutral If North Korea Attacks First," Reuters, August 10, 2017.

168 *Chinese president Xi:* Eric Talmadge and Jonathan Lemire, "Xi Calls for Calm after Trump Says US Is 'Locked and Loaded,'" AP, August 12, 2017.

168 *He stated that the United States:* David Nakamura and Anne Gearan, "In U.N. Speech, Trump Threatens to 'Totally Destroy North Korea' and Calls Kim Jong Un 'Rocket Man,'" *WP,* September 19, 2017.

168 *In October, he tweeted:* @realDonaldTrump, October 1, 2017, https://twitter.com/realDonaldTrump/status/914497877543735296.

168 *The National Security Strategy:* National Security Strategy of the United States of America, December 2017, https://www.whitehouse.gov/wp-content/uploads/2017/12/NSS-Final-12-18-2017-0905.pdf.

168 *"running out of time":* Steve Holland, "World 'Running Out of Time' on North Korea, Trump to Tell Asia: White House," Reuters, November 2, 2017.

168 *The potential for war:* Alex Pappas, "H. R. McMaster: Potential for War with North Korea Increases 'Every Day,' *Fox News,* December 2, 2017.

169 *"North Korea is ruled":* National Security Strategy of the United States of America, December 2017.

169 *Amid ongoing tweets:* @realDonaldTrump, October 7, 2017, https://twitter.com/realDonaldTrump/status/916751271960436737.

169 *McMaster commented:* Jason Le Miere, "U.S. Prepared to Launch

'Preventive War' against North Korea, says H. R. McMaster," *Newsweek,* August 5, 2017; Jeff Daniels, "Defense Secretary Mattis Urges US Army 'to Be Ready' with North Korea Military Options," CNBC, October 9, 2017; Eli Watkins, "Tillerson on North Korea: Diplomacy Will Continue 'Until the First Bomb Drops,'" CNN, October 16, 2017.

169 *"[Trump] is ready":* Sophie Tatum, "Graham on North Korea: 'We're Headed to a War If Things Don't Change,'" CNN, November 29, 2017.

170 *The murder of Kim Jong Nam:* Conor Finnegan and Meghan Keneally, "Timeline of Otto Warmbier's Saga in North Korea," ABC News, June 19, 2017.

172 *Tokyo, with a population:* Kathleen McInnis, Andrew Feickert, Mark Manyin, Steven Hildreth, Mary Beth Nikitin, Emma Chanlett-Avery, and Catherine Theohary, "The North Korean Nuclear Challenge: Military Options and Issues for Congress," Congressional Research Service Report for Congress, R44994, November 6, 2017, https://fas.org/sgp/crs/nuke/R44994.pdf.

172 *North Korea's chemical weapons:* Yochi Dreazen, "Here's What War with North Korea Would Look Like," Vox, February 8, 2018.

173 *After spending a decade researching:* Susan Southard, *Nagasaki: Life after Nuclear War* (New York: Viking, 2015).

173 *Roberta Cohen, a leading:* Paul Park, "Unpacking the Unthinkable: Experts Discuss North Korea Scenarios," The Brookings Institution Order from Chaos Blog, April 26, 2018, https://www.brookings.edu /blog/order-from-chaos/2018/04/26/unpacking-the-unthinkable -experts-discuss-north-korea-scenarios/.

174 *"to see massive trade disruptions":* Ibid.

174 *Just days after Trump's "Rocket Man":* "Full Text of Kim Jong-un's Response to President Trump," *NYT,* September 22, 2017.

175 *Kim reiterated his ownership:* "Kim Jong Un's 2018 New Year's Address"; full text is at https://www.ncnk.org/node/1427.

176 *Not one to sit around:* @realDonaldTrump, January 2, 2018, https:// twitter.com/realdonaldtrump/status/948355557022420992.

176 *The U.S. ambassador:* Pamela Falk, "Nikki Haley Says North Korean Regime 'Will Be Utterly Destroyed' If War Comes," CBS News, November 30, 2017.

176 *McMaster said in early December:* Alex Pappas, "H. R. McMaster: Potential for War with North Korea Increases 'Every Day,'" Fox News, December 2, 2017.

177 *The Bulletin of the Atomic Scientists:* @BulletinAtomic, January 25, 2018, https://twitter.com/BulletinAtomic/status/956550260318285824.

177 *In its statement:* Barbara Goldberg, "'Doomsday Clock' Closest to Midnight Since Cold War over Nuclear Threat," Reuters, January 25, 2018.

177 *Credible media reports:* Zachary Cohen, Nicole Gaouette, Barbara Starr, and Kevin Liptak, "Trump Advisers Clash over 'Bloody Nose' Strike on North Korea," CNN, February 1, 2018.

177 *The threat of a conflict:* Maria Perez, "Chilling Video: Child Placed in Storm Drain during Hawaii Missile Scare," *Newsweek,* January 15, 2018.

THIRTEEN: THE METAMORPHOSIS

179 *Moon was the son:* "Moon Jae-in: South Korea's President with Humble Roots," BBC, April 26, 2018; S. Nathan Park, "The Man behind the North Korea Negotiations," *The Atlantic,* March 12, 2018.

180 *Kim even brought:* Michelle Ye Hee Lee, "How My North Korean–Born Grandparents Taught Me about Loss, Memory and the Power of Pyongyang Cold Noodles," *WP,* June 8, 2018.

180 *The picture of the two leaders:* "Korean Summit Sparks Cold Noodle Craze," BBC, April 27, 2018.

180 *Kim Jong Un's image rehabilitation:* "Kim Jong Un's 2018 New Year's Address."

181 *Moon came into office:* Park, "Man behind North Korea Negotiations."

181 *Following Trump's "fire and fury":* Alex Ward, "The President of South Korea Has a Strong Message for Trump," Vox, August 17, 2017.

181 *A month later:* Lee Sun-young, "Moon Calls for UN Role in North Korea Crisis," *The Korea Herald,* September 21, 2017.

182 *Moon faced the challenge:* "Moon Jae-in's Five-Year Road Map Unveiled," *The Korea Herald,* July 19, 2017.

182 *Kim also said he was willing:* "Kim Jong Un's 2018 New Year's Address."

182 *The leadership in Seoul:* Steve George and Taehoon Lee, "South Korean Leader Welcomes North Korean Olympic Participation," CNN, January 2, 2018.

182 *Alarmed by Trump's tough talk:* Rachel Premack, "South Korea Is Getting Seriously Worried about Low Olympics Ticket Sales," *Forbes,* December 14, 2017.

182 *A declassified CIA memo:* Central Intelligence Agency, "South Korea: Terrorist Threats to the Seoul Olympics," memorandum, May 3, 1988, https://www.cia.gov/library/readingroom/docs/CIA-RDP90 T00100R000201120001-7.pdf.

183   *Critics charged that:* Hyonhee Shin, "Ski Lift: North Korea May Capitalize on Joint Olympics Training Visit," Reuters, January 21, 2018; Anna Fifield, "South Korea Went Gaga over a North Korean Singer. Just Wait until the Rest Arrive," *WP,* January 22, 2018.

183   *And as the Koreas engaged:* "U.S. Has No Plans to Meet N.K. Officials around Olympics: State Department," Yonhap News Agency, January 4, 2019.

183   *Secretary of State Tillerson:* Carol Morello, "North Korean Nuclear Weapons Crisis at a 'Tenuous Stage,' Tillerson says," *WP,* January 16, 2018.

183   *Meanwhile, Kim dispatched:* Josh Rogin, "The United States and South Korea Now Openly Disagree on North Korea," *WP,* February 8, 2018.

184   *Van Jackson, an Asia specialist:* Van Jackson, *On the Brink: Trump, Kim, and the Threat of Nuclear War* (Cambridge: Cambridge University Press, 2018), 173.

185   *Soon after the Olympics:* Foster Klug, "North Korean Dictator, Seoul Envoy Have 'Openhearted Talk,' " AP, March 5, 2018.

185   *Buoyed by Kim's comments:* Choe Sang-Hun and Mark Landler, "Raising Hopes, North Korea Offers to Talk about Its Nuclear Arsenal," *NYT,* March 6, 2018.

185   *Beijing welcomed the development:* Choe Sang-Hun and Mark Landler, "North Korea Signals Willingness to 'Denuclearize,' South Says," *NYT,* March 6, 2018.

185   *And so did President Trump:* @realDonaldTrump, March 6, 2018, https://twitter.com/realdonaldtrump/status/971025582061424640?lang=en.

185   *Trump then stunned:* Anna Fifield, David Nakamura, and Seung Min Kim, "Trump Accepts Invitation to Meet with North Korean Leader Kim Jong Un," *WP,* March 8, 2018.

185   *In the meantime:* "Panmunjom Declaration"; full text is at http://documents.latimes.com/panmunjom-declaration-peace/.

186   *Kim's actions:* The White House, "Joint Statement of President Donald J. Trump of the United States of America and Chairman Kim Jong Un of the Democratic People's Republic of Korea at the Singapore Summit," June 12, 2018, https://www.whitehouse.gov/briefings-statements/joint-statement-president-donald-j-trump-united-states-america-chairman-kim-jong-un-democratic-peoples-republic-korea-singapore-summit/; Ingrid Melander, "North Korea Leader Sincere, Must Be Rewarded for Move to Abandon Nuclear Weapons: South Korean President," Reuters, October 14, 2018.

186   *But as Jackson pointed out:* Jackson, *On the Brink,* 175.

186 *After all, the South Korean envoys:* Nick Allen, Nicola Smith, Chris Graham, Neil Connor, Julian Ryall, and Rob Crilly, "Donald Trump to Meet Kim Jong-un: President Says 'Deal Very Much in the Making' after Day of Mixed Messages," *The Telegraph,* March 10, 2018; @realDonaldTrump, March 8, 2018, https://twitter.com/realdonald trump/status/971915531346436096?lang=en.

187 *The Republican chairman:* U.S. House of Representatives, Committee on Foreign Affairs, "Chairman Royce Statement on North Korea," press release, March 8, 2018, https://republicans-foreign affairs.house.gov/press-release/chairman-royce-statement-north -korea-2/.

187 *And Senator Lindsey Graham stated:* @LindseyGrahamSC, March 8, 2018, https://twitter.com/lindseygrahamsc/status/971917045674766336.

187 *The president and these officials:* Heuer, *Psychology of Intelligence Analysis,* 132.

187 *"When another country's actions":* Ibid., 139.

187 *U.N. sanctions cut off:* U.S. Mission to the United Nations, "Fact Sheet: Resolution 2375 (2017) Strengthening Sanctions on North Korea," September 11, 2017, https://usun.usmission.gov/fact-sheet -resolution-2375-2017-strengthening-sanctions-on-north-korea/.

188 *North Korea does not publish:* Daniel Shane, "North Korea's Economy Just Had Its Worst Year in Two Decades," CNN, July 20, 2018.

189 *When Moon Jae-in was elected:* Bae Hyun-jung, "Full Text of Moon's Speech at the Korber Foundation," *The Korea Herald,* July 7, 2017.

189 *The former chief of staff:* S. Nathan Park, "Moon's Secret Weapon Is Sunshine," *Foreign Policy,* May 19, 2017.

189 *He said in his 2018 New Year's address:* "Kim Jong Un's 2018 New Year's Address."

189 *At a rare party meeting:* Anna Fifield, "North Korea Says It Will Suspend Nuclear and Missile Tests, Shut Down Test Site," *WP,* April 20, 2018.

190 On the day of Kim's speech to the party: @realDonaldTrump, April 20, 2018, https://twitter.com/realdonaldtrump/status/987463564305 797126?lang=en.

190 *In response to skepticism:* @realDonaldTrump, April 22, 2018, https://twitter.com/realdonaldtrump/status/988126197619068928 ?lang=en.

190 *As a result of Kim's:* "South Korea Turns Off Loudspeaker Broadcasts into North," BBC News, April 23, 2018; Choe Sang-Hun, "South Korea Hands Kim Jong-un a Path to Prosperity on a USB Drive," *NYT,* May 10, 2018.

190 *And China, for its part:* Joonho Kim, "North Korean Workers Return

to China in Defiance of UN Restrictions," Radio Free Asia, April 4, 2018, https://www.rfa.org/english/news/korea/workers-0404201813 4944.html.

190 *For the first time:* Ben Westcott, "Chinese Foreign Minister Meets with Kim Jong Un amid Warming Ties," CNN, May 3, 2018.

191 *Kim almost certainly relished:* Kanga Kong, "Kim Jong Un Now Has a Nearly 80% Approval Rating . . . in South Korea," *Time,* May 2, 2018.

191 *His reported sense of humor:* Michael Madden, "Koreas Summit: Five Key Moments from the Kim-Moon Meeting," BBC News, April 27, 2018.

FOURTEEN: THE QUEEN OF PYONGYANG

192 *South Korean media consulted:* Sofia Lotto Persio, "Reading Kim Jong Un's Lips: North Korean Leader on His Marriage, Nuclear Weapons and Trump," *Newsweek,* May 2, 2018.

192 *But things got personal:* Anna Fifield, "What Did the Korean Leaders Talk about on Those Park Benches? Trump, Mainly," *WP,* May 2, 2018.

193 *The way Ri looked:* Hollie McKay, "North Korea's First Lady Ri Sol-ju Remains a Mystery," Fox News, November 15, 2017.

193 *Kim's grandfather had:* Quoted in Bronwen Dalton, Kyungja Jung, and Jacqueline Willis, "Fashion and the Social Construction of Femininity in North Korea," *Asian Studies Review* 41, no. 4 (2017), https://doi.org/10.1080/10357823.2017.1367757.

194 *And under the rule of Kim Jong Il:* J. R. Thorpe, "The Feminist History of Bicycles," *Bustle,* May 12, 2017.

194 *According to information gathered:* "N. Korean Leader's Wife Visits S. Korea in 2005: Spy Agency," Yonhap News Agency, July 26, 2012.

194 *When touring the water park:* Erica Cheung, "Ri Sol-Ju, North Korea's New First Lady, Remains a Style Mystery," *The Huffington Post,* July 25, 2012.

194 *There she is in 2014:* Michelle Mark, "The Mysterious Life of Kim Jong Un's Wife, Ri Sol Ju, Who Probably Has 3 Children and Frequently Disappears from the Public Eye," *Business Insider,* September 27, 2017.

195 *As Korea scholars Bronwen Dalton:* Dalton, Jung, and Willis, "Fashion and the Social Construction," 512.

195 *Kang is usually shown:* Ibid.

196 *The film shows Ko:* Darcie Draudt, "Family Tradition: Modern Representation and the Ideal Woman in Kim Jong-un's First Year," in *Change and Continuity in North Korean Politics,* ed. Adam Cathcart,

Robert Winstanley-Chesters, and Christopher Green (London: Routledge, 2017), 46.

196 *"ideal, selfless public servant":* Suzy Kim, "Revolutionary Mothers: Women in the North Korean Revolution, 1945–1950," *Comparative Studies in Society and History* 52, no. 4 (2010): 761.

196 *In their article:* Dalton, Jung, and Willis, "Fashion and the Social Construction," 507.

196 *Her glamour, esteemed position:* Rosie Perper, "Kim Jong-un's Wife, Ri Sol-ju, Just Had Her Status Upgraded as North Korea Tries to Show It Has a Normal 'First Couple,'" *Business Insider,* April 16, 2018.

197 *Ri's role as the First Wife:* Draudt, "Family Tradition," 47.

197 *John Park, a Korea expert:* Tom O'Connor, "Who Is Kim Jong Un's Wife? You Know Melania Trump, Meet North Korea's First Lady, Ri Sol Ju," *Newsweek,* September 27, 2017.

197 *A smiling, appreciative Kim:* Justin McCurry, "From Missiles to Moisturiser: Kim Jong-un Visits North Korean Cosmetics Factory," *The Guardian,* October 30, 2017.

198 *One defector told the online periodical* Daily NK: "Report: Killer Heels Go Down a Storm in North," *Daily NK,* July 31, 2014.

198 *Suki Kim, the journalist:* Kim, *Without You, There Is No Us,* 187.

198 *Defectors from North Korea:* Liberty in North Korea, "The Jangmadang Generation," video, accessed January 10, 2019, https://www.nkmillennials.com/?_ke=eyJrbF9lbWFpbCI6ICJvbmVmcmVla29yZWFAeWFob28uY29tIiwgImtsX2NvbXBhbnlfaWQiOiAibXpQNERlIn0%3D.

198 *A North Korean source put it this way:* Kang Mi Jin, "Hairstyles and Hallyu as Security Steps Back," *Daily NK,* July 31, 2014.

199 *Whether emboldened by:* Jesse Johnson, "Holy Smokes: South Korean Envoy Reportedly Told Kim to Kick Cigarette Habit," *The Japan Times,* April 9, 2018.

199 *Instead, lovely Ri:* Ibid.

200 *The* South China Morning Post: Yujing Liu, "Kim Jong-un Wife's Fashion Sense a Hit with China's Public," *SCMP,* March 28, 2018.

200 *On Weibo, one of China's biggest:* Christina Zhao, "Kim Jong Un Wife's Stylish Fashion Sense Is a Hit in China," *Newsweek,* March 28, 2018.

200 *Another post compared her:* Liu, "Kim Jong-un Wife's Fashion Sense."

200 *Ri also garnered favorable attention:* Jung Da-min, "Two Former Singers Hit Right Note in Pyongyang," *The Korea Times,* September 18, 2018.

201 *The couple have at least one:* Tom O'Connor, "Who Are Kim Jong

Un's Children and Does North Korea Have an Heir?," *Newsweek,*
December 30, 2017.

FIFTEEN: WHEN TRUMP MET KIM

203 *When Trump, who had once dreamed:* O'Brien, *TrumpNation,* 53.

203 *Trump's biographers:* Kranish and Fisher, *Trump Revealed,* 352.

204 *There was a triumphant:* Carol Morello, Anna Fifield, and David Nakamura, "North Korea Frees 3 American Prisoners Ahead of a Planned Trump-Kim Summit," *WP,* May 9, 2018.

204 *Trump tweeted on April 30:* @realDonaldTrump, April 30, 2018, https://twitter.com/realDonaldTrump/status/990928644100034561.

204 *A Pew Research Center poll:* Pew Research Center, "Public Supports U.S. Talks with North Korea; Many Doubt Whether Its Leaders Are 'Serious,'" May 10, 2018, http://www.people-press.org/2018/05/10 /public-supports-u-s-talks-with-north-korea-many-doubt-whether -its-leaders-are-serious/.

204 *A CNN poll that was taken:* Grace Sparks and Jennifer Agiesta, "CNN Poll: Three-Quarters Approve of Trump's Plans to Meet with Kim Jong Un," CNN, May 10, 2018.

204 *South Koreans also:* Jessica Kwong, "Donald Trump and Kim Jong Un Approval Ratings Reach Highest Ever Marks in South Korea, Poll Finds," *Newsweek,* June 2, 2018.

204 *For Trump, his decision:* Ryan Nobles, "House Republicans Nominate Trump for Nobel Peace Prize," CNN, May 2, 2018.

206 *"fill[s] gaps in":* Heuer, *Psychology of Intelligence Analysis,* 70.

206 *"Minds are like parachutes":* Ibid., 65.

206 A Tradecraft Primer: U.S. Government, *A Tradecraft Primer: Structured Analytic Techniques for Improving Intelligence Analysis,* March 2009, https://www.cia.gov/library/center-for-the-study-of-intelligence /csi-publications/books-and-monographs/Tradecraft%20Primer -apr09.pdf.

207 *As* The New Yorker's: Patrick Radden Keefe, "How Mark Burnett Resurrected Donald Trump as an Icon of American Success," *The New Yorker,* January 7, 2019.

207 *Trump dismissed reports:* Shane Harris, "Testimony by Intelligence Chiefs on Global Threats Highlights Differences with President," *WP,* January 29, 2019.

207 *The media reported:* Shane Harris, Josh Dawsey, and Ellen Nakashima, "Trump Grows Frustrated with Coats, Leading Some to Fear He Might Be Fired," *WP,* February 19, 2019.

207 *In November 2017:* The White House, "Remarks by President

Trump to the National Assembly of the Republic of Korea, Seoul, Republic of Korea," November 7, 2017, https://www.whitehouse .gov/briefings-statements/remarks-president-trump-national -assembly-republic-korea-seoul-republic-korea/.

208 *Speaking from the Oval Office:* Cristina Maza, "Trump Promises North Korea Can Be 'Very Rich' with Kim Jong Un in Power," *Newsweek,* May 17, 2018.

208 *"What Chairman Kim":* "Transcript: Secretary of State Mike Pompeo on 'Face the Nation,'" May 13, 2018, https://www.cbsnews.com /news/transcript-secretary-of-state-mike-pompeo-on-face-the -nation-may-13-2018/.

208 *"Vision is my best asset":* Plaskin, "Donald Trump."

208 *Before the meeting with Kim:* Brian Bennett and Tessa Berenson, "President Trump 'Doesn't Think He Needs' to Prepare Much for His Meeting with North Korea's Kim Jong Un," *Time,* May 16, 2018.

208 *A Republican adviser admitted:* S. V. Date, "In Trump's Zero-Sum World, the Summit Already Has a Winner, and It's Not Trump," *HuffPost,* June 1, 2018.

208 *And less than a week:* John Wagner, "'It's about the Attitude': Trump Says He Doesn't Have to Prepare Much for His Summit with North Korea's Leader," *WP,* June 7, 2018.

209 *Apparently, the White House had not:* Eliana Johnson, "Trump and Bolton Spurn Top-Level North Korea Planning," Politico, June 7, 2018.

209 *"I truly believe North Korea":* @realDonaldTrump, May 27, 2018, https://twitter.com/realdonaldtrump/status/1000831304836018176 ?lang=cn.

209 *Before the second summit:* The White House, "Fact Sheet: President Trump Is Committed to Achieving Transformational Peace for the United States, the Korean Peninsula, and the World," February 21, 2019, https://www.whitehouse.gov/briefings-statements/president -trump-committed-achieving-transformational-peace-united-states -korean-peninsula-world/.

209 *Four months later:* The White House, "Remarks by President Trump and President Moon of the Republic of Korea in Joint Press Conference," June 30, 2019, https://www.whitehouse.gov/briefings -statements/remarks-president-trump-president-moon-republic -korea-joint-press-conference/.

210 *A senior North Korean official:* "North Korea: Full Response to US Remarks on Trump-Kim Summit," BBC News, May 16, 2018.

210 *"improvising was his strength"*: Woodward, *Fear,* 230–31.

211 *Kim told a Politburo meeting:* Jonathan Cheng, "North Korea's Kim Jong Un Confirms Summit with U.S.," *WSJ,* April 9, 2018.

212 *Kim's success in winning:* Rick Noack, "China's Official Release on Kim Jong Un's Visit, Annotated," *WP,* March 28, 2018.

212 *Kim must have been:* Ibid.

213 *In late 2017, Kim dispatched:* Anna Fifield, "North Korea Taps GOP Analysts to Better Understand Trump and His Messages," *WP,* September 26, 2017.

213 *In an interview:* "Transcript: Secretary of State Mike Pompeo on 'Face the Nation,'" May 13, 2018.

213 *Kim almost certainly:* Zachary Cohen, Nicole Gaouette, and Kaitlan Collins, "Trump Replaces H. R. McMaster as National Security Adviser with John Bolton," CNN, March 23, 2018.

214 *Those qualities in the two men:* Joshua Berlinger, "North Korea Warns of Nuclear Showdown, Calls Pence 'Political Dummy,'" CNN, May 24, 2018.

214 *Instead, President Trump canceled:* "Trump's Letter to Kim Jong-un to Cancel Summit: Read It in Full," *The Guardian,* May 24, 2018.

214 *Kim then sent:* Joon-bum Hwang, "Kim Yong-chol's Washington, DC, a Positive Signal for 2nd NK-US Summit," *The Hankyoreh,* January 21, 2019.

215 *But then in what probably:* The White House, "Remarks by President Trump after Meeting with Vice Chairman Kim Yong Chol of the Democratic People's Republic of Korea," June 1, 2018, https://www.whitehouse.gov/briefings-statements/remarks-president-trump-meeting-vice-chairman-kim-yong-chol-democratic-peoples-republic-korea/.

215 *Sentosa Island in Singapore:* "Sentosa Island," Lonely Planet, accessed January 18, 2019, https://www.lonelyplanet.com/singapore/singapore-city/sentosa-island.

216 *At the luxurious:* Diane Leow, "5 Things You Might Not Know about Singapore's Capella Hotel, Venue of the Trump-Kim Summit," ChannelNewsAsia, June 6, 2018.

216 *Kim waved to the crowds:* Lauren Said-Moorhouse, "Kim Jong Un Goes for Surprise Nighttime Walk Ahead of Summit," CNN, June 11, 2018.

216 *Later, in a more intimate scene:* "'A Scene from a Sci-Fi Movie': What Kim Told Trump about Their Meeting—Video," *The Guardian,* June 12, 2018, https://www.theguardian.com/world/video/2018/jun/12/a-scene-from-a-sci-fi-movie-what-kim-told-trump-about-their-meeting-video.

217 *During the nearly hour-long:* "'Will He Shake the Hand of Peace?' Here's the Video President Trump Showed to Kim Jong Un," *Time*, June 12, 2018.

217 *Although Trump said:* "Trump-Kim Summit: Journalists to Work from F1 Pit Building's Media Centre," *The Straits Times*, June 6, 2018.

218 *"As an example":* The White House, "Press Conference by President Trump," June 12, 2018, https://www.whitehouse.gov/briefings -statements/press-conference-president-trump/.

218 *The communiqué, widely panned:* The White House, "Joint Statement of President Donald J. Trump of the United States of America and Chairman Kim Jong Un of the Democratic People's Republic of Korea at the Singapore Summit."

218 *The communiqué fell far short:* U.S. State Department, "Joint Statement of the Fourth Round of the Six-Party Talks," September 19, 2005, https://www.state.gov/p/eap/regional/c15455.htm.

219 *Trump crafted a narrative of success:* Everett Rosenfeld and Nyshka Chandran, "Trump Says North Korea Will Keep Its Promises, and the US Will Stop War Games," CNBC, June 12, 2018.

219 *Instead, he made gratuitous comments:* "Press Conference by President Trump," June 12, 2018.

219 *And the president seemed:* Ibid.

219 *On the way back:* @realDonaldTrump, June 13, 2018, https://twitter .com/realDonaldTrump/status/1006837823469735936.

220 *Although certainly in line:* Heuer, *Psychology of Intelligence Analysis,* 116.

220 *Trump emphasized his confidence:* The White House, "Remarks by President Trump in Press Gaggle," June 15, 2018, https://www .whitehouse.gov/briefings-statements/remarks-president-trump -press-gaggle/.

220 *After having declared:* Matt Spetalnick, "U.S. Identifies North Korea Missile Test Site It Says Kim Committed to Destroy," Reuters, June 20, 2018.

220 *At the summit, Kim ignored:* Charlie Campbell, "Kim Jong Un Promises 'Major Change' after First Ever Summit between Leaders of U.S. and North Korea," *Time,* June 12, 2018.

221 *As President Trump stood:* "'We Decided to Leave the Past Behind.' Read What President Trump and Kim Jong Un Said While Signing Joint Agreement," *Time,* June 12, 2018.

221 *Washington and Seoul continue to:* Benjamin Haas, "North Korea Is Still Developing Nuclear Weapons, Says IAEA," *The Guardian,* August 22, 2018; Kirsti Knolle, "No Indication North Korean Nuclear

Activities Stopped: IAEA," Reuters, August 21, 2018; Zachary Cohen, "New Satellite Images Reveal Activity at Unidentified North Korean Missile Base," CNN, December 6, 2018.

221 *As the Trump administration:* Donna Borak and Zachary Cohen, "John Bolton Says North Korea Failure to Meet Commitments Requires Second Kim-Trump Summit," CNN, December 4, 2018.

221 *Vice President Pence similarly:* Tsuyoshi Nagasawa, "Trump-Kim Talks to Cover 'Concrete' Denuclearization, Pence Says," *Nikkei Asian Review,* January 21, 2019.

222 *As if in frustration:* "N Korea Commentary Discusses US Ties, Denuclearization," *BBC Monitoring Asia Pacific,* December 22, 2018.

222 *To underscore what he wants:* "Kim Jong Un's 2019 New Year's Address"; full text is at https://www.ncnk.org/resources/publications /kimjongun_2019_newyearaddress.pdf/file_view.

222 *President Moon touted:* "Cheong Wa Dae Hails NK Leader's Address," Yonhap News Agency, January 1, 2019, https://en.yna.co.kr /view/AEN20190101003600315; @realDonaldTrump, January 1, 2019, https://twitter.com/realDonaldTrump/status/1080240049780940800.

223 *He smiled contentedly:* Ben Westcott, James Griffiths, Meg Wagner, and Veronica Rocha, "President Trump Meets with Kim Jong Un," CNN, February 28, 2019.

223 *Like Trump, Kim miscalculated:* See Jung Pak, "The Good, the Bad, and the Ugly at the US–North Korea Summit in Hanoi," The Brookings Institution Order from Chaos Blog, March 4, 2019, https:// www.brookings.edu/blog/order-from-chaos/2019/03/04/the-good -the-bad-and-the-ugly-at-the-us-north-korea-summit-in-hanoi/.

224 *Four months after Hanoi:* @realDonaldTrump, June 28, 2019, https:// twitter.com/realdonaldtrump/status/1144740178948493314.

CONCLUSION: THE METASTASIS

225 *In November 2018:* Lee Tae-hee, "EBS Under Fire for Kids' Kim Jong-un Puzzle Kit," *The Korea Herald,* November 26, 2018.

226 *In fact, if you look:* U.S. Senate Select Committee on Intelligence, "Statement for the Record: Worldwide Threat Assessment of the US Intelligence Community," January 29, 2019, https://www.dni .gov/files/ODNI/documents/2019-ATA-SFR---SSCI.pdf.

228 *And luckily for Kim Jong Un:* McEachern, "Centralizing North Korean Policymaking," 39.

228 *Senator Lindsey Graham:* Ellen Mitchell, "Graham on North Korea: 'We're Headed toward a War If Things Don't Change,'" *The Hill,* November 29, 2017.

228 *Nikki Haley, the U.S. ambassador:* Ambassador Nikki Haley, Re-

marks at an Emergency UN Security Council Briefing on North Korea, September 4, 2017, https://usun.usmission.gov/remarks-at -an-emergency-un-security-council-briefing-on-north-korea/.

228 *Secretary of Defense:* David Sanger and Choe Sang-Hun, "North Korean Nuclear Test Draws U.S. Warning of 'Massive Military Response,'" *NYT,* September 2, 2017.

229 *"When one is firmly equipped":* "2013 Plenary Meeting of the WPK Central Committee and 7th Session of Supreme People's Assembly," http://www.nkeconwatch.com/2013/04/01/.

230 *"as a peace-loving nuclear power":* "Kim Jong Un's 2018 New Year's Address."

230 *Evans Revere, a former top Asia expert:* Evans Revere, "2017: Year of Decision on the Korean Peninsula," Brookings Institution Report, March 2, 2017, https://www.brookings.edu/research/2017-year-of -decision-on-the-korean-peninsula/.

230 *"Once an observer":* Heuer, *Psychology of Intelligence Analysis,* 11.

231 *For some of these peace advocates:* Sarah Lazare, "Liberals Go Hardline on Korea: An Interview with Christine Ahn," Verso, June 19, 2018, https://www.versobooks.com/blogs/3889-liberals-go-hardline -on-korea-an-interview-with-christine-ahn.

231 *They and others have argued:* @GBrazinsky, December 13, 2018, https://twitter.com/GBrazinsky/status/1073249132029140992.

232 *Some academics insist:* John Delury, "Kim Jong Un Has a Dream. The U.S. Should Help Him Realize It," *NYT,* September 21, 2018.

232 *Sheila Miyoshi Jager.* Sheila Miyoshi Jager, "What Trump Needs to Know about North Korea's History," *Politico Magazine,* August 9, 2017.

233 *For Kim Jong Un:* Cited in Josh Smith, "'Treasured Sword': North Korea Seen as Reliant as Ever on Nuclear Arsenal as Talks Stall," Reuters, November 13, 2018.

233 *Following the sixth nuclear test:* Seungmock Oh, "DPRK Media Highlights Rallies Celebrating Completion of State Nuclear Force," NK News, December 11, 2017.

234 *Jager concisely sums up:* Sheila Miyoshi Jager, *Brothers at War: The Unending Conflict in Korea* (New York: W. W. Norton, 2013), 7.

235 *A panel of former security officials:* Central Intelligence Agency, *Exploring the Implications of Alternative North Korea Endgames,* January 21, 1998.

235 *Richard Bush, a Brookings scholar:* Richard Bush, "The Real Reason a North Korean Nuclear Weapon Is So Terrifying—and It's Not What You Think," The Brookings Institution Order from Chaos Blog, August 9, 2017.

236 *Over the years, Beijing's leaders:* "China Urges Calm on Korean Peninsula after DPRK, ROK Exchange Fire," *Global Times,* April 1, 2014; "China's President Xi Jinping Calls for Calm, Restraint on Korean Peninsula in Meet with North Korean Envoy," *The Straits Times,* June 1, 2016; "China Calls for Restraint after US Bomber Flyover of ROK," CCTV, September 14, 2016, http://english.cctv.com /2016/09/14/VIDEmJR6zavbLb6u2R8svplg160914.shtml.

237 *Xi Jinping's first visit:* Joshua Berlinger, "Xi Jinping and Kim Jong Un Pledge 'Peace and Stability' during Historic Pyongyang Visit," CNN, June 20, 2019.

237 *Russia, too, has been:* "China and Russia Call for Easing of North Korea Sanctions," ChannelNewsAsia, September 27, 2018.

237 *Moscow's 2014 cancellation:* "Russia Forgives North Korean Debt," VOA News, June 17, 2014.

237 *All previous U.S. administrations:* Michael Rosenwald, "The U.S. Did Nothing after North Korea Shot Down a Navy Spy Plane in 1969. Trump Vows That Won't Happen Again," *WP,* November 7, 2017; Andrew Glass, "Truman Leaves Nuclear Option on the Table in Korean War, Nov. 30, 1950," Politico, November 30, 2017; Amanda Erickson, "The Last Time the U.S. Was on 'the Brink of War' with North Korea," *WP,* August 9, 2017; Jesse Johnson, "Obama Weighed Pre-emptive Strike against North Korea after Fifth Nuclear Blast and Missile Tests near Japan in 2016, Woodward Book Claims," *The Japan Times,* September 12, 2018.

237 *As recounted in Van Jackson's* On the Brink: Jackson, *On the Brink,* 61–62.

238 *"North Korea's fundamental liabilities":* Pollack, "Economic Cooperation with North Korea."

238 *In 2017, North Korea's number two:* William Brown, "Sanctions and Nuclear Weapons Are Changing North Korea," *The Asan Open Forum,* December 5, 2017, http://www.theasanforum.org/sanctions -and-nuclear-weapons-are-changing-north-korea/.

238 *Inter-Korean trade plummeted:* South Korea Ministry of Unification, "Inter-Korean Exchanges and Cooperation," accessed January 25, 2019, https://www.unikorea.go.kr/eng_unikorea/relations/statistics /exchanges/.

238 *According to market research firm IHS Markit:* John Miller, "The Trade Numerologist: Trading with North Korea," IHS Markit, October 5, 2017, https://ihsmarkit.com/research-analysis/the-trade -numerologist-trading-with-north-korea.html.

239 *North Korea's trade deficit:* Lee Kil-seong, "N. Korea's Trade Deficit with China Hits Record," *Chosun Ilbo,* January 16, 2019.

239 *In 2018, as a result of:* Lee Jeong-ho, "North Korean Trade with Biggest Partner China Dives 48 Percent amid Sanctions," *SCMP,* July 19, 2019.

239 *North Korea's economy overall:* South Korea's central bank estimates as reported in Sam Kim and Jon Herskovitz, "North Korea Likely Suffering Worst Downturn since 1990s Famine," Bloomberg, July 16, 2019.

239 *North Korea does not publicize:* "Regime Squeezes North Korean Workers in China for Funds," *Daily NK,* February 28, 2019; Tae-jun Kang, "North Korea's Internal Struggles Hint That Sanctions Are Working," *The Diplomat,* April 8, 2019; Benjamin Katzeff Silberstein, "The North Korean Economy and U.S. Policy: Stability under 'Maximum Pressure,'" in *Joint U.S.-Korea Academic Studies,* ed. Gilbert Rozman (Washington, D.C.: Korea Economic Institute, 2019), 276–301.

242 *Ryan Hass, the former China director:* Jung H. Pak and Ryan L. Hass, "Beyond Maximum Pressure: A Pathway to North Korean Denuclearization," The Brookings Institution Foreign Policy Brief, December 2017, https://www.brookings.edu/wp-content/uploads/2017/12/north_korean_denuclearization.pdf.

243 *The importance of coordinated:* United Nations, *Report of the Panel of Experts Established Pursuant to Resolution 1874 (2009),* March 5, 2019, https://www.undocs.org/S/2019/171.

244 *"Information dissemination is significant":* Baek, *North Korea's Hidden Revolution,* 216–17.

245 *In his memoir:* Clapper, *Facts and Fears,* 50.

245 *While touting his good:* "On Socialist Construction and the Internal and External Policies of the Government of the Republic at the Present Stage," April 12, 2019; full text is at https://www.ncnk.org/resources/publications/kju_april2019_policy_speech.pdf/file_view.

246 *In April 2018, he observed:* Simon Denyer and John Hudson, "North Korea Announces Firing of Tactical Guided Weapon," *WP,* April 17, 2019.

246 *The following month:* Jihye Lee, "North Korea Confirms Kim Jong Un Ordered Rocket-Launch Drill," Bloomberg, May 3, 2019; Adam Taylor, "The Full Text of North and South Korea's Agreement, Annotated" *WP,* April 27, 2018.

246 *In July 2019:* Joshua Berlinger, "Kim Jong Un Seen Beside Apparent Submarine in State Media Photographs," CNN, July 23, 2019.

246 *Three months later, in October 2019:* Idrees Ali and Phil Stewart, "N. Korea Test Was of Short- to Medium-Range Ballistic Missile: Pentagon," Reuters, October 3, 2019.

246 *In all, as of December 2019:* Choe Sang-Hun, "North Korea Fires 2 Projectiles in First Test Since Latest Talks Stalled," *NYT,* October 31, 2019.

246 *We should expect:* "KCNA Releases Detailed Report on N. Korea Party Plenum," *BBC Monitoring Asia Pacific,* January 1, 2020, accessed via LexisNexis.

247 *His warnings about:* Heuer, *Psychology of Intelligence Analysis,* 10.

247 *Heuer, who passed away:* Ibid., 4.

SELECTED BIBLIOGRAPHY

Armstrong, Charles K. "The Destruction and Reconstruction of North Korea, 1950–1960." *The Asia-Pacific Journal* 7, no. 0 (March 16, 2009). https://apjjf.org/-Charles-K.-Armstrong/3460/article.html.

Baek, Jieun. *North Korea's Hidden Revolution: How the Information Underground Is Transforming a Closed Society.* New Haven, Conn.: Yale University Press, 2016.

Bishop, Isabella Bird. *Korea and Her Neighbours: A Narrative of Travel, with an Account of the Recent Vicissitudes and Present Position of the Country.* 1898. Reprint, Seoul: Yonsei University Press, 1970.

Boot, Max. *Invisible Armies: An Epic History of Guerrilla Warfare from Ancient Times to the Present.* New York: Liveright, 2013.

Brown, William A. "North Korea's Economic Strategy, 2018." In *A Whirl-wind of Change in East Asia: Assessing Shifts in Strategy, Trade, and the Role of North Korea,* vol. 29, *Joint U.S.-Korea Academic Studies,* ed. Gilbert Rozman. Washington, D.C.: Korea Economic Institute, 2018, 326–41. http://www.keia.org/sites/default/files/publications/kei_jointus-korea_2018_180801_final_digital.pdf.

Cathcart, Adam, Robert Winstanley-Chesters, and Christopher Green, eds. *Change and Continuity in North Korean Politics.* London: Routledge, 2017.

Central Intelligence Agency. *The North Korean Succession: An Intelligence Assessment,* October 1978. https://www.cia.gov/library/readingroom/document/cia-rdp81b00401r002100110012-7.

———. *North Korean Military Capabilities and Intentions: A Special National Intelligence Estimate,* May 23, 1979. https://www.cia.gov/library/readingroom/document/0001171647.

————. *North Korea: The Dynasty Takes Shape,* March 3, 1982. https:// www.cia.gov/library/readingroom/document/cia-rdp08s02113r0001 00210001-5.

————. *North Korea: A Sociological Perspective,* January 1983. https:// www.cia.gov/library/readingroom/document/cia-rdp84s00553r0001 00010001-7.

————. *Exploring the Implications of Alternative North Korean Endgames,* January 21, 1998. https://www.cia.gov/library/readingroom/docs /DOC_0001085294.pdf.

————. "The Korean War Controversy: An Intelligence Success or Failure?" Last updated June 25, 2015. https://www.cia.gov/news -information/featured-story-archive/2015-featured-story-archive /korean-war-intelligence-success-or-failure.html.

Cha, John, and K. J. Sohn. *Exit Emperor Kim Jong-il: Notes from His Former Mentor.* Bloomington, Ind.: Abbott Press, 2012.

Cha, Victor. *The Impossible State: North Korea Past and Future.* New York: HarperCollins, 2013.

Chanlett-Avery, Emma, and Sharon Squassoni. "North Korea's Nuclear Test: Motivations, Implications, and U.S. Options." Congressional Research Service Report for Congress, RL33709, October 24, 2006. https:// fas.org/sgp/crs/nuke/RL33709.pdf.

Chanlett-Avery, Emma, Liana Rosen, John Rollins, and Catherine Theohary. "North Korean Cyber Capabilities in Brief." Congressional Research Service Report for Congress, R44912, August 3, 2017. https:// fas.org/sgp/crs/row/R44912.pdf.

Choe, In Su. *Kim Jong Il: The People's Leader.* Vol. 1. Pyongyang: Foreign Languages Publishing House, 1983.

Clapper, James R. "Statement for the Record. Worldwide Threat Assessment of the US Intelligence Community." Senate Committee on Armed Services, April 18, 2013. https://www.dni.gov/files/documents /Intelligence%20Reports/UNCLASS_2013%20ATA%20SFR%20 FINAL%20for%20SASC%2018%20Apr%202013.pdf.

Clapper, James R., with Trey Brown. *Facts and Fears: Hard Truths from a Life in Intelligence.* New York: Viking, 2018.

Collins, Robert. *Marked for Life: Songbun, North Korea's Social Classification System.* Washington, D.C.: Committee for Human Rights in North Korea, 2012. https://www.hrnk.org/uploads/pdfs/HRNK _Songbun_Web.pdf.

————. *Pyongyang Republic: North Korea's Capital of Human Rights Denial.* Washington, D.C.: Committee for Human Rights in North Korea, 2016. https://www.hrnk.org/uploads/pdfs/Collins_PyongyangRepublic _FINAL_WEB.pdf.

Cumings, Bruce. *Korea's Place in the Sun: A Modern History.* New York and London: W. W. Norton, 1997.

Dalton, Bronwen, Kyungja Jung, and Jacqueline Willis. "Fashion and the Social Construction of Femininity in North Korea." *Asian Studies Review* 41, no. 4 (2017). https://doi.org/10.1080/10357823.2017.1367757.

Demick, Barbara. *Nothing to Envy: Ordinary Lives in North Korea.* New York: Spiegel & Grau, 2009.

Downs, Jim, ed. *Why We Write: The Politics and Practice of Writing for Social Change.* New York: Routledge, 2006.

Eckert, Carter J., Ki-baik Lee, Young Ick Lew, Michael Robinson, and Edward W. Wagner. *Korea Old and New: A History.* Cambridge, Mass.: Harvard University Press, 1990.

Everard, John. *Only Beautiful, Please: A British Diplomat in North Korea.* Stanford, Calif.: Walter H. Shorenstein Asia-Pacific Research Center, 2012.

Fahy, Sandra. *Marching through Suffering: Loss and Survival in North Korea.* New York: Columbia University Press, 2015.

Fifield, Anna. *The Great Successor: The Divinely Perfect Destiny of Brilliant Comrade Kim Jong Un.* New York: PublicAffairs, 2019.

Fischer, Paul. *A Kim Jong-Il Production: The Extraordinary True Story of a Kidnapped Filmmaker, His Star Actress, and a Young Dictator's Rise to Power.* New York: Flatiron Books, 2015.

Gause, Ken E. *North Korean House of Cards: Leadership Dynamics under Kim Jong-un.* Washington, D.C.: Committee for Human Rights in North Korea, 2015.

Greitens, Sheena Chestnut. *Illicit: North Korea's Evolving Operations to Earn Hard Currency.* Washington, D.C.: Committee for Human Rights in North Korea, 2014. https://www.hrnk.org/uploads/pdfs/SCG -FINAL-FINAL.pdf.

———. *Dictators and Their Secret Police: Coercive Institutions and State Violence.* Cambridge: Cambridge University Press, 2016.

Ha, Matthew, and David Maxwell. "Kim Jong-un's 'All-Purpose Sword': North Korean Cyber-Enabled Economic Warfare." Foundation for Defense of Democracies, October 2018. https://www.fdd.org/analysis /2018/10/03/kim-jong-uns-all-purpose-sword/.

Haggard, Stephan, and Marcus Noland. *Hunger and Human Rights: The Politics of Famine in North Korea.* Washington, D.C.: U.S. Committee for Human Rights in North Korea, 2005. https://www.researchgate .net/publication/40904797_Hunger_and_Human_Rights_The _Politics_of_Famine_in_North_Korea.

Halberstam, David. *The Coldest Winter: America and the Korean War.* New York: Hyperion, 2007.

Hassig, Ralph, and Kongdan Oh. *The Hidden People of North Korea: Everyday Life in the Hermit Kingdom.* Lanham, Md.: Rowman & Littlefield, 2009.

Hastings, Justin V. *A Most Enterprising Country: North Korea in the Global Economy.* Ithaca, N.Y.: Cornell University Press, 2016.

Hawk, David, and Amanda Mortwedt Oh. *The Parallel Gulag: North Korea's 'An-jeon-bu' Prison Camps.* Washington, D.C.: Committee for Human Rights in North Korea, 2017.

Heer, Paul J. *Mr. X and the Pacific: George F. Kennan and American Policy in East Asia.* Ithaca, N.Y., and London: Cornell University Press, 2018.

Hermes, Walter G. *Truce Tent and Fighting Front: U.S. Army in the Korean War.* Washington, D.C.: Center of Military History, United States Army, 1992. https://history.army.mil/html/books/020/20-3/CMH_Pub _20-3.pdf, 501.

Heuer, Jr., Richards J. *Psychology of Intelligence Analysis.* Washington, D.C.: Center for the Study of Intelligence, Central Intelligence Agency, 1999.

Hunter, Helen-Louise. *Kim Il-song's North Korea.* Westport, Conn.: Praeger, 1999.

Huntington, Samuel. *The Clash of Civilizations and the Remaking of World Order.* New York: Simon & Schuster, 1996.

Jackson, Van. *On the Brink: Trump, Kim, and the Threat of Nuclear War.* Cambridge: Cambridge University Press, 2018.

Jager, Sheila Miyoshi. *Brothers at War: The Unending Conflict in Korea.* New York: W. W. Norton, 2013.

Jang, Jin-sung. *Dear Leader: My Escape from North Korea.* Trans. Shirley Lee. New York: Atria Books, 2014.

Kang, Chol-hwan, and Pierre Rigoulot. *The Aquariums of Pyongyang: Ten Years in the North Korean Gulag.* New York: Basic Books, 2001.

Kelly, Robert E. "A New Economy for North Korea." Centre for International Governance Innovation, August 3, 2018. https://www.cigionline .org/articles/new-economy-north-korea.

Kim, Hakjoon. *Dynasty: The Hereditary Succession Politics of North Korea.* Stanford, Calif.: Walter H. Shorenstein Asia-Pacific Research Center, 2015.

Kim, Il Sung, *With the Century.* Pyongyang: Korea Friendship Association, 2003.

Kim Il Sung: Condensed Biography. Pyongyang: Foreign Languages Publishing House, 2001.

Kim Jong Il: Brief History. Pyongyang: Foreign Languages Publishing House, 1998.

Kim, Suki. *Without You, There Is No Us: My Secret Life Teaching the Sons of North Korea's Elite.* London: Rider Books, 2015.

Kim, Suzy. "Revolutionary Mothers: Women in the North Korean Revolution, 1945–1950." *Comparative Studies in Society and History* 52, no. 4 (2010).

———. "Specters of War in Pyongyang: The Victorious Fatherland Liberation War Museum in North Korea." *Cross-Currents: East Asian History and Culture Review*, E-journal no. 14 (March 2015): 124–51. https://cross-currents.berkeley.edu/sites/default/files/e-journal/articles /s._kim.pdf.

Kranish, Michael, and Marc Fisher. *Trump Revealed: The Definitive Biography of the 45th President.* New York: Scribner, 2016.

Kretchun, Nat, and Jane Kim. "A Quiet Opening: North Koreans in a Changing Media Environment," May 2012. https://www.intermedia .org/wp-content/uploads/2013/05/A_Quiet_Opening_FINAL_Inter Media.pdf.

Kretchun, Nat, Catherine Lee, and Seamus Tuohy. "Compromising Connectivity: Information Dynamics between the State and Society in a Digitizing North Korea," February 2017. https://www.intermedia.org /wp-content/uploads/2017/02/Compromising-Connectivity-Final -Report_Soft-Copy.pdf.

Lankov, Andrei. "Kim Takes Control: The 'Great Purge' in North Korea, 1956–1960." *Korean Studies* 26, no. 1 (2002): 87–119. doi:10.1353 /ks.2002.0010.

———. *North of the DMZ: Essays on Daily Life in North Korea.* Jefferson, N.C.: McFarland, 2007.

———. *The Real North Korea: Life and Politics in the Failed Stalinist Utopia.* New York: Oxford University Press, 2015.

Lee, Hyeonseo. *The Girl with Seven Names.* London: William Collins, 2015.

Lee, Jean H. "For North Koreans, the War Never Ended." *Wilson Quarterly* (Spring 2017). https://wilsonquarterly.com/quarterly/trump-and -a-watching-world/for-north-koreans-the-war-never-ended/.

———. "Soap Operas and Socialism: Dissecting Kim Jong-un's Evolving Policy Priorities through TV Dramas in North Korea." Korea Economic Institute Academic Paper Series, November 30, 2017. http:// www.keia.org/sites/default/files/publications/lee_soap_operas_and _socialism.pdf.

Lim, Dong-won. *Peacemaker: Twenty Years of Inter-Korean Relations and the North Korean Nuclear Issue.* Stanford, Calif.: Walter H. Shorenstein Asia-Pacific Research Center, 2012.

Lim, Jae-Cheon. *Kim Jong Il's Leadership of North Korea.* London and New York: Routledge, 2009.

Manyin, Mark. "Kim Jong-il's Death: Implications for North Korea's Stability and U.S. Policy." Congressional Research Service Report for Congress, R42126, January 11, 2012. https://fas.org/sgp/crs/row /R42126.pdf.

Martin, Bradley K. *Under the Loving Care of the Fatherly Leader: North Korea and the Kim Dynasty*. New York: Thomas Dunne Books, 2006.

McEachern, Patrick. "Centralizing North Korean Policymaking under Kim Jong Un." *Asian Perspectives* 43, no. 1 (2019): 35–67. doi:10.1353 /apr.2019.0001.

McInnis, Kathleen, Andrew Feickert, Mark Manyin, Steven Hildreth, Mary Beth Nikitin, Emma Chanlett-Avery, and Catherine Theohary. "The North Korea Nuclear Challenge: Military Options and Issues for Congress." Congressional Research Service Report for Congress, R44994, November 6, 2017. https://fas.org/sgp/crs/nuke/R44994.pdf.

Myers, B. R. *The Cleanest Race: How North Koreans See Themselves—and Why It Matters*. Brooklyn, N.Y.: Melville House, 2010.

Nanto, Dick K. "North Korean Counterfeiting of U.S. Currency." Congressional Research Service Report for Congress, RL33324, June 12, 2009. https://fas.org/sgp/crs/row/RL33324.pdf.

National Intelligence Council. *North Korea: Likely Response to Economic Sanctions*, December 10, 1991. https://www.cia.gov/library/reading room/docs/DOC_0005380437.pdf.

———. *Foreign Missile Developments and the Ballistic Missile Threat to the United States through 2015*, September 1999. https://www.dni.gov/files /documents/Foreign%20Missile%20Developments_1999.pdf.

Nikitin, Mary-Beth. "North Korea's Nuclear Weapons: Technical Issues." Congressional Research Service Report for Congress, RL34256, April 3, 2013. https://fas.org/sgp/crs/nuke/RL34256.pdf.

Oberdorfer, Don. *The Two Koreas: A Contemporary History*. New York: Basic Books, 2001.

O'Brien, Timothy L. *TrumpNation: The Art of Being the Donald*. New York: Grand Central Publishing, 2016.

Park, Yeonmi. *In Order to Live: A North Korean Girl's Journey to Freedom*. New York: Penguin Press, 2015.

Pollack, Jonathan. *No Exit: North Korea, Nuclear Weapons and International Security*. New York: Routledge, 2011.

Ra, Jong-yil. *Inside North Korea's Theocracy: The Rise and Sudden Fall of Jang Song-Thaek*. Trans. Jinna Park. Albany: State University of New York Press, 2019.

Sanger, David E. *The Perfect Weapon: War, Sabotage, and Fear in the Cyber Age*. New York: Crown, 2018.

Schnabel, James F. *Policy and Direction: The First Year*. Washington, D.C.: Center for Military History, United States Army, 1992.

Singer, Peter W., and Emerson T. Brooking. *LikeWar: The Weaponization of Social Media.* Boston: Houghton Mifflin Harcourt, 2018.

Southard, Susan. *Nagasaki: Life after Nuclear War.* New York: Viking, 2015.

Suh, Dae-sook. *Kim Il Sung: The North Korean Leader.* New York: Columbia University Press, 1988.

Terry, Sue Mi. "North Korea's Strategic Goals and Policy towards the United States and South Korea." *International Journal of Korean Studies* 17, no. 2 (Fall 2013). http://www.icks.org/data/ijks/1482461379_add_file_3.pdf.

Thae Yong-ho. Testimony to the U.S. House Committee on Foreign Affairs, November 1, 2017. https://docs.house.gov/meetings/FA/FA00/20171101/106577/HHRG-115-FA00-Wstate-Yong-hoT-20171101.pdf.

Tudor, Daniel, and James Pearson. *North Korea Confidential: Private Markets, Fashion Trends, Prison Camps, Dissenters and Defectors.* Tokyo: Tuttle Publishing, 2015.

U.N. *Report of the Detailed Findings of the Commission of Inquiry on Human Rights in the Democratic People's Republic of Korea,* February 7, 2014. https://www.ohchr.org/EN/HRBodies/HRC/CoIDPRK/Pages/ReportoftheCommissionofInquiryDPRK.aspx.

———. *Report of the Panel of Experts Established Pursuant to Resolution 1874 (2009),* February 27, 2017. https://www.undocs.org/S/2017/150.

———. Ambassador Nikki Haley, Remarks at an Emergency UN Security Council Briefing on North Korea, September 4, 2017. https://usun.usmission.gov/remarks-at-an-emergency-un-security-council-briefing-on-north-korea/.

———. *Report of the Panel of Experts Established Pursuant to Resolution 1874 (2009),* March 5, 2018. https://www.un.org/ga/search/view_doc.asp?symbol=S/2018/171.

———. "2019 DPR Korea: Needs and Priorities," March 6, 2019. https://www.undp.org/content/dam/unct/dprk/docs/DPRK_NP_2019_Final.pdf.

———. *Report of the Panel of Experts Established Pursuant to Resolution 1874 (2009),* August 30, 2019. https://undocs.org/S/2019/691.

UNICEF. "Multiple Indicator Cluster Survey 2017 Democratic People's Republic of Korea," June 2018. https://www.unicef.org/eap/sites/unicef.org.eap/files/2018-06/2017%20DPRK%20MICS%20Survey%20Findings%20Report_July%202018.pdf.

U.S. Congress, House Committee on Armed Services. "Statement of General Curtis M. Scaparrotti, Commander, United Nations Command; Commander, United States—Republic of Korea Combined Forces

Command, United States Forces Korea," 113th Congress, 2nd sess., April 2, 2014. https://docs.house.gov/meetings/AS/AS00/20140402/101985/HHRG-113-AS00-Wstate-ScaparrottiUSAC-20140402.pdf.

U.S. Department of State. "Democratic People's Republic of Korea 2018 Human Rights Report." https://www.state.gov/wp-content/uploads/2019/03/DEMOCRATIC-PEOPLE%E2%80%99S-REPUBLIC-OF-KOREA.pdf.

U.S. Department of the Treasury. "Treasury Designates Banco Delta Asia as Primary Money Laundering Concern under USA Patriot Act," September 15, 2005. https://www.treasury.gov/press-center/press-releases/Pages/js2720.aspx.

———. "Treasury Sanctions Additional North Korean Officials and Entities in Response to the North Korean Regime's Human Rights Abuses and Censorship Activities." Press release, January 11, 2017. https://www.treasury.gov/press-center/press-releases/Pages/jl0699.aspx.

U.S. Federal Bureau of Investigations. "Update on Sony Investigation." Press release, December 19, 2014. https://www.fbi.gov/news/pressrel/press-releases/update-on-sony-investigation.

U.S. Government. A Tradecraft Primer: Structured Analytic Techniques for Improving Intelligence Analysis, March 2009. https://www.cia.gov/library/center-for-the-study-of-intelligence/csi-publications/books-and-monographs/Tradecraft%20Primer-apr09.pdf.

U.S. Mission to the United Nations. "Fact Sheet: Resolution 2371 (2017) Strengthening Sanctions on North Korea," August 5, 2017. https://usun.usmission.gov/fact-sheet-resolution-2371-2017-strengthening-sanctions-on-north-korea/?_ga=2.127536526.220785168.1569552870-707405175.1564779131.

———. "Fact Sheet: Resolution 2375 (2017) Strengthening Sanctions on North Korea," September 11, 2017. https://usun.usmission.gov/fact-sheet-resolution-2375-2017-strengthening-sanctions-on-north-korea/.

———. "Fact Sheet: Resolution 2397 on North Korea," December 22, 2017. https://usun.usmission.gov/fact-sheet-un-security-council-resolution-2397-on-north-korea/?_ga=2.15513014.1072312274.1569553067-221063855.1568833043.

U.S. National Geospatial-Intelligence Agency. "Developments in North Korea's Sinuiju City under Kim Jong-un," April 21, 2018. https://pathfinder.geointservices.io/public_page/u-developments-in-north-koreas-sinuiju-city-under-kim-jong-un/.

U.S. Office of the Director of National Intelligence. "Unclassified Report to Congress on the Acquisition of Technology Relating to Weapons of Mass Destruction and Advanced Conventional Munitions, 1 January to

31 December 2006. https://www.odni.gov/files/documents/Newsroom /Reports%20and%20Pubs/Acquisition_Technology_Report_030308 .pdf.

U.S. Office of the Secretary of Defense. "Report to Congress: Military and Security Developments Involving the Democratic People's Republic of Korea," 2017. https://fas.org/irp/world/dprk/dod-2017.pdf.

U.S. The White House. "Remarks by President Trump to the National Assembly of the Republic of Korea, Seoul, Republic of Korea," November 7, 2017. https://www.whitehouse.gov/briefings-statements /remarks-president-trump-national-assembly-republic-korea-seoul -republic-korea/.

———. *National Security Strategy of the United States of America*, December 2017. https://www.whitehouse.gov/wp-content/uploads/2017/12 /NSS-Final-12-18-2017-0905.pdf.

———. "Remarks by President Trump on the Administration's National Security Strategy," December 18, 2017. https://www.whitehouse.gov /briefings-statements/remarks-president-trump-administrations -national-security-strategy/.

———. "Remarks by President Trump after Meeting with Vice Chairman Kim Yong Chol of the Democratic People's Republic of Korea," June 1, 2018. https://www.whitehouse.gov/briefings-statements/remarks -president-trump-meeting-vice-chairman-kim-yong-chol-democratic -peoples-republic-korea/.

———. "Joint Statement of President Donald J. Trump of the United States of America and Chairman Kim Jong Un of the Democratic People's Republic of Korea at the Singapore Summit," June 12, 2018. https://www.whitehouse.gov/briefings-statements/joint-statement -president-donald-j-trump-united-states-america-chairman-kim -jong-un-democratic-peoples-republic-korea-singapore-summit/.

———. "Press Conference by President Trump," June 12, 2018. https:// www.whitehouse.gov/briefings-statements/press-conference -president-trump/.

———. "Fact Sheet: President Trump Is Committed to Achieving Transformational Peace for the United States, the Korean Peninsula, and the World," February 21, 2019. https://www.whitehouse.gov/briefings -statements/president-trump-committed-achieving-transformational -peace-united-states-korean-peninsula-world/.

———. "Remarks by President Trump and President Moon of the Republic of Korea in Joint Press Conference," June 30, 2019. https:// www.whitehouse.gov/briefings-statements/remarks-president-trump -president-moon-republic-korea-joint-press-conference/.

War Crimes Committee of the International Bar Association. "Report: Inquiry on Crimes against Humanity in North Korean Prison Camps," December 12, 2017. https://www.ibanet.org/Article/NewDetail.aspx ?ArticleUid=8ae0f29d-4283-4151-a573-a66b2c1ab480.

Wit, Joel, Daniel Poneman, and Robert Gallucci. *Going Critical: The First North Korean Nuclear Crisis.* Washington, D.C.: Brookings Institution Press, 2004.

Woodward, Bob. *Fear: Trump in the White House.* New York: Simon & Schuster, 2018.

Worden, Robert L. *North Korea: A Country Study.* 5th ed. Washington, D.C.: Library of Congress, Federal Research Division, 2008.

INDEX

———■———

Jung H. Pak has held senior positions at the CIA and the Office of the Director of National Intelligence, where she led the U.S. intelligence community's analysis on Korea issues. She is currently a deputy assistant secretary of state for East Asian and Pacific Affairs at the U.S. Department of State. She has written for *The Atlantic, Foreign Policy, USA Today,* and *The Washington Post,* and is frequently interviewed by major print media, as well as for television, documentaries, and podcasts. A graduate of Colgate University, Pak received her PhD in U.S. history from Columbia University and studied in South Korea as a Fulbright Scholar.

Twitter: @junghpak1